THE Shark
CHRONICLES

AN OWL BOOK

Henry Holt and Company   New York

THE Shark
CHRONICLES

*A Scientist Tracks
the Consummate Predator*

John A. Musick and
Beverly McMillan

Henry Holt and Company, LLC
Publishers since 1866
115 West 18th Street
New York, New York 10011

Henry Holt® is a registered trademark of
Henry Holt and Company, LLC.

Library of Congress Cataloging-in-Publication Data
Musick, John A.
    The shark chronicles : a scientist tracks the consummate predator /
John A. Musick and Beverly McMillan—1st ed.
        p. cm.
    Includes index.
    ISBN 0-8050-7359-0 (pbk.)
        1. Sharks.   I. McMillan, Beverly.   II. Title.

QL638.9 .M86 2002
597.3—dc21   2002022654

Henry Holt books are available for special promotions and premiums.
For details contact: Director, Special Markets.

First published in hardcover in 2002 by Times Books

First Owl Books Edition 2003

An Owl Book

Designed by Paula Russell Szafranski

Printed in the United States of America

1   3   5   7   9   10   8   6   4   2

This book is dedicated to the memory of
Julian Anthony Penello, Wise Trawler Captain.
Tony "gave something back" to the sea and its fishes.

Contents

Authors' Note

As readers will discover, this book is presented in the voice of just one of us—John (Jack) Musick. We chose this writing strategy in part to limit confusion that might arise if there were two alternating "storytellers," and in part because so much of the research and so many of the stories told here come from Jack's professional lifetime of working with and on behalf of sharks. Even so, from its conception to its completion, this book was a full collaboration between a scientist and a science writer, and a husband and wife, who share an abiding fascination with sharks and concern for their future.

THE Shark
CHRONICLES

Prologue

Fishing vessel Cape May
Ambrose Channel approach
to New York harbor
July 1961

It was hot as hell down in the fo'c'sle and a great relief to climb
the ladder up to the main deck where a fresh breeze was
blowing cool salt spray over the starboard rail. We approached
the first buoy, the one with the long bamboo pole and red flag
that marked the end of our longline.

The line itself was about a mile and half in length and to it
were attached one hundred dropper lines—the gangions.
Each of those were perhaps a dozen feet long with a short,
thin steel cable at the end and a moderate-sized hook. We had
baited the hooks with whole menhaden and then set out the
line to fish for four hours. As we retrieved the end buoy we
began to haul the line back using a specially designed mechanical line-hauler that automatically coiled the line into wash
tubs as it was pulled in.

Jack Casey handled the gangions at the rail while a Cajun
commercial fisherman nicknamed Dago ran the line-hauler.

I was assigned the duty of gaffing each shark as it came in on the line. The first few hooks came up empty, the baits probably consumed by crabs.

The fourth gangion, however, surged against the main line, revealing a large fish somewhere below the surface. Casey grabbed the taut gangion, untied it from the main line, and snubbed it down over the rail to prevent the fish from sounding. He slid the gangion aft along the rail to me. The fish, a shark, broke the surface—a twisting, thrashing sandbar six feet long and weighing about 120 pounds. The bow of our old wooden fishing vessel bucked into the sea, which was kicking up white caps in the afternoon breeze. With some difficulty I thrust the tooled steel gaff into the shark's mouth, pulling up sharply to impale the writhing animal through its gills. Then I looped the short rope tied to the gaff handle onto an iron snaphook attached to a line hanging from an overhead boom and threaded through a series of blocks down to a bronze capstan. There, one of the crew hoisted the thrashing animal up into the air and across the deck, letting it fall into a crude pen made by cordoning off part of the deck with knee-high boards. The boat continued into the waves and we continued to haul in the line, all constant motion with Casey handing successive sharks, like dogs on leashes, back to me where they were gaffed and unceremoniously swung on board. There were more large sandbar sharks, several smaller ones, and duskies, a hammerhead, and large tiger shark in the ten- to eleven-foot range. We took perhaps fifteen or twenty sharks in this set alone.

After landing our catch, the real labor of measuring, weighing, and dissecting each species proceeded. It is difficult to describe what it is like to try to weigh a half-ton tiger shark by lifting a large scale—with the shark attached below and the boom line attached above—into the air, where the whole lot swings back and forth across the rolling deck. Or what it's like to thrust my hand into the voluminous, slimy body cavity to pull out the bulbous stomach, which in turn must be slit open to discover what the stinking, partially digested contents might reveal about the great animal's diet. I remembered to check for parasites internal and external, then after removing the entire digestive tract made a complete exam of the reproductive system to determine whether the animal was mature, or if female, whether she was pregnant or had recently pupped. Finally I cut out a six-inch section of the vertebral column from under the dorsal fin to save so that the age of the shark might be determined later back in the laboratory. These chores I did methodically and carefully to procure the maximum amount of scientific information from each and every specimen. To sacrifice these magnificent animals without making such an effort would be a crass and unethical act.

During the course of that summer in 1961, we captured many other species, including makos and a few six- to eight-foot great white sharks. The sheer biomass of those apex predators, just five miles off the beaches of northern New Jersey and an hour's run from New York City, was astounding. We found that the catch was not unusual, and that those subtropical sharks were regular summer residents along the mid-Atlantic coast. We gained knowledge about shark distribution and abundance, diet, reproductive biology, and age and growth patterns that was groundbreaking both scientifically and personally. The sheer seasonal abundance of sharks was a revelation, and for me began a lifelong shark odyssey that has led me around the world.

In those early, revelatory days aboard the *Cape May,* little could I imagine that four decades later shark populations would be decimated worldwide, mostly because of overharvesting, and that I would be spending much of my time trying to save and restore this ancient group of animals who have been masters of time for more than 400 million years. To that end, this book will tell the story of sharks' evolutionary journey through time and space and examine their elegant adaptations to life at the top of marine food webs.

The lives of sharks in today's world are intertwined not only with those who see them as a necessary source of protein or an easy source of wealth, but also with researchers whose professional lives, like mine, have been dedicated to understanding how sharks function as organisms and as important components of complex ecosystems. Many of those men and women grace these pages, and their work and that of many others continues to be vital to the long-term survival of sharks. That survival is far from guaranteed, and so recounted here too is the curious and increasingly disastrous relationship of sharks to our planet's ultimate predator—*Homo sapiens*.

1 *In the Beginning*

Montana state route 87 heads north from Billings across a great, rolling prairie spotted with gray-green sagebrush. The Big Snowy mountains to the west foretell the distant Rockies, but at the moment gray curtains of rain obscure nearly the entire arc of the horizon. Bev, my wife and writing partner, peers through the steely light at a road map while quarter-sized raindrops plop on the windshield of our rented Subaru station wagon. Our destination is Bear Gulch, a sixteen-mile-long, fossil-rich limestone schism in the belly of Montana's 147,138 square miles. By dint of the sheer number of species represented there, it is one of the most productive sites on the planet—perhaps *the* most productive site—for shark fossils. Wonderfully preserved remains of animals that lived and died some 320 million years ago have been unearthed there, and together they have painted a detailed portrait of an instant in time when tropical seas teemed with a diverse assembly of sharks and other marine life, when amphibians and insects were the reigning terrestrial animals, and dinosaurs were still a hundred million years in the future.

In his elegant book *Discovering Fossil Fishes,* paleontologist John Maisey called sharks "one of evolution's greatest success stories." He was referring to the fact that living sharks represent a lineage of fishes that apparently has traversed the better part of half a billion years. Sharks are often called primitive, but to me they are astonishing creatures, exquisitely adapted to their lives as apex predators, sleek of body and in wondrously efficient motion from the moment of birth to the moment of death. As the Subaru's wipers thunk against the rain, I run down my mental list of the questions one needs to try to answer in order to understand the evolutionary trek of sharks. What were those first, inconceivably ancient sharks like, and where did their journey start? How did they get their remarkably powerful and uniquely mobile jaws? What other transformations in body form and functions filled the shadowy gap between those dim times and the vibrant hours of Bear Gulch? What came later?

Evolution, shark or otherwise, is change in a line of descent over time. Its main driving forces are genetic variations and the subsequent winnowing of traits through natural selection. Success has been measured by genetic fitness—the number of successful offspring that survive to pass on their genes to future generations. Evolution, then, is like some huge numbers game in which chance genetic changes are expressed in an individual as altered traits that in turn render the individual either better or less adapted to survive and reproduce. Better adapted individuals have higher fitness and their genes will be favored, whereas the opposite is true for individuals that are less well adapted. For centuries, naturalists have been reading the tales of biological failures and successes in the fossil record.

The seeds of early shark evolution were planted with the appearance of animals with a backbone: the vertebrates. We see the prelude in famous fossil localities like British Columbia's Burgess Shale, in rock strata laid down about 540 million years ago in the heart of the

Cambrian period of the Paleozoic era. By then, animals had been evolving in Earth's seas for about a billion years, but all the different forms were invertebrates—a motley if remarkable assortment of worms, slugs, and shelled creatures. That thousand million years of evolution had added muscles, sensory organs, and some other complexities to their small, soft bodies, but they did not have much in the way of an internal skeleton, a requirement for growing large. Starting in the middle Cambrian, however, animal evolution shifted gears. Certain animals developed a new adaptive trait—a flexible, incompressible rod running much of the body's length. The rod, a notochord, became one of four defining features of an evolving animal lineage called the chordates. The other three traits were a nerve cord running above the notochord, a muscular "throat" (a pharynx) perforated by a series of slitlike openings, and a tail.

When chordates arrived on the scene, it was the beginning of a new world order. One lineage that evolved from early forms were animals with the biological capacity to build a case of bone or cartilage in the head that protects the brain and closely allied sensory structures such as eyes. That wasn't all the ability to make a cranium could do. Adults developed from embryos that had a mass of tissue called the neural crest. It contained cells genetically equipped to guide the formation of certain other key cell types, as well as the cranium, as the animal grew. Those new possibilities included cells that could form body-building materials such as cartilage and, later, bone. Bone is a tissue imbued with channels for blood vessels and nerves. Cells that make it use minerals, especially calcium and phosphate, to assemble it. Cartilage, by contrast, is a solid but pliable tissue that resists compression, like a hard rubber ball. It, too, however, can be mineralized and so become even more rigid.

The ability to make cartilage shaped the flow of vertebrate evolution, birthing the lineage of the first fishes. The oldest fossil forms currently known, from the famous Chengjiang deposit in Yunnan, China, date to about 540 million years ago and have a cartilage skull and what appear to be cartilage supports for gills and fins. The "backbone" in these animals was a flexible notochord, the eventual foundation for a more elaborate internal skeleton. Early groups of vertebrates also evolved a dermal skeleton of mineral-hardened scales and bony plates generated by cells in the skin. Even living terrestrial vertebrates have vestiges of this ancient "skin skeleton"; human facial bones and teeth, which develop from the same embryonic tissue that produces our skin, are examples.

For the first hundred million years, all vertebrates were fishes. The earliest forms were agnathans, fishes whose mouths lacked the internal support of jaws. By about 450 million years ago, the reigning agnathans were roughly trout-sized fishes called ostracoderms. The name translates roughly as "shell-skinned," and the group's hallmark was its impressive dermal skeleton. Many ostracoderms had heads encased in a shield of interlocking bony plates, with the rest of their teardrop-shaped bodies sheathed in a chain mail of bony scales. Others, though, were built differently, and there is one group that is particularly intriguing. These long-extinct jawless fishes, called thelodonts, didn't have a bulky bony head shield but instead were covered entirely by coarse scales. The scales also lined their gills and the inside of the mouth, and in the most ancient thelodonts they were elaborate. Like a dermal parfait, each one consisted of a large inner pulp cavity overlain by a mineral-hardened material called dentine, which in turn was crowned by a glistening, thin, but extremely hard, blanket of enameloid, a substance akin to our own tooth enamel. This sort of multilayered scale is called a placoid scale (or dermal denticle), and it closely resembles the scales not only of living sharks but of virtually every fossil shark scale ever dug up. Fossilized placoid scales found in Colorado in the mid-1990s were in strata 455 million years old, although there wasn't enough other material found with them to determine what sort of fish they came from. Around the same time, however, a paleontologist named Mark Wilson working in the Northwest Territories of Canada discovered whole fossil thelodonts with triangular dorsal fins, large forked tails, and signs of a stomach—a food-storing organ that usually is associated with animals who can eat bulky meals because they have jaws for grabbing food. Jawless fishes in general, including the living hagfishes, are thought to be—and to always have been—bottom feeders that consume small prey. Wilson's thelodonts prompt questions that nobody has been able to credibly ask before. Did some thelodonts evolve jaws? And was their line, with its characteristic placoid scales, the progenitor of sharks?

Sharks and their relatives—rays, skates, and the bizarre chimaeras, known variously as ghost sharks, spookfishes, and ratfishes, among other names—make up the animal class Chondrichthyes, fishes with a cartilaginous skeleton. On this drippy day, driving over rolling prairie, I ponder the fact that we fish types know almost nothing for certain about their early origins. What is clear is that a handful of characteristics that define chondrichthyans seem to have been in place virtually from the beginning. One of these is the placoid scale. Since the teeth of sharks and their kin have the same basic architecture, this type of scale probably was the foundation from which chondrichthyan teeth evolved. Another characteristic is the absence of a swim bladder. Chondrichthyans are the only major group of fishes lacking this organ, which holds gas and so enables other kinds of fishes to be neutrally buoyant—basically, to stay afloat when they're not moving forward. But with no swim bladder, a shark must swim—or sink. The lack of a swim bladder probably has influenced the evolution of other shark features, such as their large fins and unelaborated body shape. Its influence may even be reflected in the chondrichthyan cartilaginous skeleton. For a long time it was supposed that the cartilaginous frame of a shark is simply an archaic feature, evolved before animals could make bone and never altered. In fact, though, it's more likely that it is an evolutionary specialization that makes the skeleton strong, light, and elastic, all of which translates into less energy needed to move the body. Chondrichthyans manage sex differently, too. A female's eggs are fertilized inside her body, and a male has claspers, which are grooved extensions of his pelvic fins that funnel sperm into a female's urogenital tract during mating.

. . .

Despite the downpour, we are making good time toward our meeting with Dick Lund, a paleontologist and longtime friend who has been disinterring Bear Gulch fossils since the site was discovered in the early 1960s by a rancher searching for flat rocks with which to construct a backyard patio. At precisely half past four in the afternoon the rain begins to lighten and a few moments later we pull into the gravel parking lot of a squat roadside café. A mélange of older SUVs and pickup trucks clusters by a windowless door; with a tug on the handle it opens into a darkened saloon. Near the back wall, at a table illuminated by a single, low-hung light, six aging cowboys are playing poker. At the bar, already washing the outcrop dust down their throats with cold beers, are Lund, his coinvestigator Dr. Eileen Grogan, and this year's small band of volunteers.

"Hey, bucko!" Eileen calls, striding over for hugs all around. "Can I buy you a beer?" A compact, intense New Yorker in her thirties, Eileen is one of my former graduate students. Her Irish copper curls are cropped short, and I notice that along with her decidedly hard-used field gear she's wearing pearl earrings. Grinning widely, Dick unfolds from a bar stool. Sixtyish with an animated face, a rounding midriff, and thinning sand-colored hair, like Eileen he is attired in a dust-crusted chambray shirt with sleeves rolled up to the elbows, jeans creased into dusty furrows, and battered hiking boots.

It's been more than a year since we've seen one another, but the conversation turns quickly to the reason for our meeting. Bev and I basically just want to get a feel for Bear Gulch. We want to see first-hand the limestone deposits whose trove of remarkable fossils is substantially filling in the spotty mosaic of shark evolution, and we want to get a sense of how paleontologists do their fossil-finding work. Plus, I'd like to find a fish. Tucked away in the Subaru is a geologist's pick I have owned since I was a boy, and I have been harboring fantasies of discovering a substantial Bear Gulch fossil myself.

Dick's crew, a thirty-something graduate student named Bryan, a vacationing, middle-aged accountant named Myra, and Bill, a retired oil company lobbyist, immediately take the measure of these plans.

"The goal," says Myra, beginning our education, "is not to find the fish but to move the rock." She smiles. "Move enough rock and you'll find the fish." In fact, as the next two days will teach both me and Bev, moving rock, tons of it, is the essence of fossil-hunting at a locality such as Bear Gulch, where the remains of ancient organisms are sand-wiched between rock strata that vary in thickness from less than ten to hundreds of feet. In a few localities the layers may be exposed on the surface of the Earth, then plunge downward perhaps thousands of feet. Only by accidents of geological upheaval—the tectonic events that bring the Earth's crustal plates into collision—do many fossil deposits find their way to surface layers where fossil hunters can hope to find them.

Simultaneously nursing a beer and a cigarette, Dick recalls a question once posed to him by a local rancher whose land includes a section of the Bear Gulch Limestone.

"How *did* them fish get between them rocks?" the rancher had earnestly asked the erudite paleontologist from New York. The query went to the heart of how the Bear Gulch Limestone originated and over a vast span of geologic time became such an extraordinary fossil locality. The area early Montanans named Bear Gulch is a deep, narrow canyon carved through a deposit of limestone. The chalk-colored rock, mostly lime (calcium carbonate) in its chemical makeup, exists in thin, horizontal layers, so that the steep walls of the canyon appear to be built of stacked, jagged limestone pancakes that have been sheared off with a giant serrated knife. The limestone sits like a lens on older, clay-rich rock known as the Heath Shale. Hundreds of millions of years ago, during a part of the Paleozoic called the Carboniferous period, neither the Heath Shale nor the Bear Gulch Limestone existed. Neither did Montana, at least not as we think of it today. At the time, shifting of the Earth's crustal plates was coalescing nearly all of the planet's land masses into the encompassing continent of Pangaea. Land that would become the north central plains of North

America lay roughly along the equator. This future Montana was a tropical landscape and a good part of it lay submerged under a shallow, tropical sea that stretched eastward to what today is the state of Virginia. With fishes already evolving for a couple of hundred million years, the sea's warm waters were lush with marine life, including many different species of early sharks. At one coastal point, a four-mile-wide bay opened inland east to west roughly sixteen miles, covering an area about twenty miles square. For whatever reason, possibly due to monsoonlike rains, many times over along the shore of the fingerlike bay, inflows brought masses of silty, lime-rich mud surging into the dappled water. Each sudden rush of mud buried in an airless tomb whatever life chanced to be there at the moment. Fish in the water column as well as those on the bottom were caught in a suffocating curtain of suspended sediment. Given enough time, the compressing weight of mud and the lack of oxygen (which would have prevented most microbial decay) created ideal conditions for the preservation of dead animals and plants. Water infiltrating the remains brought with it dissolved minerals. This slow mineralization and accumulating pressure gradually yielded rock having the shape and form of the once-living tissues—that is, it made fossils.

When one chips away at the layered Bear Gulch Limestone, most of the resulting fragments come away in thin sheets, each one representing a flow of mud into the ancient bay. When an animal was overcome by the inundation, its remains came to rest on top of one sediment layer as they were simultaneously being covered over by the limey mud flowing in above, which formed a new layer. Geological analysis shows that the bay existed for a mere two-thousand-year blip of Earth's history. But during its short life the repeated mud flows regularly extinguished the lives of fishes, plants, and other residents and encased their corpses between layers of forming rock.

I don't know if the pragmatic Montanan accepted Lund's interpretation of these primeval events, but a standing joke among those of us who work on living sharks is that to reconstruct a fossil fish from a piece of rock, as paleontologists must do, often takes a bit of imagination. At the bar I mention the time when Eileen was presenting a paper on Bear Gulch fishes at a major scientific meeting. Proudly showing a slide of one of her prize fossil finds and pointing out the fine points of its anatomy, Eileen had paused to ask rhetorically, "Now what do we see here?" Before she could continue, several ichthyologists in the audience had shouted out, "A rock!"

The story elicits a ripple of chuckles. "That's right," says Bill. "Believing is seeing." Everybody laughs. Then Bev and I head for a nearby town to find a motel, and the crew head back to the vacant Boy Scout camp where they have been living in tents for several weeks. Driving into my first Montana sunset, I hear Bill's words again. Despite Myra's admonition about the fundamental task of simply moving rock, I am excited about the possibility of finding a fish. Tomorrow in Bear Gulch I have every intention of believing.

The Bear Gulch Limestone produces fossils that are 320 million years old, and by any measure of time my mind can compass, a 320-year-old fish is ancient. Yet by the time the Carboniferous period rolled around, chondrichthyan fishes had already existed for at least 130 million years, diversifying into forms that could exploit many ecological niches—the ecologist's catchall term for an animal's total way of life, from its feeding strategies to its breeding habits. Rock strata from the two preceding geological periods—the Devonian and, before it, the Silurian—have yielded evidence, in the form of teeth, scales, spines, and some remarkably complete skeletons, that by the beginning of the Carboniferous shallow-water marine communities included a multitude of sharks. Some species of Carboniferous sharks even were adapted to freshwater rivers and streams, as are modern bull sharks and some stingrays. The detailed preservation of many Bear Gulch fishes provides us with a rare picture of how diverse the sharks and their relatives had already become by the Carboniferous.

Even so, in those old times sharks were different from modern ones in significant ways. Consider a 375-million-year-old specimen of *Cladoselache*. Roughly paraphrased, its name means cladodont shark. The ancient Greeks used the word *seláchios* to designate sharks and rays. Cladodont translates as "branched tooth" and refers to a now-disappeared tooth type that persisted in various sharks more or less unchanged for about 250 million years. The tooth base is a half-moon, and from it rise several pointed cusps, the tallest in the center, the others in pairs to the side. Each cusp had a separate pulp cavity. The kind, number, and arrangement of an animal's teeth make up its dentition, and a cladodont's dentition was adapted for piercing the body of a prey animal that would most likely be swallowed whole, often headfirst. It was a far cry from anything one would see in most shark mouths today. Cladodonts also were primitive in some other features. The jaw was limited to simple open-close movements, being short and too firmly attached to the cranium for more flexible operations. Many ancient sharks also had fin spines in front of the first dorsal fin—one made of bone, instead of the modified placoid scales that would become the standard recipe for modern shark spines.

Yet no one examining its petrified remains could doubt that *Cladoselache* is a shark. Its body is long and slender, and like a mako shark its tail has the scimitar shape of a swift and agile swimmer. It has powerfully built, cartilage-reinforced pectoral fins and two prominent dorsal fins, which provided maneuverability and stability. Clearly, starting from jawless ancestral origins, 150 million years of natural selection had refined chondrichthyan features into a formidable fish.

In fact, throughout the Devonian sharks were evolving rapidly, with many new species appearing within a short span of geological time. Such a blossoming of species is called an adaptive radiation, and it correlates with repeated incursions into new environments, as new forms are able to either fill open niches or displace other kinds of organisms. Evidence for a flamboyant radiation of sharks in the Devonian comes mainly from fossil shark teeth. The matchhead-sized teeth from a diminutive species named *Leonodus* are the earliest fossil shark teeth found thus far, and they come from rocks dating from near the beginning of the Devonian, about 410 million years ago. With their pulp cavity and classic structure, they are easily recognizable as shark teeth. In later strata, cladodont teeth are the most common finds, but there are numerous other types, too. Some of the older fossil teeth have two main cusps; some in later Devonian strata have three prominent peaks alongside other, smaller ones, or several pointed cusps of equal size, or cusps shaped like claws. These are just a few of many possible examples, and what they point to is a time long before the Bear Gulch bay when new kinds of sharks were steadily arising, each with its own particular feeding strategy.

Early Devonian rocks in Bolivia and Brazil have recently produced fragments of fossilized shark crania with features that paleontologists usually associate with some of the earliest bony fishes. The similarity hints that we may be getting close to figuring out what the first cranium looked like.

At the end of the Devonian, global climate was changing and a wave of extinction was washing through the Earth's seas. But while the curtain was coming down on many lineages (including early forms of jawed bony fishes), a group of cladodont sharks called stethacanthids was just beginning to flourish. The fossil record doesn't provide many clues as to what mix of features allowed them to thrive while other sharks went extinct, but it has revealed remarkable stone portraits of some stethacanthids. What is most notable is that males had a prominent bony spine or other adornment of the first dorsal fin. The males of *Stethacanthus,* an early form, boasted a thick, curved spine crowned by what looks like an inverted wire brush. The "brush" actually consists of modified fin rays and scales; that is, the components of a fin, but remodeled into a structure that might have been used to attract female sharks. Stethacanthid teeth had a spacious base crowned with one tall cusp surrounded by several smaller ones. Extrapolating from fossil teeth that rise nearly two inches from base to tip, paleontologists have estimated that some stethacanthids must have been at least eighteen feet long and had a mouth spanning several feet. If the estimates are accurate, in their time ancient stethacanthid sharks would have been the largest predators in the sea.

In Late Devonian lagoons and seas, stethacanthids swam alongside different groups of small ctenacanth ("comb spine") sharks. Generally no more than a couple of feet long, ctenacanths sported fin spines studded with row upon row of slender nubs, like the teeth of a comb.

Invading freshwater habitats, and probably dominant predators there, were assorted eel-like xenacanth sharks. Their most striking feature was an elongated, slender body—up to twelve feet long. Xenacanths also had distinctive teeth with two elongated cusps spread like the arms of a crab's open claw—dual rapiers that were well suited to preventing a live and struggling meal from escaping.

The Devonian gave way to the Carboniferous, and by the middle of that period when the Bear Gulch bay was open and available, the roll call of cartilaginous fishes had lengthened. The roster included a new group, holocephalans, "whole-headed" fishes with an immobile upper jaw fused to the brain case and a flaplike operculum over the gill openings. There were two basic holocephalan branches, the chimaeras and various sharklike paraselachians. (The "para" in this case is from the Greek for "next to.") Males had pelvic claspers, but chimaeras also had evolved a cephalic clasper perched conspicuously on the top of the head. Observations of living chimaeras have shown that the male can use his cephalic clasper to hold on to the female's pectoral fin while mating. The other chondrichthyans were elasmobranchs, whose basic distinguishing features included an increasingly strong and mobile jaw, multiple gill slits, teeth that were steadily shed and replaced, and male claspers associated with the pelvic fins. Carboniferous elasmobranchs in turn subdivided into cladodont sharks—which by then had been around for nearly 100 million years—and hybodonts, "hump-toothed" sharks that were the vanguard of a new lineage that increasingly would dominate the shark universe over the next hundred million years. Among other trends evident in hybodont fossils is evolutionary change in shark dentition. In many species the front teeth were still sharp, piercing weapons, but lateral to them were shorter and rounder teeth suited for handling food differently. Some hybodonts had flat teeth specialized for crushing. In others an evolutionary shift halted the shedding of certain teeth, which instead were retained in whorls that spiraled like a wound watch spring. Male hybodonts had two sturdy, curved spines perched like horns on either side of the head.

Early hybodonts and cladodonts both had a simple, cartilaginous, rodlike backbone with poorly mineralized vertebrae. But shark researchers class hybodont sharks as euselachians, or true sharks, for they may have been the well from which the lineage of modern sharks and rays would spring. Alternatively, that honor may go to ctenacanths.

"The bay opens to the east," Dick Lund is saying, flicking ashes from his cigarette by way of punctuation and pointing in the direction of North Dakota. "That way, there's the mouth." After an early breakfast at the café we are getting a grand tour of the Bear Gulch outcrops in Dick's battered sky blue Suburban. The morning is a breathtaking amalgam of open, blue sky and rolling gray-green prairie unzipped in places by rocky ridges. Lund has been piecing together the parameters and ecology of the ancient bay for thirty years, and at the moment it seems to be more real to him than the wildflowered ridge upon which we are standing.

"No part of the bay is more than about twenty-six meters deep—eighty, ninety feet, at most," he is saying. "All around the shallower portions there were arborescent sponges. Invertebrates are also represented by cephalopods, worms, shrimps, bivalves, many others. All over the place. Around the southern margin we've found beautiful specimens of filamentous algae, which would have floated at or near the surface. There's lots of algae, period. The primary productivity here must have been tremendous." Primary productivity refers to the rate at which plants and other photosynthetic organisms capture and store energy from the sun in their body tissues. It is a rough measure of how much food there is for an ecosystem's animals. The Carboniferous bay Dick Lund is describing was a place of plenty.

Back in the truck we negotiate a narrow track across high pastureland as Dick continues his narration of the bay's ecology. "To the southwest, we have evidence that there was some freshwater inflow to the western head of the bay, but we've found only a few fresh- or brackish-water species in that general area and no evidence that fishes from those environments were carried down into the bay after they died.

[17]

"On the other hand . . ." he pauses for effect and to light another cigarette, "the fossil *marine* fauna of the Bear Gulch Limestone is like no other assemblage of Carboniferous fish faunas anywhere in the world. This fossil fauna is unique in the remarkable quality of its preservation as well as in its contents. There are more species here than anywhere else, and there are no known ecologically, chronologically, or preservationally equivalent fossil chondrichthyan faunas that compare with what we've got here."

Every so often we are forced to stop and pass through a post-and-wire gate. The third and final gate before we enter Bear Gulch bears a hand-lettered sign: NO TRESPASSING WITHOUT PERMISSION. It witnesses the fact that Bear Gulch slices entirely through private land. By all accounts, the landowners whose terrain encompasses Bear Gulch are only too happy to ward off trespassing fossil hunters with the persuasive power of a shotgun. Lund and his crew, known with some affection by the locals as "the diggers," have worked hard to gain the trust of ranchers upon whose goodwill Lund's research depends. Lund receives no financial gain from the fossils he removes, which are analyzed and interpreted either by Lund himself or by experts at other universities and museums. Lund also is expected not to include too many outsiders in his operations there. In fact, our arrival was timed to coincide with the departure of ten-year veterans Bill and Myra, only two days before the entire crew will end their summer of work and disperse.

The track turns down into a canyon, Bear Gulch itself. Ahead is an outcrop where the crew has recently been working. A talus slope of discarded limestone shards flares down from the lip of a shelf created as the crew has slowly worked its way into the bowels of the outcrop, which accords with a location in the upper reaches of the ancient bay. We follow the track down the near face of the canyon, continue up on the opposite side, and park just behind the excavated shelf.

"All right," says Eileen as we emerge from the vehicle into the rising heat of the day. "Let's go fishing."

Gloves, water bottles, hand picks, brushes, and small, flat, steel pry bars the diggers call "wunderbars" emerge from the back of Dick's truck along with Tully, Eileen's mixed-breed pooch. Bryan shoves tools into a backpack and descends to another crop nearby. He has not found a fish for several days and wants to work alone, at what I soon learn is a furious pace of moving rock punctuated by mild curses. Bev and I follow Dick and Eileen down onto the nearer shelf, a broad, almost perfectly flat platform of limestone that juts out about four feet below the canyon top. The tons of rock removed to create it have formed a river of sharp limestone scree that cascades downward thirty or forty feet—the equivalent of truckloads of rock moved entirely by human muscle power, mostly Dick and Eileen's, in the course of a day or two. The platform thus created I gauge to be about twenty feet long. The distance from its inner wall to its rim appears to be seven or eight feet at most. Eileen refers to this circumscribed work surface as the "dance floor," and at its edge the canyon opens out broadly to a vista of rolling rangeland and wandering cows.

The day is heating into a shimmering blend of sun and sky and Dick is anxious to begin work. "What you're going to do here is whack and stack," he says, indicating a pile of shards at the platform's rim that have not yet been launched onto the scree below. "That way if you find something and need to go back and look for its counterpart, you're not going to have to scramble down the cliff hoping like hell you can find it."

When a geologist's pick strikes laminated rock such as that of the Bear Gulch Limestone, with luck the rock's layers will split apart horizontally. If fossilized remains are present between the layers, the top layer—the mud flow that originally covered the organic material—may not come away cleanly but instead may carry a portion of the fossil, or a scientifically valuable mirror-impression of same, with it. For this reason it is vital for a serious fossil hunter intent on "moving rock" to resist the urge to toss away what seem to be barren shards.

Each of us sets to work in a section of the outcrop, selecting a point near the rim and moving in toward the back wall, essentially removing limestone the way one would pull up tiles from a floor. With each strike of the pick, fissures open up in the platform, freeing pieces of the limestone ranging in size and shape from dinner plates to doormats.

The larger slabs, most more than an inch thick, are levered up using a wunderbar. Exposed layer upon layer, they are like the pages of a book. As instructed, I scrutinize the edges as well as each freshly revealed surface for dark, telltale signs of once living organisms squashed within. Despite my hopes, none reveals a fish of any type. In fact, as midday approaches, most of the pages of this particular book seem to be blank. After an hour of "tink-tinking"—Eileen's eponymous term for the striking of pick on stone—the first and pretty much the only fossil matter to appear are coprolites—fossilized feces.

"Could be shark shit," Dick says. "Feces are probably the most abundant fossils in most beds, which makes sense if you think about it."

For the next hour or so we collectively turn up more coprolites and a few uninteresting bits of fossilized shrimp remains. But though there are still no fishes in my book, and the heat continues to intensify, I begin to come across other small treasures: bits of fish scale and cartilage and ancient cephalopods, some straight and others coiled. It occurs to me that I am looking at modest ancestors of exceedingly lovely creatures such as the chambered nautilus. Every so often we pause to kick stacks of barren rock over the platform rim and sweep the dance floor. After lunch we drive to a different site where the pickings may be better and where there are trees to provide shade. My conviction that the afternoon will bring my fish is strong as ever. After the great mass extinction at the end of the Devonian, a burst of adaptive radiations greeted the Carboniferous. The essence of adaptive radiation, I think to myself, is being in the right place at the right time with the right stuff. It's a beautiful if scorching day, and my fish will come.

In the new sequence of outcrops we are now exploring, the limestone of the Bear Gulch interweaves with exposed areas of the bay-encompassing Heath Shale. In places, horizontal slices of the dark, oily shale slide off the underlying rock almost as easily as cards from a deck, and some hold specimens of early bony fishes called paleoniscoids. Through the early afternoon I work next to Eileen. I have collected fossils before; coastal Virginia where I live regularly spits out fossil shark teeth. But the fossils here are different—not only much older, and qualitatively richer in the information they can convey, but they simply represent different kinds of creatures, many if not most of which have long ago ceased to have any direct living descendants.

As the day has progressed, my eye for fossil material has grown steadily more attuned to the differing contours and textures that signal things, or minuscule parts of things, that millions upon millions of years ago were alive. I have learned to tell the difference between a shiny black spot of mineral and the equally black, glistening spot that denotes a single tiny fish scale. An instant glance discards the rounded, mineralized eddies of the ancient bay's muddy floor but fixes on the rounded, compressed shells of aquatic Carboniferous snails. Brushing fine gray dust from pages in this amazing book I am reading, I distinguish relatively recent impressions of plant material from the mineralized remains of algae that flourished and nourished the Bear Gulch bay's smallest animals, forming the basis of a marine food web that could sustain a community of life dominated by comparatively large and predatory vertebrates.

But still no fish. Believing may sometimes be necessary, but obviously it is not sufficient.

Bev's luck, and perhaps her eyes, are better. Near the top of a shale outcrop she finds shards that assemble, puzzlelike, into a four-inch, intact paleoniscoid. Its rear body and scales are sharply etched, although its head at some point has been turned to spaghetti by plant roots in search of mineral nutrients. Even in its damaged and paleontologically not very useful state, she clearly considers it a triumphant advance beyond my modest trove of scales, snails, and coprolites.

Soon another paleoniscoid turns up. It is in the hands of a local rancher who has putted in on an ATV, stopped to chat with Dick, and absentmindedly picked up a rock from a ledge where Lund and Bryan have once again been furiously plowing through rock. When he zooms away, the fossil fish goes into a tray in the back of the truck that holds our combined gleanings. The rancher's casual find will turn out to be the best the day has to offer.

To escape the sun, which now is steadily broiling us to a turn, Bev and I follow Eileen as she walks up canyon and bushwhacks her way into a shaded limestone fissure where days earlier she discovered a jaw fragment several inches long, from a fish as yet unidentified. It may be a form entirely new to science. The weathering walls of the narrow passage are crumbling, and the stony jaw was simply there, exposed, as she passed by. Her practiced eye grasped its import instantly, and it will be one of the more valuable discoveries of the summer.

Under yellow light at a round Formica table, Bev is listening to a tape-recording of a discussion of key events in shark evolution we had two days earlier while driving to meet Dick and Eileen. "Vertebrate jaws originally evolved from gill arches—skeletal elements that supported the gills," I hear myself say over the sound of the Subaru's wipers clunking away against the rain. "The jaw then became a hinged tool for grasping prey." On reflection, my explanation had been oversimple. How the vertebrate mouth came to include a jaw has been a central and passionately debated puzzle, heating up even more with the suggestion that thelodonts may have had jaws and been ancestral to sharks.

Jawed animals are collectively termed gnathostomes ("jawed mouth"), and undisputed fossils of jawed fishes first appear in strata that are about 420 million years old. This places the jaw's debut during a Paleozoic period called the Silurian, although it could have been earlier. Jaws were world-changing, the anatomical equivalent of the silicon chip. They didn't just expand vertebrate options for feeding, allowing animals to seize and disable larger prey. Once they were equipped with teeth, jaws allowed animals to chew or manipulate food in new ways, or to otherwise use their mouth to advantage. Jaws with teeth also could be a potent defensive weapon. The evolution of jaws was a shift that fundamentally changed the dynamics between predators and prey in the ocean world. The possibility that the first jaws graced the mouth of an ancestral shark is exciting.

Fossil discoveries around the world confirm that sharks were definitely swimming in Silurian waters, along with at least two other groups of jawed fishes. One group, acanthodians, were a lineage of mostly slender, pan-sized animals, all of which had bony spines in front of their fins and at least some of which had bone in other body parts, such as the cranium. A second group, placoderms, had tanklike armor: a dermal skeleton that sheathed the head and forebody with bony plates. Some were nearly twenty feet long. Both placoderms and acanthodians had bone in their jaws, whereas shark jaws were cartilaginous. In each of the three groups the jaw was built slightly differently. This observation, and the fact that existing and extinct, but recent, fishes display nearly a dozen basic jaw architectures, has led paleontologists to argue about what the earliest functional jaws were like—an argument that Bear Gulch might settle.

In a living shark, the upper and lower jaws consist of cartilage segments. Viewed straight on—the way we often see trophy shark jaws mounted on walls—these cartilages frame the shark's mouth with a curving arch. Ligaments and muscles firmly but flexibly suspend the upper cartilages from the brain case (the chondrocranium). Buttressing the jaw from behind is the hyoid arch, built of a curving row of abutting pieces of cartilage. At either side of the skull the outer ends of the arch attach at boxlike capsules that house a shark's inner ears. In addition to its bracing function, the hyoid arch also provides attachment points for muscles that open and close the jaws. The whole arrangement is flexible enough that the shark jaw can project back to front or expand side to side. In most species, four or five additional arches, each one built of curved, needle-shaped pieces of cartilage, support gill openings. This anatomy is found as well in ancient fossil forms; it is hundreds of millions of years old.

Jawless fishes like ostracoderms had cartilaginous arches supporting their gills, plus other cartilage struts embedded in the soft tissue of the mouth. Lampreys and hagfishes, the only living jawless species, are both built according to this ancient plan. But how did those parts—or some other ancient ones—coalesce into a structure with such world-changing possibilities?

Recently, when an American anatomist named Jon Mallatt peered into the recesses of vertebrate history, he saw a jawless mouth slowly being remodeled from the inside out. Mallatt has proposed that originally the mouths of jawless fishes were supported by a small cartilage arch. Well behind it were gill arches used, as they are today, in breathing. Over millennia, however, elements of the two first sets of gill arches were transformed, becoming longer and bulkier, encroaching on the primitive mouth—becoming, respectively, the upper and lower jaws and the hyoid arch. When early versions of these jaw components were finally in place, mouth opening and closing movements used in breathing could easily be co-opted for grasping food. And as the hyoid arch evolved into an ever more sturdy buttress, feeding could become more aggressive. Thus, more or less, the jaw may have been born.

Absent from Mallatt's anatomy lesson is a picture of a jaw that is structurally pliant enough to have spawned all the different jaw arrangements that evolved in fishes, including the unusually mobile modern shark jaw, and that is where Bear Gulch comes in.

One fossil Bear Gulch paraselachian is a fish named *Debeerius ellefseni*. A smallish animal with a rounded, pointy snout, a dorsal fin waving like a flag from a fat spine, and splotches of darkly pigmented skin extending from the top of its head to its tail, *Debeerius* has a skull with the primitive shape of a chimaera's while the types and arrangement of its teeth are sharklike. Its jaw is a versatile, nonsharky anatomical scheme called autodiastyly—a self-supported (auto), double-hung affair (diastyly). Like the "jaw" of a toy-soldier nutcracker, the upper jaw cartilage of *Debeerius* was stoutly suspended from the brain case at two anchor points. This secures the jaw to the cranium and creates a strong tool for crushing shellfish so their soft bodies could be eaten. The sturdy cartilage that in sharks makes up the hyoid brace was only a promise in *Debeerius*, waiting for the day when the survival value of forceful encounters with prey would promote its repurposing into a buttress. These details are worth knowing because, from the parts of *Debeerius*'s curious jaw and the relative positions they held, one can credibly posit the evolution of every basic type of chondrichthyan jaw. In fact, from *D. ellefseni* one can credibly trace the evolution of *every other type of jaw known to exist.* Specimens from the Bear Gulch Limestone provide the only known examples of a jaw yielding so many plausible possibilities.

If you want to know what the first jaw looked like, you probably don't have to search any further than *Debeerius.* As chondrichthyans evolved, that original plan was modified. In the holocephalan lineage the fusion of the upper jaw and cranium resulted in an arrangement anatomists call holostyly. In most sharks and other elasmobranchs a scheme called hyostyly emerged: the connections between the jaw and brain case became more movable, while the hyoid and attached muscles provided the necessary mechanical support at the back of the jaws, favoring a greater range of motion. All this remodeling had various consequences, but one of them was that sharks could take larger prey.

It is just after 8:00 A.M. on our second day, the morning air once again clear with the firm promise of heat. This morning Eileen has invited me along to a crop beyond the previous day's shale deposits where in recent days she has been moving a prodigious amount of rock. The resulting platform excavated into the canyon wall is roughly six feet by seven. As our picks strike stone they liberate slabs several feet long, almost as wide, and as thick as my wrist. Once again, albeit cautiously, hope surfaces that I will find a fish, and sure enough when one of the wrist-thick limestone pages turns, the elongated contour and shiny scales of a six-inch paleoniscoid come into view. While not a shark, in my mental hierarchy of fossil finds it ranks well above cephalopods and coprolites.

In the rising stack of ash-colored limestone I find myself imagining a world in which the mix of fishes in the sea was dramatically different from any known today. This portrait is one of the key contributions of Bear Gulch fossils to our understanding of what the world of large marine animals was like in the Carboniferous. Since Dick Lund began excavating fossils from Bear Gulch in 1968, well over five thousand specimens encompassing hundreds of extinct fish species have been recovered there, along with thousands of invertebrate animals and plants. Of the Bear Gulch fishes, only about 40 percent are bony like the little paleoniscoid now safely tucked into a collecting tray. It or one of its cousins might have been a forerunner of the twenty-five-thousand-plus species of teleost ("completely boned") fishes that dominate modern waters. Their heyday hadn't yet arrived, though, and wouldn't for another hundred million years. There are, however, five or six species of coelacanths, thick-bodied bony fishes with fleshy, paddlelike fins, recognizable cousins of the one rare living genus that still ekes out an existence in three Indo-Pacific localities. However, like *Debeerius,* the majority of Bear Gulch fish specimens are chondrichthyans. Lund believes this was the case in other continental shelf habitats as well. In short, if you were a vertebrate in the Carboniferous, chances were better than fifty-fifty that your flesh hung on a frame of cartilage. In that general sense, you were a shark.

If Dick Lund omits from his analysis animals known only from fossil teeth or fin spines, he ends up with a roster of well over four hundred chondrichthyan species. With every hundred fossils excavated, the roster grows by at least one new species. Extrapolating from these figures, Lund has concluded that "the diversity of sharks present in the small bay was as broad as that found in similar environments today among bony fishes." In fact, by the time of the Bear Gulch bay, the lavish Carboniferous adaptive radiation was in full swing and there were at least nineteen different lineages of chondrichthyans, comprising dozens of species. To the defining chondrichthyan characters—a cartilage frame, placoid scales, claspers in males—new and sometimes bizarre variations were being added. Earlier, over French toast and eggs at the café, Dick had asserted that this explosion of change was reflected in the fact that Bear Gulch chondrichthyans had "virtually every body form you can imagine in a fish." What was happening in the Carboniferous shark world was that holocephalans were in the process of splitting off from the rest of the sharks, and each of the genetic lines of chondrichthyans was evolving different kinds of changes in the same structures. The Bear Gulch bay was a microcosm of these parallel events.

Nearly all Bear Gulch chondrichthyans thus far discovered are small by modern shark standards; specimens of only two species, both cladodont sharks, are longer than a baseball bat. Yet the comparatively pint-sized lineup includes fishes with bodies shaped like eels, paddles, ribbons, water droplets, tadpoles, and spindles wide at the center and tapering to each end—some of the latter stocky, others elongated. Tails range in shape from graceful ovals and split arcs to short and blunt, from sturdy paddlelike affairs to those with the rough contours of an arrowhead. Some of the more bizarre body shapes belonged to holocephalans called petalodonts, after their peculiar teeth with the cusps aligned like flower petals. A reconstruction of one fossil Bear Gulch petalodont, *Belantsea montana,* shows a short-bodied creature that appears to be as much fin as it is fish. Two deep, arching dorsal fins trace the outlines of fleshy humps of its back, and large fanlike pectoral and pelvic fins are attached to each side.

If this were a book about fins, the next several pages could simply enumerate the characteristics of different Bear Gulch chondrichthyan varieties—including dorsal fins that are long and low to the body or that (on a male) are forward-bending tubular affairs; others are recognizably sharky with a back-curving vee. Pectoral fins appear in the guises of triangular flaps, fans, and fleshy fingers, among others. The ten specimens of teardrop-shaped *Delphyodontos dacriformes,* a holocephalan, seem to have no appreciable fins at all. Inescapable in this welter of body shapes, tails, and fin arrangements is the conclusion that Carboniferous chondrichthyans boasted a welter of specializations for moving through the water or hovering over a sponge reef.

In the shallow, mud-bottomed Bear Gulch bay the spectrum of chondrichthyan feeding strategies rivaled that of body architectures. The mud burial of Bear Gulch organisms was so gentle, leaving bodies so undisturbed, that many fossils disclose details of the entire body, ranging from the positions of blood vessels and internal organs to dentition and the structure of the animal's jaw. Correlated with Lund's other gleanings, the information coalesces into an image of a tropical bay pulsing with roving predators and elusive prey, and of a multitude of feeding adaptations for many niches. The bay's larger cladodont sharks, including *Stethacanthus,* have formidable piercing teeth for impaling prey destined to be gulped whole. Fossils of some paraselachians display sharp, piercing teeth fused into whorls, or teeth with multiple peaks, ridges, and grooves that could hold prey tightly. Certain of the Bear Gulch sharks had different types of teeth in different parts of the jaw—for instance, small grasping ones in front, followed by piercing cuspids and grinding molars. A comprehensive dental package of catch, kill, crush. Some of the fused, rather rigid jaws of the bay's holocephalans served as platforms for broad, anvil-like teeth ideal for crushing the outer armor of snails and bivalves. It was, and still is, efficient dentition for fishes extracting a living from shell-armored creatures.

Sex also drives evolutionary alternatives, and in that regard the fossils of Bear Gulch indicate two things. First, at some early fork in the evolutionary road, cartilaginous fishes operated under conditions that favored the evolution of internal fertilization—a complicated and biologically expensive mechanism for having sex. The evolution of paired claspers facilitated the delivery of sperm to egg. No other vertebrate manages sex quite this way, which is why claspers are considered to be an ancient and defining feature of the whole chondrichthyan class. They are, however, just one of several ways Bear Gulch chondrichthyans could tell the boys from the girls. Sexual dimorphism—differences in the ways males and females are built—was common. As Dick Lund has observed with scholarly detachment, "remarkable differences in secondary sexual characters" show up in certain fossils, from dramatic sex-related variations in body size to the sizes and shapes of fins and a host of other features.

Not only do males of all species have claspers, but the cladodonts have a spine in front of the first dorsal fin. In *Falcatus falcatus* males, the fin curves forward like a unicorn's horn; one of Lund's favorite discoveries is a fossilized *F. falcatus* male and female pair who were lethally clobbered by sediments during the act of mating, the male's first dorsal fin in the female's mouth. (He once commissioned a T-shirt decorated with a drawing of the pair.) Atop their heads *F. falcatus* and other male Bear Gulch stethacanthids also had fields of large, protruding scales that look like, and probably felt like, the fine teeth of a cheese grater. A holocephalan with the mouth-filling name *Harpagofututor* had long spines that look like a set of crab claws projecting out over its eyes.

For me, the Bear Gulch bay symbolizes both a culmination and a beginning in shark history. The lineup of its wonderfully different chondrichthyans was the fruit of a 130-million-year odyssey that began, possibly with thelodonts, with the laying down of a biological scheme for animals with a light but strong cartilaginous skeleton, placoid scales that could be refashioned into teeth and other structures, internal fertilization, and other ancient chondrichthyan features. The journey may well have included evolution of the first, amazingly adaptable jaw. Possibilities bloomed in the Devonian with its roll call of stethacanthids, cladodont sharks, ctenacanths, xenacanths, and others, each suited to a specialized ecological niche in an increasingly complex aquatic world. They flowered again in the Carboniferous as holocephalans arose, flourished, and ultimately parted evolutionary company with their cousin elasmobranchs, and as hybodont sharks appeared on the stage for the first time. And while the Bear Gulch bay itself was short-lived, for millions of years beyond it chondrichthyans of all kinds would continue on successfully in the seas and in freshwater.

A new era in shark evolution dawned about 30 million years after the demise of the Bear Gulch bay. That is when, in a time frame that brackets the Permian period 290 to 250 million years ago, a wave of extinctions eliminated an estimated 95 percent of Earth's living species. The search for causes usually focuses on movements of the planet's crustal plates and accompanying shifts in climates and water temperatures, both of which would have brought to bear enormous selection pressures on marine animals. When the decimation was over, the surviving chondrichthyans had diverged onto sharply different paths. Holocephalans, so diverse in the shallow Bear Gulch bay, had been reduced to a modest handful of species; today there are fewer than thirty, nearly all living in the deep sea. Early elasmo-branchs, the stethacanthid and ctenacanth sharks, also had dwindled. As the Mesozoic era dawned, though, other kinds of sharks were evolving to fill the open ecological niches. The reign of "new sharks," the neoselachian ancestors of modern sharks, was beginning.

The route to a neoselachian body was the distillation of key physical traits as cladodont features had given way to hybodont ones. Along with differently shaped teeth, the shark snout elongated and the jaw became freer from the muscles and ligaments that had bound it to the cranium. The shark jaw now was markedly protrusible and, braced by the hyoid arch, it could move outward and sideways. Some shark forms were also evolving mineral-hardened vertebrae as cartilage cross-walls developed at intervals along the notochord, enclosing it at those places. With time, the constrictions expanded and sharks gained the physiological means to calcify them into a series of hard vertebrae that surrounded the overlying nerve cord and provided a firm internal support to which swimming muscles could attach. The shark body, increasingly streamlined, came to be sheathed in a smooth blanket of placoid scales, and fin spines slowly disappeared; of living elasmo-branchs, only the spiny dogfish and some of its relatives and Port Jackson sharks still have those relics of the primitive past.

In fossil strata younger than about 130 million years before present, the characteristic teeth of hybodont sharks vanish. We know almost nothing for certain about the demise of those animals, except that while they were fading into history a sister lineage of sleek sharks with powerful mobile jaws was gaining a foothold throughout the marine world. By the beginning of the current geological period, the Ceno-zoic, nearly all the families of modern sharks would be established.

Before the Mesozoic ended, however, two more major chapters in shark evolution were written. One was the emergence, at least 70 million years ago, of large, open-ocean sharks, the forerunners of makos and white sharks. And while Jurassic dinosaurs and mammals were evolving on land, in some other sharks certain characters were becoming transformed. The body was flattening, the tail's bulk being whittled down. Pectoral fins were enlarging into muscular and powerful propulsive engines. In the Jurassic, a new elasmobranch lineage evolved, the batoids—rays and skates. They eventually came to be built like swimming wings, the body flat and the mouth facing downward, with broad, rounded or tapering pectoral fins propelling the whole ahead of a slender, trailing tail. Today batoids comprise about six hundred living species whereas sharks are represented by only about four hundred.

By midday our digging is done and Dick is supervising preparations for closing the summer's operations. The back of his truck is crammed once again with picks, brushes, wunderbars, and gloves, plus the morning's meager tray of fossil material—the paleoniscoid fish Eileen and I found plus two more unearthed by Dick and Bryan. We retrace our track across the high pastures, through the series of post-and-wire gates to the spot where in the cool morning Bev and I had left the Subaru. Then we follow Dick's Suburban down the winding hardtop, past the modest ranch homes and wildflowers, and on into the diggers' camp. My wife and I camp simply, and we are surprised to see an elaborate tent village with crude but effective shower facilities and a finely turned out, covered kitchen. A few paces away a large canvas tent shelters the season's stone treasures awaiting packing for the trip home, which will be followed by months of painstaking analysis and cataloging. The light inside is dim but still adequate for Eileen to methodically tick off the mix of petrified fishes, scales and coprolites, shrimps and snails, her prize jaw and all the other creature remains gleaned from weeks of backbreaking excavation. In the space of two days we have been privileged to glimpse a world that existed for only a speck on the geological time scale, but which embraced a pivotal moment when sharks were taking leave of other chondrichthyans and embarking on their unique evolutionary voyage. I stop for a moment to let my fingers brush some of the cool chunks of limestone laid out on a camp table, then exit into the hot afternoon sun.

2 *The Players*

I stand pouring a bottle of ice water over Bev's cropped blond hair. We both are on the verge of heat prostration brought about by the midday sun that is toasting this scrubby expanse of Mexican desert. In the shade of a large white awning advertising Tecate beer, we are resting and rehydrating to the bright sounds of a mariachi band. These guys are the real deal, outfitted with straw cowboy hats, boots, silver belt buckles, and salsa-red shirts barely covering bulging middle-aged bellies. To one side, a bank of Mexican women are serving up stewed beef with chiles, rice, frijoles, and homemade tortillas, while children dart between wooden picnic tables and study the sweating gringos.

We are guests at a raucous lunch party at the end of a dusty track outside the hamlet of El Cién, Baja California del Sur, fifty miles northwest of La Paz where the American Elasmobranch Society is holding its annual meeting. Even the town's revolver-toting sheriff has shown up, managing to look impeccably starched and pressed in one hundred plus–degree heat. The host for our expedition, Shelton Pleasants Applegate, is one of the world's foremost authorities on fossil shark teeth, and the cactus-dotted hills around El Cién have been his laboratory. Unlike Bear Gulch fossils, however, those from El Cién are a mere 25 to 40 million years old. Because all the modern groups of sharks were present 30 million years ago, and haven't changed much since, most of the teeth one finds at El Cién are very similar to those of sharks in twenty-first-century seas. Now as then, an animal's teeth reflect its mode of obtaining food, and hence a key element of its lifestyle.

The origin of modern sharks lies somewhere in the murky recesses of the early and middle Jurassic, some 200 million years ago. Even by then, the two basic modern shark lineages, Squalea and Galea, had diverged. Sharks have recently been divided into these two lines of descent because of basic differences in their overall body form, the anatomy of their crania, and other features. Galeomorphs encompass four shark orders (the scientific names are noted in parentheses): the requiem sharks (Carcharhiniformes), the mackerel sharks (Lamniformes), the carpet sharks (Orectolobiformes), and the bullhead or Port Jackson sharks (Heterodontiformes). Squalomorphs include the cow sharks (Hexanchiformes), bramble sharks (Echinorhiniformes), dogfish sharks (Squaliformes), the angel sharks (Squatiniformes), and the saw sharks (Pristiophoriformes). Allied with this lineage are the batoids: skates and rays and their relatives (Batoidea), which collectively represent the most diverse radiation of modern elasmobranchs. When sharks swam over the terrain of El Cién, it was probably the steeply sloping bottom of a tropical sea, and paleontologists probing the now-dry earth there have found teeth from most of the major living types of sharks and some rays.

"If you're trying to construct an elasmobranch encyclopedia," Shelley Applegate is saying, "the place you've got to start is with the scientific nomenclature." A native of Virginia, Applegate speaks with a euphonious Richmond drawl. "An animal's classification encapsulates its whole evolutionary story." He is sitting at a large picnic table strewn with El Cién shark teeth, fanning himself with a paper plate and tapping both feet to the thrum of guitars. Now in his early seventies, with flowing white hair, he has spent four decades analyzing, devising, and revising the scheme of shark evolutionary relationships.

When biologists describe a creature, it is assigned to both a genus and a species—the genus being simply a set of closely related species that are similar in their outward features and underlying genetics. Closely related genera are grouped into families, and families into orders, creating a hierarchical classification. For instance, the great white shark, *Carcharodon carcharias,* is in the genus *Carcharodon.* The tradition of using a Latin binomial to name a species was started by the eighteenth-century Swedish naturalist Carl von Linné, whose own name was latinized to Linnaeus. At the time, knowledge of elasmobranchs was so sparse that the Swede simply assigned all sharks to one genus, *Squalus,* and all rays and skates to another, *Raja.* (In fact Linnaeus based his fish classification on one devised by his ichthyologist friend Peter Artedi who, as legend has it, met an untimely death by drowning in an Amsterdam canal after a night of reveling.) Moving beyond the genus level, *C. carcharias* belongs in the family Lamnidae. Advancing another step, different lamnid families are grouped in the order Lamniformes, the mackerel sharks. Because evolutionary relationships are postulated in part by comparing the physical features of living creatures, classification above the species level can be a tricky and often controversial business. Classifications noted here may reflect only one of several respectable views on the subject of where a given species of shark fits in the overall scheme.

Sharks whose remains are found at El Cién were part of the third great elasmobranch adaptive radiation—a mid-Cenozoic burst of new species in the geologic-time equivalent of an eye blink. Today approximately 360 species of living sharks and 456 species of batoids have been recognized, but because new ones are still being discovered, the total number of living elasmobranch species probably tops out at about a thousand. Of the approximately ten orders of modern sharks, nearly all have representatives at El Cién. Most are galeomorphs, like nurse sharks, great whites, thresher sharks, tiger sharks, and hammerheads. One bit of history shared by most of these animals is that they evolved and diversified in the Earth's warm or temperate seas.

Prime examples are sharks of the order Carcharhiniformes, which swim in tropical waters everywhere on the planet and account for more than half of living sharks. Probably best known are the streamlined requiem sharks that dominate tropical coasts. This family includes the tiger and bull sharks, sandbars and duskies, lemon sharks, blue sharks, silky sharks, spinners, oceanic whitetips, sharpnose sharks, and a host of others. Most are medium-sized to large—in the three- to eight-foot range—although some, including the feared tigers and bulls, grow much larger.

The requiem shark resumé is packed with superlatives. For example, the blue shark ranges over more of the world ocean than any other chondrichthyan, consuming masses of squid and small fishes. In the course of a year, a single animal may migrate around an entire ocean basin. Any mariner who has spent much time at sea has observed blues cruising along, their front dorsal fin and graceful arched tail breaking the water's surface, the dark blue skin of the shark's slender back blending to brilliant blue on the sides and pure white below.

The most infamous of all elasmobranchs, next to the great white, are tiger and bull sharks. Tiger sharks (*Galeocerdo cuvier*) can exceed eighteen feet. Such large adults regularly leave the tropics in summer and migrate to temperate latitudes when the water there warms. Then they turn up even as far north as the Ambrose entrance channel a few miles from where the Statue of Liberty overlooks New York harbor. Bearing faint dark vertical bars along their sides (which fade with age), tiger sharks have big, blunt heads and broad, serrated, backward-curving teeth.

Tiger sharks occasionally interpret humans as potential prey, but by educated estimates bull sharks (*Carcharhinus leucas*) may be the culprits in more attacks than any other shark (although they are officially ranked third in shark-attack records). One reason is that they inhabit shallow water along coasts and rivers, where people are also. Bull sharks are famous for their ability to spend long periods in the brackish or fresh water of warm rivers like the Amazon, and in a few freshwater lakes. In the 1730s, John Atkins, a British sea captain on a slave-trading voyage to West Africa, recorded encounters with sharks in a river emptying into the eastern Atlantic from Sierra Leone. "Shirks [*sic*] very much infest the mouth of this river," he wrote in his log. "The most bold and ravenous of the watery tribe . . . we have catched three in less than half an hour." With a nondescript gray, chunky body, a mature bull shark is the middle linebacker of the shark world. Its small, piggy eyes peer out over a short, blunt snout, and its upper jaws sport erect, triangular, heavily serrated teeth. Its body may measure eight or nine feet long, and eight or nine feet in circumference—the equivalent of a ninety-six-inch waist. Along with other carcharhinids, such as sandbar and dusky sharks, tiger and bull sharks have been objects of intensive and often devastating fisheries.

Hammerhead sharks are also carcharhiniforms, and teeth from at least three species have been sifted from the dirt at El Cién. Hammerheads and their sister species, the bonnetheads, have the basic carcharhinid body plan but have evolved a cephalofoil—the striking, flat, lateral extensions of the head. In cross section the "hammer" looks like a wing, and like a wing it provides lift and maneuverability as the animal swims. The most bizarre member of this group is probably the winghead shark (*Eusphyra blochii*), an odd, almost T-shaped little species found along coasts of India, Southeast Asia, and northern Australia, and whose head is nearly half as wide as its three-foot body is long. By contrast, the great hammerhead (*Sphyrna mokarran*), a stingray connoisseur, can reach eighteen feet in length. Other species generally fall somewhere in between.

• • •

Other carcharhinid groups include catsharks, false catsharks, weasel sharks, and houndsharks. Catsharks, named for their oblong, catlike eyes, are small, slender sharks with two dorsal fins set way back on the body. Many have chainlike or spotted markings, like a child's connect-the-dots game. They are adapted to cold, usually deeper water along the outer continental shelf and slope, with some species living two thousand feet or more beneath the surface. I once observed a common species, the misnamed chain dogfish (*Scyliorhinus retifer*), on a dive in the submersible *Alvin* off the Virginia coast. The little twelve- to fifteen-inch sharks spent most of their time resting on the sandy bottom at six hundred feet. Catsharks are common in aquaria because they are small and relatively inactive, and they do well in captivity. The false catshark (*Pseudotriakis microdon*) is a skinny, rubbery, deepwater animal the color of dark cocoa and can grow up to twelve feet long. It has an unusual, elongated first dorsal fin that calls to mind the xenacanth sharks of 260 million years ago. Apparently false catsharks aren't fussy eaters; on a research cruise to the Canary Islands, I culled a Coke can and a potato from the stomach of one we captured on a deep longline.

What houndsharks lack in size—only the largest come close to six feet—they make up for as a commodity. Each year millions of tons are caught and sold for their meat, for the oil in their livers, to be ground up into meal for animal feed, and for their fins, which are sold for shark fin soup. Weasel sharks, all denizens of tropical Indo-Pacific ocean coasts, physically resemble their cousin requiem sharks, like sandbars and tiger sharks. One weasel shark genus, *Hemipristis,* once flourished over a wide swath of the world ocean; its teeth are plentiful at El Cién and in fossil deposits of similar age elsewhere. Today, though, just a single survivor, the "fossil shark" (*Hemipristis elongatus*), occurs in the Indian Ocean, where it is widely harvested in artisanal fisheries.

Of all lamniforms, the family that draws the most public interest is Lamnidae, the mackerel sharks. Modern lamnids include mako sharks, salmon sharks, porbeagles, and the notorious great white shark. The latter is the largest living predatory fish, but it pales in comparison with its ancestors. Throughout the Middle Ages, and perhaps even earlier, people living on and around the Mediterranean island of Malta would occasionally find peculiar objects that tapered to a point from a thick and broad base, the angled edges studded with tiny serrations. The strange rocks came to be called "tongue stones" and could cover a person's palm. In the 1660s, a physician named Nicholas Steno, who spent his spare time dissecting animals that included Mediterranean sharks, was observant enough to propose that tongue stones were actually fossilized shark teeth. In fact, Steno had stumbled on the remains of *Carcharodon megalodon,* a giant-toothed white shark that reached an astonishing length of perhaps fifty-six feet. "Megalodon," as shark aficionados call it, is an extinct lamnid and the elasmobranch equivalent of *Tyrannosaurus rex.* The largest *C. megalodon* tooth found to date, now in the Field Museum of Natural History in Chicago, is nearly five inches wide at its base and about six and a half inches tall.

The teeth of today's white sharks are proportionately huge triangular cutting tools edged with deep serrations, designed to carve great chunks of blubber and muscle from seals, whales, and dolphins. The sharks themselves probably can grow to about twenty-one feet, although their maximum size isn't known for sure. In fact, we shark scientists haven't begun to really understand much of their basic biology. What *is* known relates largely to their habitat. For instance, white sharks are rare in the tropics because they are adapted to patrol temperate continental and island shelves, from cooler northern waters off Japan, California, and Nova Scotia to the southerly coasts of South Africa and Australia. Although groups of great white sharks sometimes aggregate when they happen on rich food sources such as a seal colony or a whale carcass, sightings and meager tracking data suggest that for the most part great whites navigate the oceans alone. Attacks on humans have spurred studies of white shark feeding behavior, but reliable data on other potentially revealing topics are harder to come by. Simple things we don't know, for example, include how abundant great whites are; where, how, and how often they reproduce; or how far they range in their seasonal movements.

Turbo-charged swimmers with immensely strong jaws, great whites are effective hunters of their large natural prey. The qualifier "natural" is important, because while white shark meals encompass marine animals from seals, sea lions, and porpoises to other sharks, large bony fishes, sea turtles, and carrion, large land mammals such as humans are *not* the sort of prey white sharks have evolved to hunt. The fact that people, surfboards, and small watercraft sometimes draw the notice of white sharks (or any shark) is a fluke, the artifact of a recent ecological revolution—the coastal invasion of recreational humans—for which neither the sharks nor the humans have been prepared.

The license plate on my field vehicle reads ISURUS—the genus of the shortfin mako shark (*Isurus oxyrinchus*), also a lamnid and surely the most beautiful shark in the sea. Cobalt blue above, pure white beneath, makos can grow large, to ten feet or more, and have a forbidding set of teeth befitting their role as hunter of agile tunas, bluefish, and even swordfish. The day before our group trek to El Cién, my friend José Castro, a natural-born collector whose research specialty is shark reproduction, had accompanied Shelley Applegate out to the site and picked up a heavy, curved fossil tooth about two inches tall, which had graced the jaw of a now-extinct mako. The next morning, while the rest of us scrabbled in the dirt, José strolled around with the impressive tooth in his pocket. Torpedolike swimmers, makos have endeared themselves to the sportfishing fraternity because, when hooked, they run like tunas and jump like marlin. More than one hooked *Isurus* has vaulted into the cockpit of its would-be captor's boat, wreaking havoc while the crew bailed overboard.

If the mako's body is a torpedo, the round, deeper torso of its cousin the salmon shark (*Lamna ditropus*) suggests a battleship's artillery round. Ranging throughout the cold North Pacific, where Pacific salmon are a prime food source, the largest salmon sharks measure in at about nine feet long. On the other side of North America, in the cold North Atlantic, and also in the cool southern Indian Ocean, the similarly large and round-bodied porbeagles (*Lamna nasus*) hunt pelagic schooling fishes like herrings. Porbeagles themselves have been one of the most heavily hunted sharks, especially by long-liners who have marketed the fine meat (much like swordfish) and more recently the fins. In the 1960s in the Atlantic, Norwegians exploited the fishery to the point of collapse. After a thirty-year respite, in the late 1990s, history predictably repeated itself in the western Atlantic when Canadian and American commercial fishermen did the same.

Mexican waters have always held sharks. According to José Castro, who spent several months researching the matter, ancient Mayans may even have bequeathed the word "shark" to the English-speaking world, from their word *xoc* (pronounced shock), meaning a shark of large size. Twenty years and thousands of shark teeth after Shelley Applegate first began exploring it, the rocky earth of the El Cién formation is still spitting out shark teeth. Several hours before the mariachis and lunch appeared, Bev, I, and the others had trooped behind Applegate's ample straw-hatted figure to an expanse of small hills and gullies. Even in the building morning heat, he had kept up an amiable patter of instructions.

"The mad-scramble Easter egg method is a time-honored way of finding exposed teeth—a good method if you are a single-tooth postage-stamp shark toothologist," he had suggested. "Don't turn over large rocks or logs unless you're interested in meeting a rattlesnake. Those who want to can use a sieve to sift through shovels full of dirt—that's the more *scientific* method. Save any other curious objects, like fossil shells. They can help us understand the paleoenvironment. Anybody who finds a natural set of teeth wins a grand prize. Associated sets are more likely, but still rare; we've been over this area a lot. Drink your water. We're all in this together, so look out for your neighbor."

Teeth, which tell us so much about how an animal makes its living, are generally the only part of a shark calcified enough to hold up during fossilization, and they are the most common of all fossils, as well as the most common remnants of living sharks. Rarely, whole sets of shark teeth turn up in fossil deposits; more commonly, teeth from dead sharks are scattered by scavengers or currents. Add to this the fact that sharks have been shedding and replacing their teeth for most of their history and the inevitable conclusion is that there are a lot more fossil shark teeth around than there ever were sharks to begin with. Despite this obvious reality, over the years shark paleontologists would find differing teeth and on that slim basis describe new species. The so-called type specimen—the evidence deemed sufficient to propose the existence of a shark species—was a tooth in a tray in a museum.

Shelley Applegate was one of the first researchers to be discomfited by this state of affairs. He reasoned that different teeth in a shark's mouth are adapted for slightly different functions, so they naturally differ slightly in size and shape. For instance, lateral teeth, in the sides of a shark's jaw, have a different form and food-handling function than do teeth farther forward, which are literally on the front lines during prey capture. With an eye educated in dusty southeastern fossil beds, in the 1960s Applegate convinced the National Science Foundation to fund a project in which he would prepare a detailed description of the characteristics of different tooth types in the jaw of the modern sand tiger shark (*Carcharias taurus*), then compare them to fossil teeth from the sand tiger's extinct forerunners. In the summer of 1962 I had played a minor part in that scholarly adventure by helping Shelley collect sand tigers off the coast of New Jersey. Later we rendezvoused for a trip to Venice, Florida, where there had been a commercial shark fishery during World War II. With a puny budget and ridiculously crude equipment, we had set out in a small wooden skiff equipped with a cooler of beer, a bucket of bait, a short ten-hook longline, and a loaded shotgun. After several beers' worth of fishing, the afternoon became memorable when a huge bull shark slammed one of our hooks and promptly began towing us toward the center of the Gulf of Mexico. At the time, the shotgun seemed an ideal tool for dispatching the shark, but as I took aim and fired the skiff lurched sharply in a swell and I lost my footing. The next thing I knew, I was lying on my back in bilge water in the bottom of the boat, staring up at a gaping hole blasted in the gunwale. With a second shot the hook pulled out, leaving me and Shelley to watch with a mix of relief and consternation as the shark escaped into the shadowy green water.

Other fishing expeditions were more successful, and Shelley Applegate ultimately was able to delineate both the large and subtle differences in the full set of a modern sand tiger's teeth. He went on to develop a method for reliably assembling *fossil* shark teeth into sets. The eventual outcome was a wholesale overhaul of museum shark-tooth trays. In the case of the Lamniformes, for instance, Applegate sorted through fossil teeth that supposedly represented more than a thousand different species and discovered that they actually represented tooth *sets* of just a few dozen. The work not only revamped the way paleontologists approached their exploration of fossil sites, but also helped spur new thinking about the evolutionary relationships among the sharks that swim in the seas today.

At 10:30 A.M. it is beginning to seem, at least thermally, like a morning in hell. Under Shelley's guidance, our little group has begun scouring a pebbly hillside. I adopt a search technique that involves slowly walking from one likely looking spot to the next, hoping to spy obvious shark teeth lying on the surface. Bev quickly opts for the detail-oriented, sit-and-sift method. Finding a chubby ocotillo, she plops in its sparse shadow and proceeds to scour every square inch of sand around her. Then, on to the next ocotillo. Her initial discovery is a three-quarter-inch-long sand tiger tooth the color of butterscotch. Its arched base nearly intact, the tooth's slender central cusp spikes upward buttressed on either side by a small cusplet. I will eventually turn up a respectably stout, gracefully curving mako tooth, a *Hemipristis* specimen, and my own cache of sand tiger teeth.

Plentiful in the ancient seas of El Cién, sand tigers still strongly resemble the ancestral creatures from which all modern mackerel sharks probably evolved. Large but slightly soft-muscled, they have long, recurved, awl-like teeth that are perfectly adapted for capturing smaller fishes. Sharks often bear different common names in different parts of the world; sand tigers, for instance, are known as ragged-tooth sharks in South Africa and in Australia as gray nurse sharks. The species is protected in both countries, as well as along the east coast of the United States because human harvesting has reduced its numbers to the point of population collapse. Found in most of the world's shallow, warm-temperate and coastal seas, sand tigers are among several sharks that are highly vulnerable to fishing pressure because females produce only a couple of pups once every year or two.

Some other lamniforms elude common preconceptions of what a shark looks like. The crocodile shark (*Pseudocarcharias kamoharai*) is a compact oceanic animal with huge green eyes adapted for the dim, midocean "twilight zone" where it lives. The flabby goblin shark (*Mitsukurina owstoni*) lives close to the bottom in cold water down to about fifteen hundred feet. A weird pinkish white, it has a bizarre long snout that juts out like a fleshy, pointed paddle over a jaw full of thin teeth that call fishhooks to mind. Also in this order is the recently described *Megachasma pelagios,* the megamouth shark. Discovered in 1976, these big, open-ocean filter feeders have a bulbous head protruding from a sausage-shaped torso, while a massive and gracefully tapering caudal fin brings up the rear. The largest megamouths captured thus far have measured around sixteen feet long, their mouth a three-foot-wide cavern with scores of tiny teeth and a multitude of gill rakers that are used to sieve shrimp and other planktonic animals from the water. Megamouths apparently spend most of their lives negotiating the water column between depths of 150 and 1,000 feet. The first, unlucky one to be caught, in the central Pacific Ocean, had become tangled in parachutes deployed as sea anchors by a U.S. Navy ship.

Other huge lamniforms are the basking sharks (*Cetorhinus maximus*), which can grow to thirty feet or more. Basking sharks spend part of their time at high latitudes in cool regions of the ocean; an early description of one species came from a Norwegian naturalist who examined a specimen caught off the Norwegian fishing port of Trondheim in 1765. Then as now, basking sharks migrate north-south and on- and offshore as the seasons change, spending summers in higher latitudes and winters in more temperate ones. The group's common name comes from the fact that basking sharks often cruise slowly at the surface, sometimes in large schools, ram feeding as their gaping mouths passively gather in plankton like giant pool skimmers. This surface-swimming behavior, coupled with the conspicuous size of basking sharks, has made them pathetically easy targets for harpoon fisheries.

Close to noon, my thoughts have turned to cold beer and the sparkling Sea of Cortez, by the crow's reckoning just a skip and a jump to the southeast. A day earlier Bev and I had chartered a small Mexican *panga* for a day of fishing. Just at dawn we'd met the captain and his mate and sped out of the cove in front of our hotel—a tile-roofed stucco edifice called the Perla—and for the next hour we'd motored quietly, catching bait fish for the live well and watching the round hills across the bay turn chameleonlike from black to marine blue to pink and finally tan. Later, after scoring five big, iridescent dorados and sharing the skipper's lunch of fish tacos, we had turned for port when a large, dark, elongated form rocketed into the air a hundred yards away. The fish rotated its body in a short spiral as it completed its arc back into the sea. I realized I was seeing an event few shark researchers ever witness in the flesh: the legendary acrobatics of a breaching thresher shark, famously photographed by the writer and avid sport fisher Zane Grey in the 1930s.

Even when they are not vaulting skyward, thresher sharks are easy to recognize because their tails are almost as long as the rest of their bodies. The common thresher (*Alopius vulpinus*) and bigeye thresher (*Alopius superciliosus*) live in both the Atlantic and Pacific oceans, a species called the pelagic thresher (*Alopius pelagicus*) is found only in the Pacific, and there is genetic evidence—DNA from tissue removed from a fish that wasn't examined more closely—that a fourth, still undescribed, species may exist there also. The bigeye is a deepwater fish, and like a lot of fishes that have evolved where there isn't much light, it has huge eyes that look a little like giant marbles. Behind each orb is an elaborate network of blood vessels—a *rete mirabile* or "wonderful net"—that may help keep the shark's brain warm in cold water, as a similar anatomical adaptation does in swordfishes. A thresher's long tail is a hunting adaptation. Using it initially like a hockey stick to herd schooling fishes into a close formation, the shark then slaps its tail into the school. With luck (for the shark) the strike will be hard enough to stun at least a few fish, which the thresher can consume at leisure on its next pass. When we catch threshers on the longline, very often they're hooked in the tail because they've come up to slap the bait.

Some of the most primitive of all modern sharks belong to the galeomorph order Orectolobiformes—carpet sharks. Limited almost entirely to the Indo-Pacific, carpet sharks generally have small mouths and short sensory barbels dangling from their nostrils. Examples are wobbegongs, reef sharks that go back 150 million years to the Jurassic. A wobbegong's flattened physique, beginning with its vertically compressed head and body, is part of a suite of adaptations that help suit it to the life of an ambush predator. Mottled skin and a fringe of skin flaps on either side of the head help break up the shark's profile— an important advantage for a would-be ambusher that, depending on the species, can grow up to twelve feet long! Wobbegongs also have broad, fleshy pectoral fins that they use like fat arms to help ease themselves across the bottom or from pool to pool in shallows. Other shallow-water bottom dwellers are the chunky, tannish nurse sharks. Nocturnal hunters, when daylight streams onto the reef these animals sometimes pile atop each other on the bottom like sleeping puppies. In the entire Atlantic Ocean there are only two orectolobiforms, the nurse shark *Ginglymostoma cirratum* and the whale shark *Rhincodon typus*.

The whale shark is strikingly different from any other shark on Earth. Not only are these the largest fish in the ocean, reaching lengths of up to sixty feet, but when a whale shark's wide mouth opens it forms a cavern into which clouds of plankton, squid, and small schooling fishes are sucked and then swallowed while the water in which they were swimming is flushed out through the shark's comb-like gillrakers. Famous for their white spots and soaring upper tail fin, whale sharks range through the tropical waters of the world ocean, often traveling at or near the surface. They migrate thousands of miles across the open sea and into coastal areas where dozens may congregate if the feeding is good.

The fourth and final galeomorph order, Heterodontiformes, was discovered in the 1790s off Port Jackson, Australia, where a shark representing this order's lone family, Heterodontidae, was collected. Port Jackson sharks (*Heterodontus portusjacksoni*) and their relatives are also called bullhead sharks because they all have some version of a short, blunt, club-shaped head without a whisper of streamlining. They look incredibly ancient, partly because they are one of only two living shark orders to have spines (the other being spiny dogfishes, Squaliformes) in front of their dorsal fins. When you look at a bullhead, you know from the shape of its head, its downward-pointing mouth, its short, fat body, and its chunky, mollusk-crushing teeth that this must also be a benthic animal, adapted for life near the bottom.

My field notes from the winter of 1968 contain the following entry:

> *Fishing vessel* Sea Breeze
> *30 miles east of Ocean City, Maryland*
> *February 1968*

The big trawl winches groaned loudly and the cables popped and snapped under the strain of hauling back several tons of fish in our trawl net. As the net was brought alongside and the big wood and steel doors were hooked into place, we realized that the net was hanging straight down, a dead weight full to the mouth with spiny dogfish. Had our catch consisted of bony fishes like sea bass or porgies, the rising net would have popped to the surface before it reached the boat because the gas-filled swim bladders that such fish possess would have expanded like balloons as the pressure decreased. Instead, these dogfish, each weighing eight to ten pounds and several tons in the aggregate, were like so many bricks in a bag. This catch was so large we could not begin to lift the net on board without destroying it or the tackle used to hoist it. So, we detached the stout bull rope tied on one end to a trawl door and on the other to a heavy rope that encircles the cod end of the net, and began to slowly haul the bag to the surface. Once we had the bag we untied the line that cinched the cod end shut, like opening the strings of a purse. As the cod end opened, the sharks swam out by the thousands, free again.

Scrawled in blue ink, these words were written as my coworkers and I were discovering that spiny dogfish (*Squalus acanthias*) then made up an average of 50 percent of the biomass in our trawl catches—mind-boggling abundance. These are small sharks, with spines in front of their dorsal fins. Like most squaloids, they are denizens of cold water, spending summers in the Gulf of Maine and even farther north in the Gulf of St. Lawrence and the Grand Banks. The species occurs globally in cold temperate latitudes and once upon a time may have been the most abundant species of shark on Earth. Overfishing now has robbed them of that distinction, but in part because the spiny dogfish inhabits temperate coastal areas and has long been the target of fisheries, it still is probably the best-known representative of the Squalea, the second great lineage of elasmobranchs. Most other squalomorphs are limited to the dim depths of the world's continental slopes, the bathyal zone, where, as in high latitudes, the water is always cold.

Beyond ecological differences, squalomorphs differ markedly from galeomorphs in certain body features. For instance, like many Paleozoic elasmobranchs, the sharks in the order Hexanchiformes—cow sharks and their distant relatives, the frilled sharks—have six or seven gill slits but only a single dorsal fin. The various species of cow sharks have a blocky physique, can grow up to fifteen feet long, and live mostly in deep water. Frilled sharks (*Chlamydoselachus anguineus*) seem to prefer deep canyons and the submerged edges of continents.

Their six-foot bodies are sinuous and eely, and their mouths are located at the tip of the snout like those of cladodont sharks—elasmobranchs that were extinct by 320 million years ago. A frilled shark's gill slits run like ruffles under its head from one side to the other.

Dogfishes and their relatives (Squaliformes) all lack an anal fin and many have fin spines. The group's size range is enormous, from sleeper sharks (*Somniosus microcephalus*) that can grow large enough (roughly twenty feet) to consume an entire reindeer carcass, to the spined pygmy shark (*Squaliolus laticaudus*), a peewee species that barely tops six inches. The almost as tiny cookiecutter shark (*Isistius brasiliensis*) and much larger kitefin are known for their snub noses, powerful jaws, and dentition that can remove a neat spherical chunk of blubber or flesh from prey like whales and swordfishes.

The upper continental slope in most tropical and temperate seas is dominated by small to medium-sized dogfishes, like the gray gulper shark (*Centrophorus granulosus*). Its close relatives include fishes like *Deania*—the bird-beaked shark named for its elongate pointy snout—and the lantern sharks (in the genus *Etmopterus*), some of which are less than a foot long. Their coal-colored skin is pitted with photophores, tiny light-producing organs that may be used as beacons to locate suitable mates in the nearly lightless depths where lantern sharks live. In deep tropical waters, prickly dogfishes (*Oxynotus bruniensis*) are the cartoon characters of the shark world, with a camelback, unusually large, thick scales that make their skin coarse and thorny, and two broad, high dorsal fins that trail aft like banners from thick fin spines. Odd as such features are on a small fish, such a deep body and large fin spines probably are effective adaptations for deterring predators.

Two orders of squalomorphs, the saw sharks (Pristiophoriformes) and the angel sharks (Squatiniformes), have been tied closely to the batoids. Saw sharks encompass a handful of uncommon deepwater species. They have a short, slender body, broad pectoral fins, and a long, tapered snout studded with many thin teeth of different sizes. Twin barbels that hang down from the snout like a mustache probably sense chemical stimuli from prey. By contrast, the tropical, coastal angel sharks are adapted to ambush their piscine prey. They have a flattened body with huge winglike pectoral fins that extend up to the sides of the head, an adaptation for covering themselves with sand on the bottom. Together with a mouth positioned at the tip of the snout and eyes essentially on the top of the head, the angel shark physique seems to bridge the basic body designs of sharks and rays.

One hundred and forty million years ago in the Jurassic, when dinosaurs were multiplying across the land and the first birds were taking to the air, a fork in the path of elasmobranch evolution began the rise of the batoids, whose flattened body plan allowed them to radiate into new adaptive zones in the oceans. Today hundreds of different elasmobranchs, including the rays and skates, are classified as batoids, and from all the evidence it seems that this encyclopedic group's adaptive radiation still is steaming ahead full throttle.

A shark swims. But batoids are the birds of the elasmobranch world, with structural and functional adaptations that permit them to fly through the water. Those specializations include broad winglike pectoral fins attached to the head, and gill openings that open not on the sides but on the lower (ventral) body surface. With this basic physical plan as a starting point, batoids have evolved a panoply of body forms and can be assorted roughly into the Torpediniformes, electric torpedo rays; Pristiformes, the sawfishes; Rhyncobatiformes, the guitarfishes and their close cousins the Rhiniformes, or wedgefishes; Rajiformes, the skates and their relatives; and Myliobatiformes, the stingrays.

Batoids run the gamut from gigantic sawfishes to rays shaped like butterflies, to electric rays shaped like thick Frisbees trailing a short, thick tail. An adult torpedo ray can measure up to a yard across, and on each side of its disk, just behind the eyes, is a sizable, kidney-shaped lump—contours of paired electric organs that in large species can generate enough voltage to jolt a man onto his hind quarters. In nature the shocks are used for both defense and offense. Different species are adapted to life at seafloor, ranging from coastal waters to the deep ocean.

Sawfishes (not to be confused with saw sharks) are imposing: growing as long as twenty feet, they have an elongated, tooth-studded snout that looks roughly like the business end of a chain saw. Living close to the bottom along tropical coasts, they probably use the saw to strike fish and dig up invertebrates. Some species, like the largetooth sawfish (*Pristis perotteti*), routinely enter freshwater. This sawfish can penetrate the Amazon River, for instance, as much as a thousand miles inland from the Atlantic Ocean. Until recently, a thriving population of largetooth sawfish would run up a tributary river into Lake Nicaragua—where they were extirpated only a decade after an active fishery developed for them. In fact, most species of these remarkable elasmobranchs are in drastic decline because their habitats have been destroyed and because they are taken as bycatch in many different net fisheries.

There are more than forty species of benthic rays called guitarfishes or shovelnose rays, and in their general outlines different ones do bear a resemblance to a guitar (or banjo) or a shovel. The tapered head merges with large triangular pectoral fins, which in turn taper back to an elongated, sharklike torso bearing two short dorsal fins. In the Indo-Pacific, different species have evolved striking patterns of light and dark markings and arrays of sharp "thorns" along the midline of the back. In some places they support large fisheries, sometimes too large; off the coasts of Brazil and Argentina they have become critically endangered.

Similar in general appearance to the guitarfishes are the large-headed, blunt-snouted wedgefishes. Chunky animals that can grow to over ten feet, they sport two sharklike dorsal fins and frequent tropical coasts.

The skates and their relatives add up to more species—at least two hundred—than any other batoid group. In every ocean in the world, they cruise near the bottom along the upper continental slopes in coastal temperate areas and in the tropics as deep as six thousand feet.

Though skates tend to be small, some northern species may have disks as big around as a kiddie wading pool. A distinguishing skate feature is the long, thin, and often thorny tail with two small dorsal fins perched near its tip.

Stingrays and their kin, in the order Myliobatiformes, include some of the largest modern chondrichthyans. Their most singular trait is a whiplike tail studded with serrated, venom-spiked spines. John McEachran, my first Ph.D. student and now an internationally recognized authority on batoids at Texas A&M, once was stabbed in the foot by a stingray spine while he was collecting in the Gulf of Mexico. Loosely connected to the stingray's tail, each spine has a double row of serrations and is covered by a sheath of tissue loaded with tiny venom glands. Because its serrations point backward like the wings of nested arrowheads, the spine embedded in McEachran's flesh was difficult to pull out, and when it did emerge its venom-charged sheath sloughed off inside the resulting jagged puncture wound. The venom, which destroys the surrounding tissue, continues to work when the spine is removed. Even after his wound was debrided by a physician, McEachran's foot took months to heal because the venom's damage was so potent.

More than sixty species, most of them tropical, make up the family of true stingrays. These can be big animals—adults of some species have disks over six feet wide and weigh nearly half a ton. Stingray skin hues range from black to violet to yellow brown, arrayed in patterns from bars and leopardlike spots to fine white flecks, reticulated "mazes," and free-form blotches.

Some stingrays can tolerate a broad spectrum of salinity (that is, they are euryhaline), swimming up rivers then out to the ocean again. But one family, the freshwater stingrays, can live only in freshwater. This odd group underwent its radiation in tributaries of the Amazon River, although the family has found its way into other South American river systems as well. Nocturnal foragers, they pass the day buried along shallow sand beaches. That may be just as well, given that local people in the Amazon often kill stingrays on sight because they are considered dangerous and conveniently make good eating. If a captured animal is young enough, however, its fate may be to be sold alive to the ornamental-aquarium-fish trade. Bringing a hundred dollars or more in foreign pet stores, the little rays end up in fish tanks around the globe.

Eagle rays and cownose rays are mostly migratory creatures of coastal seas. An eagle ray's pectoral fins have an avian taper, and depending on the species its skin may be a deep purple brown, tan with stripes or spots, gray brown with a maze of ornate, darker markings, or some other striking pattern. Cownose rays get their name from their broad, fleshy snout. Species of both groups enter estuaries where females pup and sometimes raid commercial shellfish beds. Cownose rays usually travel from place to place in small schools at or near the surface, their wing tips actually breaking into the air as they swim. Because a ray's wing tips are triangular, not unlike the shape of a shark's dorsal fin, the flotillas often produce reports of shark invasions. In late summer near my home on the Chesapeake Bay, as many as ten thousand cownose rays form vast surface schools. Eventually, the huge schools migrate out of the Bay, turn south, and travel beyond Cape Hatteras, North Carolina, where they probably overwinter on the outer continental shelf close to the Gulf Stream.

A final, remarkable cadre of rays, the coal black devil rays and manta rays, dwarf all other batoids. Plying open coastal waters, these massive animals typically grow to around twelve feet across, but some become monsters twice that size—big enough to fill out the floor space of a good-sized living room. Their strange-looking cephalic lobes—fleshy flaps that extend outward in front of their eyes—are a feeding specialization that funnels plankton into the giant ray's mouth as it flaps along in slow motion, moving with deliberate grace through its watery world.

It is four o'clock and the afternoon has wound down with only a few folks heading back out to the hillsides after lunch. It's just too blasted hot. So we have eaten, examined, and compared fossil shark teeth, and every so often tried our crude Spanish on the steadfastly polite village kids. Shelley Applegate is beaming, having simultaneously amassed trays of fossils and not lost any of his novice paleontologists to heatstroke. As the village ladies pack up their pots and tablecloths and the mariachis stow their instruments, several of us squeeze onto the torn vinyl seats of a dust-caked van for the three-hour, non-air-conditioned ride back to La Paz.

As we make our way down the dirt track, back to the highway, and turn south, the thought surfaces that making a reliably complete list of living sharks and rays is going to be impossible. New species are regularly being discovered, assigned names, and allotted entries in the elasmobranch encyclopedia. The rumored fourth species of thresher shark is just one example. Most of the more recent finds are from deep waters where collecting has been sparse and consist of animals that simply aren't big enough to easily range over long distances. The outcome is geographic isolation of related populations separated by an impassable gulf of ocean. With time, a new, genetic chasm may open if the populations develop genetic differences that prevent their members from successfully interbreeding. When that happens, two species exist where once there was one.

Sometimes the identification of a new species leads to a sea change. In the 1980s the discovery off South Africa of a few small stingrays with six gill openings instead of five required the establishment of a whole new batoid family. Although rare, specimens of six-gilled stingrays have now been captured throughout the Indo-Pacific and as far east as Hawaii. They are odd-looking creatures with elongated, pointed snouts, short tails, and flabby muscles. Details of their lives are still mostly lacking, other than that they inhabit deep water, grow bath mat–sized disks of three feet or more, and probably live on shellfish crushed with their small, flat teeth.

When the van finally pulls up in front of the Hotel Perla, we are greeted by the welcome sight of a bartender on the patio squeezing limes into a pitcher. North and east of us, dusk and quiet have descended over El Cién, with its trove of teeth heralding the modern era of sharks. To the west, the sun is setting over the Sea of Cortez, and mingled with smells of fish frying somewhere, I can detect the cool salt scent of the sea borne on the evening breeze. I'm pretty sure that somewhere out there is the leaping thresher, swimming in its deepening blue world with other sharks whose lineages have survived and thrived in those selfsame waters for 40 million years. Yet even here in the relatively pristine Sea of Cortez, the future of sharks is far from certain. In the villages surrounding La Paz, racks upon racks of shark meat are set out each day to dry in the sun. Over the last several years artisanal fisheries have exploded here, and shark populations already are dwindling rapidly. If there are paleontologists a million years from now, I wonder whether they will note that in the upper Holocene, in the twenty-first-century A.D. terrain that once was a pool of Mexican ocean, sharks' teeth disappeared from the fossil record.

3 *Fearful Symmetry*

The first shark arrives only minutes after we finish setting the anchors from the open Aquasport outboard, at Triangle Rocks six miles offshore from South Bimini in the Bahamas. To Bev and me up on the gently rocking deck, it appears as a dark shape moving silently over the broken coral and white-sand bottom. Dean Grubbs, who did his doctoral work in my laboratory, is already in the water and identifies the first visitor as a Caribbean reef shark, a typical requiem shark six to seven feet long. "Here come a few more, Sonny," Dean calls. "Another reef and two smaller blacknose sharks." Sonny Gruber has brought us here along with a small group of marine biology students from the University of Miami, all of whom have come for the privilege of studying sharks in their natural environment.

Sonny trails a stout nylon line tied to an orange buoy over the stern to where it streams out for about thirty feet down-current. Then we don our snorkeling gear and are over the side into the aquamarine water. We swim to the trailing line and each of us finds a place to hold on, a dangling string of humans hanging there like so much laundry, watching the sharks circling in increasing numbers. The reef sharks are a soft gray above and white below with dusty edges on their fins. The smaller blacknose sharks are a lighter, yellowish gray with white fin edges.

After a few minutes Sonny orders the students out of the water. The rest of us, however, including a few of Sonny's staff from the Bimini Biological Field Station, remain on the line, transfixed by the sleek forms moving effortlessly around us. The sharks seem almost oblivious to our presence, ignoring us except to avoid collisions. Different individuals pass within a foot or two of us and one small blacknose actually swims between Bev's flippers.

Then Sonny throws in the first chunk of fish, the head of a barracuda. This brings an immediate response from the assembled sharks, which now number fifteen or twenty. They start to slash at the bait as each of Sonny's tosses sends two or three more pieces of fish splashing into the water. The sharks cannot be more than twenty feet from us, rushing one after the other toward the surface, rolling, grabbing the bait, and gliding away, only to turn sharply for another feeding run. Soon the surface breaks into a maelstrom of feeding sharks in apparent frenzy.

But is it? From our submerged vantage point, the answer is no. Each shark is focused purely on the food. And even though the sharks initially appear to career about haphazardly, it soon becomes obvious that their movements are elegantly controlled. No effort or attention is wasted. Not only do they ignore us humans, they also ignore the schools of yellowtail snapper, grunts, and other reef fishes that have slipped in to snap up sinking scraps. These sharks are interested only in the chunks of fish that periodically rocket into the water. Literally immersed in a scene that seems ethereal, even surreal, I don't feel any fear—only amazement at the grace of the sharks and their effortless movement through the sun-streaked, blue-green ocean. When Sonny's bait bucket is empty, the reef fish withdraw like ghosts. Then gone, too, are the sharks, as silently and magically as they had appeared.

Really, though, it's not so much magic. Reef sharks seem to have fairly small and circumscribed home ranges, and as a leading expert on shark behavior, Sonny Gruber has used this feeding station to study them off and on for ten years. Individual reef sharks probably live for twenty or thirty years. Dean Grubbs, who periodically teaches marine biology courses here, has recognized one individual with a scarred dorsal fin for eight years running. So the local sharks have come to associate the arrival of Sonny's boat—which they detect initially through sound—with food. These reef and blacknose sharks normally feed on smaller prey like fish or squid or even crabs. They have no predatory interest in larger animals such as sea turtles or humans, and thus pose little threat to people even if they may be attracted to small boats that anchor up here on Triangle Rocks. If an easy meal doesn't arrive in short order, the sharks simply lose interest and vanish.

When the Aquasport motors up and turns her bow toward the lab, I keep thinking about William Blake's poem "The Tyger" and his phrase "fearful symmetry." What the poet understood about the tiger's muscular form and harmonious functioning with nature could even more aptly be applied to sharks. In fact, it's damn near perfect. But what lies beneath those evocative words? What makes sharks sharks?

If I had to anoint one element as the signal attribute of sharks, it might well be the constellation of their features related to locomotion—how they move through the water with such grace and precision. Swimming is a constant for most sharks, because they are negatively buoyant. Crudely, it's swim or sink. Unlike most bony fishes, which are neutrally buoyant because they have a swim bladder filled mostly with oxygen, most sharks have to swim to stay aloft in the water column. Propulsion is provided by the powerful muscles lying along each side of the body. Those muscles are attached internally to the cartilaginous vertebral column and externally to the shark's thick skin, which stiffens and acts as a firm sheath, an external tendon against which the muscles contract. That contractile force pulls the shark's tail and the aft third of its body back and forth in rhythmic undulating motion. As the tail beats from side to side, the resulting vectors push the animal straight ahead, and because sharks have a heterocercal tail—the upper lobe is longer than the lower one—the tail, or caudal fin, also provides lift.

If the shark's tail produces lift, why then doesn't the shark's nose push downward? The forward part of the shark's body also is provided lift, in this case by the shark's large pectoral fins, which are shaped in cross section exactly like an airplane wing. The relationship of a fin's (or wing's) length to its average width is called the aspect ratio. Fins that are relatively long, narrow, and pointed have a high aspect ratio, yielding lower drag than fins with a low aspect ratio (such as those of a ray, which are much wider from leading edge to trailing edge). Examples of high-aspect-ratio shark fins would be the pectoral fins on blue sharks and the crescent-shaped caudal fin of mako sharks. Both of these species are pelagic and make long oceanic migrations—and thus have undergone strong natural selection for a body form that maximizes swimming efficiency. Even so, their overall body shapes, as well as their behaviors, are dramatically different. The blue shark is cigar-shaped, long and slim with an elongated upper tail lobe and pectoral fins that provide lift even when the shark is swimming slowly. In one study, a device attached to the aft end of a blue shark could measure the animal's tail beats and transmit the information through a sonic transmitter to a ship. The researchers found that blue sharks in the deep ocean save energy by using their long, graceful pectoral fins to glide down through the water column where they feed on squid, then swim back up simply by beating their tails as usual.

The mako, by contrast, is built like a big torpedo, the shark world's answer to the bluefin tuna. Its tail is large, keeled, and shaped like a crescent moon. This lunate shape provides maximum thrust with minimum drag. Natural selection has so streamlined the mako that a male's claspers fit into grooves in his body, eliminating drag that would be caused by these appendages flapping about in the streaming water as the fish swims along (an affliction most other male sharks must tolerate).

Makos also have much more red muscle than blue sharks do because makos cruise at faster speeds and use their red muscle to produce heat (but that's another story). As in the human body, the muscle mass of a fish is divided unevenly into white- and red-colored muscle. Supermarket fish fillets, which are mostly the more palatable white muscle, often will have a strip of deep crimson flesh running down the center of the fillet on the outside. Red muscle takes on that color because it is filled with myoglobin, a reddish, iron-rich protein similar to hemoglobin that has a high affinity for binding oxygen. Red muscle provides the propulsive force as a shark cruises along, requiring a steady stream of oxygen. White muscle, on the other hand, comes into play when the shark accelerates to burst speed to catch prey or avoid a predator. Swimming at burst speed requires about ten times as much energy as swimming at cruising speed, which is why there is always considerably more white muscle in the fish body. Unlike red muscle, white muscle can function when the tissue's oxygen has been depleted, building up an oxygen debt in a process that generates lactic acid. Excess lactic acid is toxic, but for sharks the strategy is possible because intensive use of white muscle is only a short-term proposition. The oxygen debt can be repaid and the lactic acid metabolized when the animal resumes its cruising mode and its red muscle kicks in again.

For makos and other active pelagic sharks, reducing drag is a key facet of swimming efficiency. Suction drag, for example, is an energy-devouring slowing effect that is manifested by the formation of eddies as the water flowing next to the shark's body—the surface-boundary layer—separates at the rear of the body and tail. It is the same phenomenon that creates little whirlpools at the end of a canoe paddle. It is no evolutionary fluke that those sharks that swim actively have an elongated body, high-aspect-ratio fins, and caudal keels that help maintain a smoother flow of water over the base of the tail.

Anyone who looks carefully at sharks notices that most have a tab at the tip of the upper caudal lobe that flaps back and forth as the tail beats, and it turns out that even that little tab is a part of the stream-lining package. I once helped a high school student, Ronnie Callis, devise an experiment to test whether the flap might affect the turbulent eddies and resulting drag that are produced by the shark's moving tail. Ronnie built a miniature wind tunnel into which he placed casts of tails from baby sandbar sharks that we had collected in Chesapeake Bay. He attached a small strain gauge to each cast and placed the casts at different angles of attack to the wind flow. He also made some tails without the extra tab. That simple experiment, carried out largely by a gifted eighteen-year-old, revealed that tails without tabs had significantly higher drag than tails with tabs, which bent with the flow. Another little bit of structural harmony.

In addition to suction drag, sharks are subjected to drag from friction that develops as they move through the water. How much friction develops—and therefore how much energy is required to overcome it—depends on the nature of the water flow over the animal's skin. The flow may be turbulent, or it may take the form of a smoother, sheetlike laminar flow. Which pattern develops is linked with a shark's swimming speed, which in turn is determined by the size of the shark. Larger sharks swim faster than smaller ones do. Comparatively smooth laminar flow correlates with more leisurely swimming. It produces less friction drag than does turbulent flow, which is associated with faster swimming. Because large pelagic sharks like makos swim at higher speeds, they are subjected to turbulent flow and higher friction drag. Yet they reduce this energetically costly drag through special features of the scales that cover their skin.

A shark is blanketed with millions of denticles—pinhead-sized placoid scales that resemble little teeth, with a toothlike pulp cavity supplied with blood vessels and nerves. Only elasmobranchs (and perhaps their jawless ancestors) have evolved this type of scale, which can take a variety of shapes. The denticles of many sharks have small ridges that run parallel to the long axis of the animal's body—architecture that suggests a role in drag reduction, but doesn't prove it. I have worked on this problem for years, beginning with a day in the early 1980s when the phone rang in my office at the Virginia Institute of Marine Science (VIMS). The caller was Dennis Bushnell, an engineer at NASA's Langley Research Center in Hampton, Virginia, who was hoping to apply drag-reducing mechanisms found in nature to airplanes and watercraft. One of his coworkers, Mike Walsh, had been experimenting with microgrooves on small, stiff, plastic sheets in wind tunnels. By manipulating the wind speed and the sizes of grooves and ridges, Walsh had been able to reduce friction drag in the system by 10 to 15 percent; he'd also derived mathematical equations that predicted the optimum sizes of ridges and grooves to lessen drag at given wind speeds. As I listened to Bushnell describe Walsh's work, the ridges and grooves on shark scales immediately came to mind, because both air and water are fluids and follow the same laws of fluid dynamics. (The viscosity, or density, of water is greater than that of air, but this fact could be accounted for in Walsh's equations.) Would shark denticles compare in drag-reducing ability to NASA's experimental microgrooves?

Bill Raschi, a graduate student in my laboratory at the time, was so intrigued by the question that he immediately postponed his other research and began collecting denticles from as many different shark species as possible. With each new specimen, he would remove a small patch of skin from beneath the dorsal fin, soak it in chlorine bleach until the denticles fell off, then prepare and mount the denticles for scanning by electron microscope, which could provide measurements of the minute grooves and ridges in microns—millionths of an inch. After several months of Raschi's labor, we had the necessary measurements of around a dozen shark species of various sizes and were nearly ready to do the analysis.

Friction drag, and in our case the dimensions of the ridges and grooves that might help reduce it, both depend on the velocity of the moving water—or, since it's the shark that's moving, the animal's swimming speed. But there hadn't been much research on swimming speed in wild or captive sharks, so my first stop was the National Aquarium in Baltimore, where sharks swim freely in a large, doughnut-shaped tank. With a stopwatch and the help of curator Juan Sabalones, I calculated swimming speeds of the aquarium's sharks, which included sand tigers and sandbar sharks. On our summer longline cruises we also began to fish for sharks with a rod and reel, the reel outfitted with a metering device to tell how fast the line was paying out. The trick was to hook a shark, then read the meter as the animal streaked away from the vessel at burst speed. Combining this work with theoretical equations relating swimming speed to shark size, within a few months we were able to estimate both cruising and burst speeds for all the sharks from which Bill Raschi had examined denticles. When Bill plugged in the values for denticle ridges and grooves and swimming speeds, the result was a revelation. The denticles of all of the fast, active, pelagic species—like the mako, silky, and blacktip sharks—had dimensions that closely fit the NASA equations for optimum drag reduction at burst speed. The ridges and grooves on our sharks' denticles were probably shaving friction drag in those animals by 10 to 12 percent—in nature, enough to bestow a real advantage in terms of the amount of energy a shark must expend as it swims through life.

Since those days, the denticle discoveries have continued. For example, conventional wisdom has been that a denticle's ridge-and-groove topography lessens friction drag simply by helping to smooth the flow of water at the shark's skin surface. Some of our more recent work has revealed that the ridges and grooves on successive scales from a shark's head to its tail are aligned in rows that actually channel the water flow in specific ways over most of the shark's body. The take-home lesson is that the mechanism by which a shark's scales reduce friction drag may be even more complex than anyone has supposed.

Another important factor controlling friction drag is the shark's surface area. When Bill Raschi began our placoid denticle research, he found few actual measurements of shark surface areas. Instead, researchers used a theoretical function of shark length squared (assuming the area to be equal to the shark's length multiplied by itself). Consequently I was determined to amass empirical data on shark surface area, and to develop accurate equations relating body surface area to length—and as it turned out, measuring the surface area of a complex three-dimensional object like a shark was simple. While we were at sea on our research vessel *Anthony Anne,* my student Chris Tabit would remove the fins from dead sharks brought up on our longline, leaving carcasses that resembled flatheaded torpedoes. Chris then marked a line midway down the side of each shark and, doing first the upper half of each animal, then the lower half, covered the shark with a sheet of clear plastic, which was then cut to form a body-fitting template. Back in the laboratory the templates were washed, dried, and weighed. Because Chris had already weighed a ten-square-centimeter sample of the plastic, all we had to do to calculate the surface area was divide the weight of the sample into the total weight of both templates for each shark and then plot length against surface area for a large size range of sharks from small smooth hounds to massive tiger sharks. With the help of Dr. David Evans, a mathematician on the VIMS faculty, we next derived a simple equation that could express this relationship. For all the sharks we studied, that equation (0.67 length times girth = area) predicted each shark's surface area with incredible accuracy: multiply a shark's length by its girth and take two-thirds of that number, and no matter what kind of shark you are looking at, you will always have a near-perfect calculation of its surface area. It was a finding that emphasized the remarkably conservative nature of the basic shark body plan, which can be traced back to the earliest Paleozoic shark. The flattened batoidlike forms are, of course, the exception.

Some of the VIMS studies on drag reduction were collaborations not only with NASA but also with engineers from Newport News Shipbuilding Company, famous maker of nuclear aircraft carriers and submarines. The United States military, particularly the navy, has been more than a little interested in sharks as models of hydrodynamic efficiency, and their interest isn't academic. Drag drains energy from submarines and torpedoes just as it does in fishes, and finding ways to reduce it means both greater fuel efficiency and an extended range of operations through the oceans.

Noise is another side effect of the drag created as water moves over a body. In a business like submarine warfare, where stealth is crucial, reducing noise associated with drag is of great value. So it is also with sharks, the silent predators. Unlike bony fishes, which actively produce sound by vibrating their swim bladders or rubbing parts of their hard skeletons together, sharks, with no swim bladder or hard bones, do not make voluntary sounds. In fact, the only sound produced by sharks is the inadvertent, very low frequency noise produced by turbulence as they swim and turn. In sharks that swim unceasingly, it appears that even these accidental sounds have been minimized by finely honed drag-reducing adaptations, making such animals the stealthiest predators in the sea.

Here are notes from my field log dated June 1975:

Submersible Alvin
Norfolk Submarine Canyon
70 miles east of Norfolk, Virginia

Today we cramped together, the three of us, into a titanium sphere a little more than six feet in diameter. This sphere is the pressurized nucleus of the research submersible *Alvin*, which externally supports manipulator arms, bright lights, 35-millimeter still and video cameras, and electric batteries to provide power; as well as cylinders full of air, other, pressurized ones that provide buoyancy, and stacks of disposable iron ballast weights. It was like being in a womb, self-contained, breathing a limited air supply, a canister of crystals absorbing our exhaled carbon dioxide. Doug Markle and I stretched out on either side of the sub's forward end, peering out of thick quartz portholes the circumference of grapefruits. Dudley Foster, our pilot (also a retired fighter pilot), sat on a small seat between us, maneuvering the craft and staring at a bank of blinking lights, gauges, and dials. Dudley controlled our position in the water column by dumping ballast or purging gas from the control cylinders.

We drifted along just above the bottom, nudged by *Alvin*'s small propellers. Fishes are surprisingly common a mile deep in the ocean at the base of the continental slope, and we saw large and small grenadiers, mud-colored eels, and black halosaurs, all hovering just above the bottom, undulating, facing into the gentle bottom current.

"Wow! What in hell was that?" Doug exclaimed as a black form suddenly darted across the lights in front of the sub. I said I thought it was a shark. Then we saw another and another, small, typical squaloids, two or three feet long, velvety black with large eyes that reflected green in the sub's lights.

The constant darting movements of those little sharks were in stark contrast to that of the bony fishes at this depth, like the grenadiers or bathysaurus, which hover above the bottom or lie directly on it. Because Markle and I previously had collected similar sharks in Norfolk Canyon with our trawl nets, we could easily identify these ones: Portuguese sharks (*Centroscymnus coelolepsis,* small dorsal fin spines) and black dogfishes (*Centroscyllium fabricii,* fin spines are large and curved). We were not surprised to see either form, but their behavior was surprising. They were not hovering like the bony fishes, something such deep-sea sharks are "supposed" to do.

Hovering, like a trout holding in a stream, is an energy-saving capability that requires neutral buoyancy: the body must be neither lighter nor heavier than the surrounding water. The swim bladder of bony fishes, with its adjustable volume of gas, affords neutral buoyancy and, because deep-sea squaloids have features that in theory provide roughly the same service, they were presumed to spend much of their time hovering as well. For starters, like all sharks they have a huge liver relative to their body size, large enough to fill much of the body cavity. All shark livers provide some buoyancy because they contain quantities of oil, but the oil in a deep-sea squaloid's liver is squalene—an extremely low density hydrocarbon that provides superior flotation. Deep-sea sharks also have evolved other body-lightening features, including muscles that contain more water than those of other sharks (and so are less dense), and less calcification of their cartilage parts. The reduced mineralization translates into less weight and a correspondingly greater tendency to float. With these modifications, squaloids don't have to swim as fast as do sharks that use their pectoral fins for lift. And because their pectoral fins are relatively small and paddlelike and are used mostly for maneuvering instead of lift, they are not subjected to nearly as much drag.

Even so, the dogfish and Portuguese sharks illuminated by the gauzy glare of *Alvin's* headlights surprised me because they had been swimming, not exploiting their neutral buoyancy to hover. Why would a fish not take advantage of an opportunity to save energy? It appears that for them and many other sharks, more or less constant motion is not optional. Most active sharks have evolved to meet their body's requirement for oxygen by "ram" ventilating their gills, opening the mouth to let water stream over the gill filaments. If even the neutrally buoyant deep-sea sharks ram ventilate, it must be an ancient adaptation. The strategy makes sense especially since most sharks have to swim to stay aloft anyway.

Besides deep-sea squaloids, the only other shark to achieve neutral buoyancy is the sand tiger. Sand tigers can hover, though they do so rarely and not with much grace: on occasion a sand tiger will gulp air at the surface and then swim back down close to the bottom, the trapped air providing the lift to keep it from sinking. In its effect this peculiar behavior parallels the swim bladder, but it's cruder and can work only if the shark is in shallow water.

Ram ventilation doesn't *have* to correlate with fast swimming, although many sharks do so. For instance, sandbar sharks must move along at a good clip to generate the lift they need to stay aloft. By contrast, the sand tigers at the National Aquarium would usually cruise along slowly, ram ventilating with their mouths agape until they made a turn, when the natural water flow through the mouth and across the gills was disrupted. In a split second, probably with internal sensors as the triggers, muscles associated with the sand tiger's mouth and gill arches would go into action, pumping water into their mouths and out their gill openings. Benthic sharks like catsharks and angel sharks, which lie still for long periods on the bottom, have a naturally lower oxygen demand, but still must actively breathe in a programmed sequence: muscle contractions shrink the mouth cavity, pushing water inside it out over the gills. Then the shark's mouth opens, other muscles expand the cavity once again, sucking in a fresh supply of water, and the cycle continues.

Other elasmobranch breathing options are geared to different lifestyles. Some sharks and all rays have a pair of vestigial gill openings, called spiracles, located behind the head on the dorsal surface. Spiracles rhythmically pump water into the animal's gullet, over its gills, and out the gill openings. They are especially useful for a benthic animal when it is lying on the bottom, because most benthic animals have their mouth tucked underneath the head. If they were to respire in the usual way they would probably suck in sediment that might clog their gills or hinder oxygen uptake and the exit of waste carbon dioxide. Many benthic elasmobranchs use their spiracles to both bring water into the gill chamber and move it out.

Locomotion also is different in the wing-shaped batoids. The pelagic rays like eagle rays and mantas literally fly through the sea, gracefully flapping their pointed wings (and ram ventilating). The more benthic forms like skates scoot over the bottom, undulating the feathery edges of their wings in rapid waves, front to back. This subtle rippling of the wing margins grades into the more obvious but slower flapping of the entire wing in pelagic species. Not surprisingly, pelagic rays that actively swim all or most of the time have the highest aspect ratios for minimizing drag. Some of the benthic batoids also can walk over the bottom by alternating movements of their pelvic fins. Skates even have special lobes on their pelvic fins, called crura, which act like little feet.

. . .

Beep-beep. Beep-beep. The monotonous sound faded, then swelled again in my earphones. It was emanating from Shirlee, a three-hundred-pound, eight-foot female salmon shark swimming fathoms below the steel deck on which I was standing. Months before Bev and I attached ourselves to Sonny Gruber's shark-watching clothesline, I had spent the better part of a week aboard the fifty-eight-foot research vessel *Montague* in Port Gravina fjord, an arm of Alaska's Prince William Sound. For much of that time my attention focused almost entirely on Shirlee, who represents her species' capacity for a physiological feat that may be unique among fishes.

Salmon sharks are broad-shouldered lamnids with large eyes and a bulletlike snout. Their body is shaped like a teardrop, with broad keels in front of the scimitar tail, an adaptation for hydrodynamic efficiency. Charcoal black above mottling to pure white below, the salmon shark has large black freckles on its belly. More robust than their cousins the makos, salmon sharks also differ markedly from their other mackerel-shark kin, the great white, in having a smaller mouth and curved, awl-shaped teeth—perfect tools for catching salmon and other piscine prey.

Beep-beep. Beep-beep. We had been tracking Shirlee for some twenty hours, beginning the previous afternoon when we placed a sonic transmitter about the size of a C-cell battery inside a dead herring and fed it to her, in an operation that reminded me of giving a biscuit to a dog. It was an adaptation of a technique developed by my student, Ken Goldman, and another member of our crew, Scot Anderson, a naturalist for Oceanic Society Expeditions. Scot and Charlie Stock of Alaska's Department of Fish and Game had perfected it for tagging salmon sharks without having to capture them. The procedure was simple. Scot and Charlie would simply motor out in an inflatable rubber boat, an eleven-foot Zodiac, and tease the sharks to the surface with herring. Scot would do this by clipping a herring to the end of his fishing line, lowering it to a depth of fifty feet where the sharks were hanging out, then quickly reeling it back to the surface. More often than not, a shark would follow the bait back to the boat, where Charlie stood poised like Ahab, tagging pole in hand, waiting to jab a dart tag into its broad back.

Then it was simply a matter of allowing the shark to catch the herring-transmitter sandwich and swallow it down. We wanted the shark to ingest the transmitter, which would send sonic signals indicating depth and temperature back to our hydrophone on the *Montague*, because while most sharks are ectothermic—their body temperature is the same as the surrounding water—we knew salmon sharks were warm-blooded. Yet neither we nor anybody else had much idea of how well they could thermoregulate and maintain the higher body temperature. With the transmitter in Shirlee's stomach, however, we could monitor her body temperature, and having already taken a temperature-depth profile, by simultaneously tracking depth we could calculate the temperature of the water in which she was swimming. We could then compare the two.

Ken Goldman, a tall, wiry figure with long red hair and matching beard, soon emerged from the *Montague*'s cramped sleeping quarters nursing a cup of strong coffee. Ken is studying shark thermoregulation as part of his doctoral work at VIMS, and this actually was his research cruise, the third of the season. I was along mostly to help out as needed and to do a little salmon fishing in the down times. Ken studied thermoregulation in great white sharks in the Farallon Islands off San Francisco for his master's degree and was trying to find out more about the phenomenon in salmon sharks, which of all the mackerel sharks live in the coldest water. In addition to tagging sharks and gathering temperature information, he was taking vertebrae and reproductive tracts from a handful of animals, hoping to add to the scientific data on these animals' age and growth patterns. And following a personal tradition of naming his research subjects after members of his family, he had named Shirlee after his mother. Throughout the previous day and all night long, we had taken turns monitoring the hydrophone and following Shirlee. My watch had begun at 5 A.M.

"How's Shirlee doing?" was Ken's immediate question.

"Ken, if she had breasts we'd have to call her a mammal," I answered, and it was almost true. To our amazement, during the entire tracking period Shirlee had been maintaining a body temperature of 78° F while swimming in water ranging from a chill 60° F at the surface down to a frigid 39° F at four hundred feet on one of her deeper excursions.

From one of the high peaks that surrounds the fjord on three sides, a herd of mountain goats had kept watch on us as we worked. The billy stood guard below while the nannies and kids grazed on sparse fodder clinging to the higher rocky slopes. Then Scot and Charlie, who had been out tagging, came putt-putting toward the *Montague* wearing embarrassed grins. The Zodiac's front air chamber was shriveled, the rubber vessel and the two fortyish men in it supported solely by its two lateral air chambers.

"We got a flat," Scot had offered, but a glance at the bow of the crippled Zodiac revealed a perfectly defined outline of a salmon shark's upper teeth. In fact, in the preceding days Scot had become fascinated with luring sharks ever closer to the boat. He would wait until one had closed to within inches of the dangling bait and then with a maniacal cackle snatch the morsel away just as the shark lunged.

"Looks like you finally pissed them off," I observed. Behind me, the rest of the crew's laughter reverberated around the fjord. Then Ken's shout broke the mood. "Shirlee just barfed up the transmitter!" The signal from the device told us that it had sunk like a stone to the bottom of 312 feet of Alaskan ice water, and in an instant it was clear that the experiment was over.

Aiming for a personal record, Scot and Charlie would ultimately tag 103 salmon sharks in three days of the *Montague*'s five-day cruise. And despite her transmitter-induced indigestion, in just twenty-four hours Shirlee added to the slowly growing body of knowledge about thermoregulation in sharks, and in salmon sharks specifically. Ken Goldman and Scot Anderson would successfully track three salmon sharks that summer, adding to a single track from the previous year.

Each fish maintained its body temperature at a more or less steady 78° F despite the fact that it was swimming in water as much as 40° colder. Temperature probes inserted into red muscle and various organs of more than thirty other salmon sharks captured by cooperating sport fishers would add even more to our understanding of this species' body-warming strategies.

The capacity to thermoregulate—essentially, to be "warm-blooded"—is another striking bit of evolutionary fine-tuning that enables certain shark species to operate as more effective predators. Studies show that makos, porbeagle, and white shark all can do so, and suggest that the threshers also can control their body temperature to some extent. This research has been provocative, because until the late 1960s, biologists thought that only mammals and birds were endotherms, able to maintain an elevated body temperature that is warmer than their surroundings. Then, led by a pioneering researcher named Frank Carey, scientists at the Woods Hole Oceanographic Institution discovered that some of the tunas and mackerel sharks could do just that. With cooperation from animals like Shirlee, we are now discovering how warm-blooded some sharks are. Like birds and mammals, Shirlee has shown us that not only can her species maintain an elevated body temperature, it can maintain a constant temperature *all the time,* an advanced type of thermoregulation called homeothermy.

How do warm-blooded sharks heat their bodies and keep them that way? In key parts of the body, they have a *rete mirabile,* a heat-exchanging "marvelous net" of tightly interlacing blood vessels. Working muscles and metabolically active organs in sharks and other fishes normally produce heat that moves into the blood in nearby veins. When the warmed venous blood reaches the shark's gills, its load of heat rapidly dissipates to the surrounding cool seawater while the blood is loading on oxygen. Thus the oxygen-replenished blood returning to the shark's body from the gills is, like seawater, cold. Enter the retes, each a circulatory crossroads consisting of a network of capillaries, incoming arterioles carrying oxygenated blood and outgoing vessels of the venous system. The vessels are packed together so tightly that in cross section a rete resembles a bloody sponge. The packing allows heat from venous blood that is moving back toward the gills to be transferred into the arriving cool arterial blood by way of a countercurrent mechanism—the different types of blood vessels are aligned so that the warm and cool streams of blood are flowing in opposite directions. This setup maximizes the opportunity for heat to move into cooler blood and warm it, and the heat transfer goes on continuously. As warmed arterial blood steadily courses through tissues delivering oxygen, its heat keeps the temperature of the tissues elevated as well.

Mackerel sharks, including great whites, have retes associated with the red muscles that run along their flanks, with the liver, and behind the eye. The latter is an especially strategic location because it warms the eyes and the brain as well. Maintaining a constant temperature in the brain ensures that the animal's neural processing isn't disrupted by sudden changes in temperature as the shark moves between shallow and deeper water. And new research on warm-blooded tunas suggests that the processing of visual signals in the retina occurs more rapidly at warmer temperatures. For a swift fish like a tuna or mackerel shark, that is a crucial adaptation. Without it, such animals would likely perceive only a blur of images as they course through their environment.

The salmon shark, champion of thermoregulation, also has a rete nestled close by its kidneys, and the one around its liver includes a capacious venous sinus filled like a hot-water bottle with warm blood. Arteries thread through the compartment like hoses through a blood-filled bag. When the shark enters warmer water, where less internally generated heat is necessary to maintain a high core temperature, its body adjusts by shunting some blood flow around the rete instead of through it—so the unneeded heat is lost.

The physical and functional demands of being warm-blooded align with other body traits as well. All lamnids, including salmon sharks, need ample oxygen for their high metabolism. So they have a large gill surface area relative to their body size and have a larger heart than other sharks of similar size. A large heart can pump blood at the necessary rate to supply enough oxygen to the tissues of these highly active sharks and maintains enough pressure to keep blood flowing through the maze of tiny capillaries in the retes, tubes so narrow that red blood cells can shoulder through them only in single file.

Likewise, a shark's body temperature can be related to its activity level. One evening Ken Goldman commented that salmon sharks chase salmon with surprising stubbornness. "Sometimes you see a dorsal fin just skimming along after a salmon, I mean really hauling," he had observed. "And when a salmon jumps, the shark just rockets after it into the air, and when that shark hits the water again it's right back on the salmon's ass. They just don't give up."

The blood of Bimini's reef sharks is the same temperature as that of the surrounding sea. Like an invisible biological fence, this fact more or less limits them to tropical habitats where the water is comparatively and reliably warm. On the other hand, salmon sharks like Shirlee have been caught in the Pacific Ocean within the expanse of latitudes bracketed by Costa Rica in the south and Nome in the north. They can be fished two thousand miles out in the Pacific or ten feet from the beach in an Alaskan fjord. This vast range reflects the ability of endothermic sharks to operate efficiently over a correspondingly wide range of environmental temperatures.

There are other profound advantages associated with thermoregulation. A shark's life processes (like those of other organisms) depend on systems of enzymes—catalytic proteins that generally are highly sensitive to temperature. They operate sluggishly or not at all if the body is too cool, and are essentially destroyed if it is too hot. Thus, by maintaining a constant, relatively warm body temperature, an endotherm enjoys a more efficient metabolism than does an ectothermic species such as a spiny dogfish. This enhanced efficiency shows up in key and measurable facets of an animal's life. For instance, in sharks and other fishes, body growth is temperature dependent. By sustaining a higher core body temperature, warm-blooded sharks can grow more rapidly than ectothermic sharks of similar size, and they mature sexually at a younger age. Thus they can become large enough to deter most of their predators sooner, and begin reproducing sooner.

Evolving into warm-blooded creatures also has allowed such sharks to expand their geographic and depth ranges considerably. Ectothermic sharks can occupy deep or shallow water, tropical or cold habitats, but lacking the ability to raise their body temperatures above that of their environment, they do not have the freedom a lamnid does to move so freely between cold and warm seas and make its life in both.

The blood contained within a shark's arteries and veins is the crimson river of its life. Retes that liberate a shark from the constraints of cool body temperature exploit the ease with which it loads and unloads body heat. Pumped by the animal's heart, the blood also circulates nutrients, hormones, and the oxygen captured from water flowing across the gills, and hauls away carbon dioxide wastes. Sonny Gruber discovered that baby lemon sharks in Bimini's lagoons can extract virtually every molecule of oxygen their blood takes on—an astounding physiological feat considering that in our own bodies 40 percent of the oxygen we breathe in never makes it to our cells. In a sense, it is wasted. Perhaps one of the things that makes sharks sharks is the fact that, overall, they are amazingly thrifty with their biological capital.

Consider how their bodies have evolved to cope with the soup of salts that envelops every marine animal. When I started working in Chesapeake Bay, the largest estuary in the United States, I soon realized that it held just three common species of sharks—a sparse line-up compared to the ocean beyond. It was also obvious that sharks were most abundant in the lower eastern quarter of the Bay, where salinity was highest. (The Bay is fed by rivers that produce a marked salinity gradient from pure freshwater in the upper Bay to full seawater [thirty-two parts salt to a thousand parts water] at its mouth.) In other words, sharks were limited to the saltiest water—and the reason why underscores another of the specializations that set sharks apart from other animals in the sea.

Fishes, like all animals, face osmotic stress—the tendency to gain or lose too much water or too many key ions like sodium, chloride, magnesium, and potassium (often lumped together as "salts"). For us humans the typical risk is losing body water by evaporation to the air; for a marine fish it is losing water through osmosis to the sea and simultaneously being inundated with salts. To maintain the necessary chemical balance in their blood, bony marine fishes drink the only water available to them—seawater—then jettison the excess salts that come with it. Some salts leave by way of the gut, while specialized cells in the gills actively pump out others. At the same time, the kidneys of a bony marine fish adjust the balance of ions in the blood to meet internal needs, removing unwanted ones by loading them into urine and hoarding those that are needed. This balancing act is also designed to conserve as much water as possible. A bony marine fish produces only a scant urine, consisting of a little water infused with unwanted ions and other wastes.

Marine elasmobranchs, by contrast, rise to the constant challenge of dehydration in a totally different way. For starters, they never drink. Instead, to take on needed water a shark's body retains substances that by rights should be excreted. This strategy effectively raises the ion content of its blood to a level higher even than that of the sea and, following the rule of osmosis (where salt goes, water follows), draws in virtually all the water a shark needs in a steady trickle across its gills. The chemicals a shark retains are trimethylamine oxide (TMAO) and the body waste urea. A shark's kidneys, it turns out, are remarkably adept at holding back urea instead of excreting it (as human kidneys do). But while having enough water isn't an issue for sharks, balancing the ions needed in their body is. Like bony marine fishes, elasmobranchs excrete some salts via their gills, but even more important in this regard is an organ found only in sharks and a few other ancient fishes, such as coelacanths: the rectal gland. Named for its location nestled against the lower intestine, this glob of glandular tissue extracts the requisite amount of sodium chloride (basically, table salt) from a shark's blood and shunts it into the gut. From there the salt is eliminated in the animal's feces.

Like the sharks in Chesapeake Bay, most sharks are limited to saltier water because that is the environment where retaining urea and TMAO works best. The strategy's effectiveness wanes in brackish

water and fails completely in fresh. Even so, some elasmobranchs—
such as freshwater stingrays and bull sharks nearly eighteen hundred
miles up the Mississippi River—have evolved the osmoregulatory ver-
satility to thrive under conditions that would quickly kill most sharks.
Like freshwater fishes, they are subject to excess water flooding their
bodies and a loss of salts to the environment, so their kidneys retain
far less urea and TMAO and manufacture a stream of watery urine. In
their gills, the cells that otherwise expel ions can reverse metabolic
gears and soak up salts from the surrounding water, keeping the necessary internal balance. Because they don't build up a potentially haz-
ardous salt load to draw in water, freshwater stingrays have lost the
rectal gland during their evolution. In species like bull sharks and
sawfishes, which regularly enter freshwater, the gland atrophies,
shriveling like a prune.

In Bimini I had thought a great deal about the characteristics that
make sharks the oceans' supreme predators. An evolutionarily ancient
osmoregulatory system is only one of them. Another is that they are
able to lead a diverse range of lifestyles, from the sluggish benthic
nurse sharks to the rocketlike makos, with a similar, conservative body
plan. Also figuring in the mix are sensory systems conveying information of a sort we humans can only try to imagine, defenses against disease that may also be profoundly ancient and that are unique today,
and the diverse and vulnerable ways sharks and their relatives reproduce. All address problems and opportunities presented by the varied
environments in which sharks have lived for so long. In biological uni-
son they are what make sharks sharks.

Some hours after our trip out to Triangle Rocks, I slipped on a
clean shirt and, with one hand in Bev's and the other clutching a fly
rod, walked to Sonny Gruber's shark lab from our little rented apart-
ment, a half mile or so down a neighboring canal. Lights were wink-
ing in the modest facility, and indeed all over the island. We planned
to stay for a few more days, to roam around a little, and talk with
Sonny about his lemon shark research, which has yielded classic data

on shark senses and behavior. For the moment, though, I was headed for a pier where the lab's small fleet of motorboats, the largest a twenty-four-footer, bobbed and tugged at their lines. It was my sixtieth birthday, already indelibly marked, and I hoped a bonefish would suck up my shrimp fly. Dean Grubbs had mentioned that a handful of the skittish creatures liked to hang out in the sea grass across from the pier, although on this balmy evening nothing seemed to stir.

I tried to concentrate on my casting, but the sharks of Triangle Rocks kept intruding. Their absolute *control* was mind-boggling. Sometimes we think we understand things when, it turns out, we have only scratched the surface.

Inside the shark lab people were hustling around making a birthday feast in my honor, with homemade conch fritters and cake. Sonny was on the VHF radio, setting up a rendezvous for me to go out in the morning with Bonefish Ray, a top Bimini guide. The waiting cake, an artful opus executed by Sonny's wife Mari and several lab staffers, featured palm trees and a mustachioed fly fisherman reeling in a fish from a lagoon of blue green icing. There were even a couple of gulls wheeling in a frosted sky. I was more than a little abashed that Mari and her helpers had gone to so much trouble, but impressed at the perfection of the scene's details. Of course, perfection always lurks in the details of things. Perhaps that truism applies as well to cakes as it does to sharks.

4 *Sex, Sharks, and Videotape*

A couple of hours past dawn, the shark's tail abruptly breaks the flat calm of the lagoon. A grayish brown back arches out of the knee-deep water, and then all hell seems to break loose—two sharks flailing and rolling, their bodies slapping the water's surface, sending up sheets of spray. A nurse shark mating event has begun, although at the moment whether it will culminate in the union of sperm and egg is anybody's guess.

Wes Pratt has been leaning against the supports of an observation platform planted into the coral rubble bottom. Now he slips his slender frame onto a yellow kayak, his paddle splashing only a little as he closes the distance to the thrashing sharks. Draped across the kayak's bow is a ten-foot dip net, its closed end clenched between Pratt's teeth; the fifty-something scientist intends to try to briefly capture the male so that a visiting National Geographic Society photographer, Kyler MacIntyre, can fit the amorous shark with an underwater camera. This male has already begun the essential foreplay of shark sex, attempting to grasp the tip of one of the female's pectoral fins in his mouth. He must quickly work his way up the fin, rolling it up in his mouth like a jelly roll until his purchase on the female is strong, before she will allow the sexual encounter to proceed. Based on years of observations by Pratt and his research partner Jeff Carrier, it's a maneuver that demands skill born of practice, and one at which only the most experienced males succeed with any regularity. A female nurse shark who doesn't want to be mated executes avoidance maneuvers. She will try to swim to shallower water, for instance, sometimes with the male in tow. She also will pivot her body sharply toward him, then roll up and over his head. The tension resulting from this pivot-and-roll can pull a loosely held pectoral fin out of the male's mouth and give her a good chance of escaping the unwanted advance.

That elasmobranch equivalent of a brush-off is what we appear to be witnessing now, for the female is clearly not cooperating. While the male does his best to hang on and improve his grip on her right pectoral fin, Pratt slips off the kayak into the churning water, readying the dip net as he goes. Jeff Carrier has waded in to help with the operation, for each of the sharks is over eight feet long and weighs in the neighborhood of 250 pounds. Suddenly the female's roll dislodges the male and Pratt lunges with the net, missing by inches. Then another lunge and another miss as the male shifts direction and barrels by Carrier. The harassed female streaks away and the luckless male hurtles off into the narrow channel that leads out of the lagoon.

It's safe to say that few people have ever seen sharks mating in nature. Reports are almost nonexistent in the scientific literature except for the collaborations of Pratt, a senior scientist with the National Marine Fisheries Service in Narragansett, Rhode Island, and Carrier, who is professor and dean at Albion College in Michigan. Every summer since 1991, however, the two researchers have been monitoring and filming nurse shark sex in the turquoise waters off Florida's Dry Tortugas National Park, taking advantage of the site fidelity of nurse sharks that faithfully return to these mating grounds year after year.

Their field laboratory is an acre-sized coral reef flat where they have erected their observation platform inside the reef, the arc of which forms the larger lagoon. Built of scrounged construction scaffolding, the platform consists of two plywood decks about four feet by six, supported by steel pipes. The lower deck stands a foot or two above the warm and shallow water—knee-deep to waist-deep, depending on the tide—while the top one is several feet above and accessed by ladderlike rungs. Altogether the platform looks like the contraption rigged by the fellow who put up drywall in my living room. The Pratt and Carrier team, including Carrier's wife Carol and Pratt's fiancée Theo, use it as anchorage for their kayaks—one the color of Pepto Bismol, the other canary yellow—and more importantly as a perch from which to spot incipient mating events. This year the National Geographic Society photographer has been occupying the lower deck with his blue, torpedo-shaped "Crittercam," a sophisticated underwater video camera that the team has been harnessing to various male sharks in order to film their comings and goings. Carrier's seventeen-foot runabout, anchored nearby, serves as a ferry between the platform and the park beach where the team has established its camp.

The Dry Tortugas are spare, beautiful, almost treeless sand isles southwest of Key West, Florida. Each research trip there spans late June to early July, the height of the breeding season for the local population of nurse sharks. The previous summer Pratt and Carrier recorded 165 nurse shark sexual encounters during that period—an average of nearly eight per day—and this year the tally will probably be about the same. Added to the observations of previous years, they have witnessed at least 500 mating events. These involve frequent attempts at copulation but few successes; this morning's aborted effort was typical. Each event lasts from a few seconds to ten or fifteen minutes, depending on the male's endurance, and at least 90 percent of the time females reject their suitors. Yet enough mating events are consummated that when the season ends, most of the mature females here will be pregnant.

During the flight down from Virginia with Bev two days earlier, I had scanned Pratt and Carrier's recently published "Summary of observed courtship and mating behaviors in elasmobranch fishes." The report is easy reading, noting observations of a meager dozen or so shark species and seven batoids. To accomplish mating, all sharks and rays copulate in some fashion, males inserting one of their two penislike claspers into the female's body. Sperm delivered into the female's reproductive tract in this way will fertilize her eggs. But as Pratt, Carrier, and other scientists have discovered, these simple facts belie a system of surprisingly complex behaviors and a reproductive strategy that puts most sharks at a major disadvantage in the modern world of intensive fisheries.

When Wes has resecured his kayak to the platform with a nylon line, he interprets the sequence we have just witnessed. The female was an animal the team had first tagged in 1995 and then recaptured shortly before our arrival, providing an opportunity to measure her and clean and check her tags before releasing her once again.

"She's yellow roto-tag 9909," he says as seawater sloshes gently at the base of the platform's supports and damselfishes dart in and out of coral hidey-holes. It's a perfect, cloudless day with no wind and excellent visibility both above and in the water. Our lips are plastered with a purple zinc oxide paste against the tropical sun's broil, the same reason we are wearing full aquatic bodysuits. "Earlier this morning," Wes continues, "we saw her refuging with another female, resting on the bottom with her fins down."

"Refuging" is the term the team has coined to describe the way female nurse sharks seem to pointedly seek respite from males when they're not inclined to be mated. "We believe that refuging females are actively avoiding males, either because they're not ready to mate, or as a means of selecting the right male to mate with. Once things got rolling she was clearly avoiding while the male was trying to grab her right pectoral fin. It was a little battle of the sexes. Sexual competition is well known in all animals. . . . If you're a female you only want the best male to mate with you. So each is trying to control the situation. In this case, the male probably was very inexperienced, because at one point I saw him accidentally grasp one of her pelvic fins, and in the end he was only able to get four or five inches of the pectoral fin. To succeed he really needed to get that whole right pectoral fin rolled up into his mouth."

Pratt and Carrier have named different parts of the lagoon, with areas that the sharks seem to favor for mating dubbed the Bedroom and the Love Nest. The Gate is the lagoon's narrow entry channel that opens from the surrounding reef system; the Parking Lot is a stretch of lagoon outside the main mating area where buoys signal boaters to keep out. On low tides, Pratt says, females sometimes pile up on the bottom there, a common resting mode for nurse sharks of either sex. Now, up on the platform's top deck, Theo is scanning the Gate with binoculars when a fin appears. She calls out that it may be 9909 again, swimming toward the Love Nest. Nearly all of the previous year's observed matings were there or in the Bedroom, which is where this morning's event took place. Other encounters almost certainly occur in deeper areas of the lagoon, but the depth increases the likelihood that they will go unrecorded by the research team. Likewise offshore. With the possibility of 9909's return, our hopes rise for another mating event, but the big female simply disappears, probably refuging once more away from the main traffic of males.

Shark sex is a variable and tricky and even risky business, especially for females. As the breeding season gets under way, a sexually mature female probably exudes a hormonal perfume that attracts males and prompts their advances. A male blacktip reef shark, for instance, will follow along behind a female, his snout aligned closely behind her vent or cloaca (the common opening of her reproductive tract and intestine). Where we are, male nurse sharks patrol inside and outside the lagoon, looking for females that, in a shark universe, seem approachable. A male may begin his approach with a slow pursuit, which the team has dubbed "following"; sometimes as many as four trail the same female. When being followed by two or more males, a female's progress into the lagoon can be bruising, as mating attempts force her against the rocky, wave-beaten shore, and it can be incredibly slow. Carrier and Pratt have logged up to six hours watching females move not much more than a quarter mile, with males relent-lessly following.

The next step toward shark mating is the male's attempt to gain a mouth-hold on the female. An amorous nurse shark male tries to grasp one of her pectoral fins. A male blue shark directs his bite either to a pectoral fin or to the back of the female's head and flanks (where, tellingly, her skin is three times thicker than the male's). Probably designed both to gain the female's cooperation and to hold her body in a suitable position, the bite can do damage ranging from scratches to deep lacerations. If a female isn't interested in mating, at this point she may discourage the male's approach by abruptly reorienting her body. The nurse shark's pivot-and-roll is one version of such avoidance behavior; an avoiding female sand tiger scoots down to the bottom to make her fins that much more difficult to grab, and may even turn and bite an obtrusive male. On the other hand, the female can signal her receptivity (or submission) by arching her body toward the male and cupping her pelvic fins under her body, a posture that may help guide the insertion of a clasper.

With mating close at hand, as a rule the male now tries to insert just one of his two claspers into the female's vent. He may also work to adjust his partner's body position to facilitate copulation. Male nurse sharks, for example, sometimes use their head to rotate the female more or less onto her back so that the top of her snout presses into the bottom and acts like a brace. In shallow water, he may try to nudge her deeper where he will have more freedom of movement, all the while maintaining his grasp on her fin. When a clasper is properly positioned, the mating usually is accomplished in a minute or two, although the timing and details vary from species to species and some sharks may copulate for fifteen minutes or more. Coupling manta rays don't even stop swimming; Japanese researcher Kazunari Yano has seen paired mantas *in copula* "flying" as usual through the water while the male squirms to place his clasper where it needs to be. But among sharks this general sequence—pursuit of the female by one or more males, then the bite, body positioning, and copulation with an acqui-escing partner—seems to be fairly standard.

From a human perspective, shark sex can seem violent, for in addition to the wounds inflicted by bites, females suffer internal damage. A male's claspers are supported by calcified cartilage that is ridged or has a barbed or gafflike tip that, like a grappling hook, embeds in the female's vagina to maintain contact. When the male withdraws his clasper after mating, the barbs or ridges can gouge or tear the female. Such injuries make it easy to tell when a female has recently mated, and in my own work I have often seen mature female sharks with red and irritated vents.

In camp, our home is crude—a backpacking tent, a cooler, two duffels holding our snorkeling gear, swimsuits, and a change of clothes, and two five-gallon water jugs, enough to last for our short visit if we are frugal. All this is arrayed at the base of a spreading tropical shrub on a white-sand bluff, with the tent facing the moat that surrounds the park's main tourist attraction, Fort Jefferson. In this nineteenth-century brick fortress, Union troops watched over inmate Dr. Samuel Mudd, the Virginia physician convicted of aiding John Wilkes Booth after he broke a leg fleeing Ford's Theatre, having just assassinated Abraham Lincoln. Kyler's tent is on the other side of a porous wall of branches over which, we will learn, black rats scuttle at night. On the lagoon side of the same squat tree, the research team lives in comparative luxury, in a pair of two-room tents bracketing a tarp-covered picnic table. Campers on the island must bring water unless they plan on drinking the Gulf of Mexico, and so abutting this domestic nucleus is a pup tent-cum-pantry that is buttressed by dozens of water jugs. In the evening cocktails may be served on the "veranda," a small folding table circled by camp chairs with an unbroken view of the harbor where sailboats rise and fall with the tide.

On the afternoon a tourist-packed Key West ferry had dropped us off, Wes, Theo, and the Carriers were out at the platform where they had been since early morning, watching and waiting with no mating attempts in evidence. As Pratt would say later, it had been an unusual, meditative day, when the activity consisted mostly of noting the rhythm of the tide, the marine equivalent of watching the grass grow. By the time the team had called it quits and paddled back to the island, Bev and I were ensconced on the veranda imbibing cocktails concocted from powdered juice mix, tepid jug water, and a dollop of spirits from an aluminum canteen. A breeze rattled palm fronds overhead while the talk turned to the tagging program that Carrier and Pratt have been maintaining for a dozen years.

"A unique part of our study," Wes observed, "is that we have a wild population of sharks that actually has some aspects of a captive one. They come back year after year, so we can revisit the group again and again." This assertion is well grounded. Because Carrier and Pratt have been studying nurse sharks in the Tortugas for so long, most of the adults in the breeding population now carry some combination of the team's external tags and internal electronic PIT (for "passive integrated transponder") tags. Some of the external tags consist of strings of color-coded beads attached to a dart propelled from a modified speargun. Others are plastic cattle ear tags; different colors are used in different years. PIT tags are inserted just under the skin beneath the base of a shark's first dorsal fin. Pratt has jury-rigged a waterproof housing for the PIT tag reader, replete with a grip and trigger, which allows him to read the tags even on nurse sharks sheltering deep underneath coral overhangs. (Another of Pratt's inventions is "Bite Buster," a plierlike contraption he uses to pry open the jaws of sharks so offended by his curiosity that they bite him. This and other home-made field tools dangle outboard from rigging he has strung along the sides of his kayak—probably the only kayak so equipped in the world.) External tags also are always attached to a dorsal fin—the first dorsal on a female, the second on a male—thus allowing tagged males and females to be distinguished during the throes of a mating event even if tag numbers can't be read. Whenever a mating event is observed, however, an effort is made to record tag numbers, first in a waterproof field log and later in a computer database. Team members also try to note distinctive natural body markings, such as a gouge on a dorsal fin.

All of this low-tech monitoring has helped Carrier and Pratt begin to fill in unknowns, such as the seasonal and long-term pace of breeding, at least for nurse sharks. For instance, says Wes, "in a given year all the tags we see on females are, for the most part, the same color. The next year the sharks we see will have a different-color tag, but again, mostly the *same* color. The following year the pattern will reverse again. So from that we can say that these sharks generally come back to breed every other year."

Many shark species seem to have a two-year breeding cycle, although I mention to Wes my hypothesis that even in those that do, if food supplies are low, some sexually mature animals, especially females, may skip a year because of the need to build up their bodily resources before reproducing. Carrier and Pratt have in fact found this to be the case with their nurse sharks, and the observation is more than just a researcher's footnote. At the very least, if fisheries managers are going to intelligently formulate and enforce catch regulations that protect the reproductive base of shark populations, they must understand the vagaries of when and where the sharks breed and how fluctuating natural conditions can affect the process.

In this operation, the tags also facilitate tracking of particular sharks. In recent years, a male whom the team named One O'Clock Notch (a reference to a gouge on a dorsal fin) has emerged as one of the more dominant males in the mating arena.

"We observed One O'Clock the very first years we were here," Jeff explains. A trim, stocky, wry man in his mid-fifties, he speaks in a resonant radio voice. "He was young then—and so were we—and in those days he didn't have much success with females. But he's much more experienced now. I guess you could say he's not a sixteen-year-old in the back of his daddy's Chevy anymore."

Bev and I laugh at this, but in fact One O'Clock's tags are now showing up frequently in the growing database of mating events and successful copulations. "He's figured it out," Jeff notes, "and more importantly, I'm gonna guess that the females have figured out that he's a desirable male . . . whatever that means in a female shark's brain."

In addition to gaining procreational advantage with experience, a male nurse shark also attempts to mate with as many females as possible, increasing the chances that his genes will pass to a new generation. Yet the drive to procreate is powerful for both sexes, and often females mate with several males, sometimes in quick succession—serial sexual encounters that may help ensure that as many of a female's eggs as possible become fertilized. José Castro, a specialist in shark reproductive biology known for his beautiful photographs of shark embryos, has found that nurse shark mothers carry embryos of different sizes—and so, presumably, of different ages. His work suggests that females ovulate several eggs over a period of a month or so, with the eggs being fertilized in sequence. Dovetailing with Pratt and Carrier's behavioral observations, genetic evidence points to multiple fathers for the litters. Another of Castro's intriguing findings is that while female sharks from temperate latitudes have well-defined breeding seasons, their close relatives living in more tropical areas may breed year-round.

Beyond avid courting, a male shark's role in making baby sharks is pretty much limited to using his claspers to deliver sperm during sex. A young male's claspers, not yet calcified, are small and floppy like limp french fries. Wes Pratt has examined a lot of claspers, including those of blue sharks and dozens of great whites, ranging from the tiny ones of newborns to those of mature males. The white sharks have what Pratt calls "short and soft" claspers until they reach the age and size (apparently around eight feet) at which sexual maturation moves into high gear. Then, steady calcification makes the growing claspers increasingly rigid; one way to tell if a male shark is old enough to mate is to gauge the hardness of his claspers. When a male great white shark reaches full maturity at a length of about sixteen feet, his claspers are hard and about fifteen inches long, about a tenth of his body length. In some skates, a mature male's claspers grow to about a third of body length, and it has been estimated that the claspers of *C. megalodon*, the extinct fifty-plus-foot white shark, were five feet long.

Another curious attribute of a male shark's gonadal equipment is that his testes change dramatically with the seasons. In a nurse shark, for instance, from the end of August to January they are inconspicuous streaks of tissue, but thereafter they plump into sausage-shaped organs producing typical elasmobranch sperm—packages of DNA that are blanketed with mucus or another gooey substance that causes them to clump like globs of translucent tapioca. When the mating season is past and sperm are irrelevant (for a male) the testes shrink again.

A lengthwise tube or groove in each clasper's upper surface is the channel for semen, the viscous mix of sperm and seminal fluid. This fluid is stored in paired chambers, the seminal vesicles, on the underside of a male's spine; in a male basking shark the chambers can jointly hold ten or twelve gallons. Other details of a male shark's reproductive plumbing include, under the skin just forward of each clasper, a bulbous siphon sac that opens into the groove near the entry point for sperm. When a male has found a receptive mate and is on the verge of copulating, his claspers start to flex like handles on a water pump—movements that indirectly pump seawater into the siphon sac. When he ejaculates, a stream of his prepackaged sperm (mixed with seminal fluid) squirts into the clasper groove and flows deep into the female's reproductive tract. Meanwhile the siphon sac's load of water is being flushed out. This flood may help wash sperm clumps into the female's body—or, alternatively, its raison d'etre may be to flush out a previous partner's sperm. Pratt and Carrier have often seen copulating females with a diaphanous ribbon of previously deposited semen trailing out behind.

A female shark's reproductive anatomy has its own quirks. Some squalomorphs have two functional ovaries, but generally a female shark has only one, typically on the right side of her body. In some species these egg factories are very productive; a mature female sand tiger, for instance, may sequester more than twenty thousand eggs, which are ovulated fifteen or twenty at a time. The ovary of a female spiny dogfish produces yolky eggs the size of Ping-Pong balls, and some sharks make even larger ova. Each liberated egg tumbles briefly into the fluid of the shark's abdominal cavity before being funneled by beating, hairlike cilia into the shark's twin oviducts (the equivalent of fallopian tubes). Beyond the split, each oviduct bulges into a shell gland (also called an oviducal gland), where eggs are fertilized and protective capsules secreted over them. Each shell gland merges with a uterus—of which, accordingly, a female shark has two. A passageway from each uterus connects with the shark's cloaca. When the female is mated, sperm swim up through her uteri and on into the shell glands, where in many, perhaps most species, an unusual fate awaits them.

Although in sharks, as with most other animals, sex is geared exclusively toward making offspring, a mated female does not necessarily become pregnant right away. Instead, in one of the unusual features of shark reproduction, she may store the sperm she has received in her shell glands, which likely secrete nutrients that keep the sperm alive until conditions, including the female's own physical readiness, are right for her next crop of eggs to be fertilized. That moment in time could be many months, even more than a year, into the future. For me this point is underscored each June by the smooth dogfish (*Mustelus canis*) that migrate just offshore from my laboratory. These are large, pregnant females, a yard long and round of belly who, having wintered in warm waters farther south, are pushing north to pup in Chesapeake Bay and beyond, where food for their newborns will be ample. As soon as the pups are delivered, these ladies will become pregnant again, despite the fact that most *Mustelus* males are hundreds of miles away. As soon as she has birthed her brood, and cued probably by hormonal changes, the sperm cached in her shell glands will become active and each gland will release the tiny swimming cells in time to fertilize a newly arriving batch of ovulated eggs before they are encapsulated. The whole sequence is a coordinated piece of choreography that helps maximize the number of litters the female will produce in her lifetime.

We think this is the standard scenario for sperm storage in female sharks, although *Mustelus* may have evolved additional insurance that eggs will be fertilized. Reproductive biologist Bill Hamlett, working in my laboratory with my student Christina Conrath, found sperm also burrowed into the uterine walls of females. It may be another way for a female to provision herself with sperm, but if so it is a strategy that has never been observed in any other shark—or, for that matter, in any other animal.

The reef lagoon where Carrier and Pratt have erected their platform is one of the few places in the world where sharks have a known, clearly delimited, area devoted to courtship and mating (which is why the two have worked with park managers to close the area). But like most other sharks, the male and female nurse sharks congregating there seem to live completely separate lives until the drive to procreate draws them together. This independence of the sexes, which we see in lots of animals, may reduce the competition for food within the population, and given the separation, a female shark's ability to store sperm and keep it healthy until the moment arrives for eggs to be fertilized may have evolved as a biological safety net. From then on, the pooled genes from sperm and egg launch the shark embryo on its development from a nondescript ball of cells into a streamlined predator. And as nature would have it, some surprising alternatives have evolved for protecting and nourishing young sharks until they are born.

Baby elasmobranchs come into the world in one of two basic ways. Like birds and reptiles, some develop encapsulated in what amounts to an eggshell, basically a thick, leathery covering that is applied by the shell gland. It surrounds both the embryo and a store of yolk, which is the only nourishment the young animal will have until it hatches. This is an ancient reproductive mode called oviparity, "birth from an egg," and we see it in skates and about 30 percent of shark species. It is the primitive condition, the way the earliest jawless fishes and chondrichthyans protected young until they were minimally ready to meet the challenges of independent life. In other species, developing young survive on a combination of yolk and additional maternally supplied food until they are born from the mother's body— the mode of live birth, or viviparity. This dichotomy is where simplicity ends, however. The viviparous elasmobranchs, including some rays and roughly 70 percent of existing sharks, have evolved a plethora of strategies for the motherly care needed to nourish fetuses in the uterus; in fact, more different ways of maternal nurturing have evolved in elasmobranchs than in any other vertebrate group. Both oviparity and viviparity are high-ticket items biologically, requiring the mother to support her developing offspring for many months, in some cases for years. This requirement for her to muster major bodily resources in order to bear young is one reason why most female sharks have to grow large before they mature sexually, and then have pregnancies as long or longer than any other animals.

Oviparous sharks have large eggs stocked with an ample supply of yellowish, lipid-packed yolk to feed the embryo. Within a day after an egg is fertilized in the shell gland, the pinpoint-sized early embryo has been coated by a gelatinous blanket and enclosed in a durable capsule. Egg capsules in general can be remarkable, even beautiful, objects—flexible but tough, resistant to corrosion from seawater, up to a foot long in some species, twisting in corkscrew shapes with coiling tendrils, or oblong with hooks at the corners. Most are deep brown or a dark rusty color. Each uterus holds one encapsulated embryo at a time, usually for just a few days. Then, perhaps as the mother selects appropriate sites, such as rock crevices, where the capsule tendrils or hooks can attach, the two eggs in her uteri are deposited. Over weeks or even months, this sequence is repeated again and again. Months or even a year may pass before the developing offspring are ready to hatch, and despite their protective housing most don't survive the raids of predators. Scientists exploring the Monterey submarine canyon off central California discovered that catsharks there deposit their eggs in communal nesting sites, a habit probably found in some other oviparous species as well.

Skates, which probably evolved from live-bearing ancestors, also lay eggs in leathery cases, the blocky "mermaid's purses" that wash up on beaches. Sizes vary; for instance, barndoor skates produce eggs so large that the cases become trapped as "bycatch" in trawl nets, as do the skates themselves. Barndoor skates have been pushed to the brink of extinction because of the huge numbers of both the animals and their egg cases that are routinely captured and discarded.

. . .

The young of live-bearing sharks grow while protected and, some-times, fed by their mother's body until they are at least marginally equipped to fend for themselves. The thing I find most intriguing about this fact is the number of different ways that have evolved for nurturing the baby sharks. Some live bearers, like nurse sharks, pro-vide only yolk for their offspring. In terms of protection, they've moved a step beyond the egg-layers, but not much. After fertilization, a cluster of fifteen to twenty embryos, each sheathed in a sheer, trans-parent capsule (analogous, perhaps, to living pearls in breathable plastic bags), takes up residence in each of the mother's twin wombs. Like a shell, the capsule around an embryo provides crucial control over the infant shark's chemical environment, because at this early point in development the tiny sharks have few functioning organs. For the next five or six months, each embryo's sole source of nourishment will be yolk, initially in an external sac attached to its gut like a yellow ball, and then absorbed into a chamber in the shark's abdomen. When the capsule eventually ruptures, the growing shark inside has suffi-cient yolk reserves to sustain it while key organ systems become fully functional. During this time, for instance, whereas the initial fluid in the mother's uterus was chemically nothing like the sea, it steadily becomes more of an ocean as the mother flushes her uterus with sea-water. Each of her young correspondingly gains the ability to hoard urea and regulate its ion-water balance. The baby sharks' senses and nervous systems also steadily become as complex and refined as those of their parents.

With variations in the details, fully a quarter of shark species, including such widely different forms as spiny dogfishes and whale sharks, support their developing young in the way just described. Steadily using up their yolk provisions for growth and metabolism, the offspring at birth will weigh 40 percent less than the yolk-filled fertil-ized egg did. Sometimes the number of yolk-supported embryos is huge: in the mid-1990s, some three hundred embryonic whale sharks were discovered in the uterus of their dead mother. Many live-bearing sharks produce large litters, but the whale shark's luckless brood still stands as a record.

We tend to think of babies of any animal as small in comparison to their parents. Yolk-fed (technically, lecithotrophic) juvenile sharks fit this stereotype, because there's no way to pack an egg with enough yolk to support the growth of a large offspring. But because the sea teems with predators waiting to devour small juveniles, from an adaptive standpoint increased birth size confers a huge advantage in terms of increased survival. The price of that advantage, which many viviparous sharks have evolved to pay, is that the mother must provide the extra nourishment her young need to grow large before birth. This matrotrophy, being "mother fed," represents a major leap forward in shark evolution and it has evolved at least three times in three quite different forms. In a phenomenon that is sometimes called "egg cannibalism," lamniforms—makos, white sharks, threshers and their relatives—feed the developing embryos in the uterus by providing an ongoing supply of yolky eggs that the embryos consume. For instance, the typical brood of eight or nine infant great white sharks subsist on ovulated, unfertilized eggs, the stern end of their bellies growing distended as if each had swallowed a lightbulb. Embryonic sand tigers have gone over the top with this strategy: by the time a developing sand tiger is a little over two inches long, it already has multiple rows of usable teeth, and the first embryo in each uterus to reach a length of about four inches promptly begins fulfilling its predatory destiny by eating its siblings, after which it depends on a conveyor belt of ova. Its mother will birth only these two precocious cannibals, which will have grown to about three feet long before they leave the security of her body. Bigeye threshers also produce a single offspring from each uterus, but we don't yet know if they are solitary winners of a shark-eats-shark race in the womb.

In rays and some sharks the strategy has been to supply only enough yolk to feed embryos briefly, and then—possibly with a hormonal signal as the trigger—to switch to a protein-rich milky substance called histotroph. As her pregnancy proceeds and her offspring's digestive system develops, the lining of a female's womb elaborates into a dense carpet of villi, fingerlike projections that envelop her young and secrete what amounts to a fluid cocoon of food around them. This arrangement provides such a feast of nutrients that a newly conceived stingray will have increased its weight three thousandfold by the time it is born.

Some of the advanced requiem sharks, like duskies, make a truly huge maternal investment in offspring, of a sort that we usually associate not with fish, but with mammals like ourselves. Rather amazingly, their evolution has remodeled the yolk sac into a placenta. Attached to the mother shark's uterine wall by what is effectively an umbilical cord, the placenta develops into a lush, complex, blood-infused organ that for the duration of her pregnancy will shuttle nutrients and other substances from her bloodstream to that of her baby and remove its body wastes. The mammalian placenta serves the same function in a pregnant woman. But whereas a woman's body usually must create a placental tether to only one infant, depending on the species a placental shark must do so for anywhere from four to a hundred young.

Like other nurturing adaptations evolved by live-bearing sharks, the placental lifeline's steady stream of nutrients allows young to grow large and emerge into the sea as capable hunters. However, their undoubtedly enhanced survival extracts a huge cost in terms of the time required for the growth of baby sharks before they are born. For example, each of a dusky shark's pregnancies will last a year and a half. A female great white shark may also have eighteen-month pregnancies once she reaches maturity at about fourteen years. In some other shark groups, factors other than the size of offspring can prolong gestation. Spiny dogfish pups are only about eleven inches long, but such sharks inhabit cold water, have a slow metabolism, and grow at a snail's pace. Females are pregnant for nearly two years, equal to the gestation time of an elephant. The record for longest pregnancy of any animal on Earth, an estimated three-plus years, is held by the frilled shark, which also lives in cold water and develops slowly. Again and again, as we learn more about how long it takes for different sharks to produce young, we see the same time-demanding pattern.

Over the millennia, reproductive strategies like these have served sharks well in terms of increasing the survivorship of new generations, but in today's human-dominated world, such a leisurely reproductive program cannot compensate for aggressive harvesting.

In the natural world we often see a trade-off between making the biological investment required to produce a few, robust offspring, or instead to make a slew of more vulnerable young of which only a few will survive. In the sea generally, body mass and death rate tend to be inversely proportional; that is, the smaller you are, the greater the number and kinds of hungry mouths that can consume you. Dusky shark litters usually range from around three to a dozen pups, that of a blacktip reef shark only three or four, those of several species only two—but all are large enough and equipped physiologically to escape most of the dangers that await newborns in the ocean. Blue shark females, by contrast, birth about sixty small, squirmy offspring that are much more likely to become somebody's lunch.

At half past nine on our first night in camp, after a supper of reconstituted dry food and a workday that had begun fourteen hours earlier, Jeff Carrier had opened a laptop computer on the picnic table and begun reviewing the previous day's tag data. The computer's battery had just been recharged in the park rangers' quarters (where the accommodations are enviably less rustic than our own); in the darkening evening the little screen's glow enveloped Carrier's stubbly beard in a bluish light, the only real competition for which was an almost translucent bubble of moonlight.

One of the patterns revealed by the Tortugas tagging program is that, unlike female nurse sharks, which seem to return to mate only if they have not done so the previous year, most of the males show up year after year, persistent in the attempt to pass on their genes. Some have been fitted with ultrasonic transmitters like the ones Ken Goldman stuffed into the herring he fed to salmon sharks in Alaska. The transmitters' signals are detected by bottom monitors Carrier has placed at various locations in and outside the lagoon; every few days he pulls the monitors and downloads their stored contents into the laptop, whereupon the information becomes translated into data points plotted on a map of the study area etched on the computer's screen. With time, and in combination with field observations, the result is a growing sense of the daily rhythms of this small population of nurse sharks as they go about the making of a new generation. For instance, Pratt and Carrier now know that whereas females often seem to settle into the protected area, using it as a place to shelter and rest, males enter it only when they are chasing mates and depart when the effort is over. Exiting the lagoon at its shallow mouth, they move into deeper water along the edge of the reef. Where they go and what they do there is a minor and manageable mystery among the many unknowns in the vast realm of shark reproduction.

"We want to know, for example," explained Carrier, "after a mating event in the lagoon, do they go to another mating site we don't know about? Maybe." Females taking refuge in the lagoon often arrive bleeding with fresh bite marks, sometimes deep ones—which suggests that the little lagoon is not the only part of the reef system where mating events take place. "But," Jeff continues, "it also seems likely that— not unlike males of other species—if mating ends in copulation, there could be a need for physiological replenishment afterward."

Signals from the transmitters, and video footage from Crittercam, are indeed helping pinpoint underwater sites where males hang out between forays into the lagoon, sometimes merely resting on the bottom in as much as seventy feet of water. Of themselves these may not seem like remarkable facts, until we consider how incredibly rare it is to have such an intimate look at the lives of any wild animals. "In a way," says Carrier, "we're given an opportunity by these animals to see so much of what goes on in their lives. It's something for which I personally feel grateful."

Experience is also shedding light on possible human impacts on shark matings. Our first day out at the platform we had seen a few nurse sharks, including some two-foot juveniles, but there was no apparent mating activity. After the next morning's failed attempt, the day crept along with only an occasional tarpon sighting to relieve the monotony. Tired of cooking our brains on the reef, Bev and I gave up the watch in the early afternoon and went snorkeling, learning later that shortly after our departure there had been another mating event, this one consummated. We wondered if the excessive or insensitive presence of people might deter these sharks from their mating mission.

"There's no doubt in my mind," Jeff Carrier confirms, when the question is posed. "That's why the lagoon area is closed to people during the mating season. In the old days, swimmers or boaters would come through when we'd be watching a mating event, and it would immediately break up."

Bev asks if the researchers are concerned about their own impact on the sharks. "We do worry about our disruptive effects," admits Pratt. "That's what the kayaks are all about and why we tiptoe around and sit on towers. . . . I like it best and I think we're at our best when we have a minimal team here."

"But we know from experience when to go in and when not to," Carrier adds. "The early phases of courtship are most critical, right up to the point where the grasp is made by the male. If you do anything prior to that time, you'll break up 'following behavior' that might be occurring, or some of the other precopulation things. I don't know if there's an elasmobranch correlate of foreplay, but that may be about as close as it gets." But once a male has started working on his grasp, both sharks seem more concerned with the ensuing courtship stages than with human perturbations. The day before we arrived, Pratt and Carrier had approached a pair of coupling sharks, attaching both a sonic transmitter and Crittercam to the male. Far from being unduly distressed by the paraphernalia, within twenty minutes he was back trying to mate another female while Crittercam recorded the entire sequence.

Even low-tech videos of nurse shark matings are engrossing to watch, partly because for so long we have known so little about this aspect of sharks' behavior. Using video cameras outfitted with hydrophones and underwater still cameras, Pratt and Carrier have obtained extraordinary film and photographs of the various phases of courtship and mating events. At scientific meetings I have been fascinated by some of these images. One that persists in my mind is a female nurse shark nearly nine feet long, rolled onto her back in water only a few feet deep, her pelvic fins cupped and her snout pressed against the coral rubble bottom, absolutely motionless while her partner completes their union. Both animals' tails are thrust into the air and the blue green water's surface is sparkling.

More advanced equipment can also provide a wealth of data. Using a video camera rigged with light-emitting devices (LEDs), Pratt and Carrier have observed that nurse sharks actively mate at night, maybe more so than during daylight. (Some investigators believe that, in general, nurse sharks are nocturnal animals.) Its depth sensors track how deep males go when they leave the lagoon, and its microphones have even picked up the sounds of males munching their way up a female's pectoral fin.

Beyond the purely scientific value of this sort of knowledge, it may well be crucial to intelligent efforts to manage fisheries that target sharks. If we know when and where even a few kinds of sharks mate, what the triggers are and the sequence of steps, and how often male and female sharks engage in this most primal of behaviors, we can at least begin to delimit places where, and times when, the sharks should be left to their reproductive business. We may also be able to protect key coastal locations all over the world where shark pups spend their vulnerable first weeks of life.

Indeed all over the world shark researchers are asking necessary questions, and with so much left to learn, well they might. Only a tiny corner of the puzzle includes nurse sharks in the Dry Tortugas, and even that still has major pieces missing, including understanding the effects of environmental factors such as lunar cycles and water temperature, the almost unknown role hormones play in shark reproductive cycles, and the full complexity of the social interactions that shape the making of new generations of sharks.

Shortly before Bev and I were to pack up our gear and board the ferry back to Key West, Wes Pratt remarked that "By being here and interpreting for others what we find, hopefully we can ultimately do some good for the animals."

"I daresay we know more about shark mating behavior than any other investigators, and we know virtually nothing," Jeff Carrier added. "The more we study, the more we continue to raise questions. It's a lot more complicated than anybody thought."

5 *Eye, Ear, Nose, and Snout*

Research vessel Pierce
Mid-Atlantic Ridge, north of the Azores
October 1986

The wave took me by surprise, rolling up over the stern out of
the dark and knocking me off my feet. I groped for the safety
wire strung across the stern, but felt the rushing water carrying me overboard toward a roiling, black sea. Then, as if by
some supernatural force, I was snatched back from the brink.
Standing there on the heaving deck smiling down at me was
Steve Branstetter, dressed out, as I was, in sea boots and dripping oilskins. "Kinda cold for a swim tonight," he grinned.
"Thought you might want to stay aboard."

The above-described incident, noted in my field log, took place
virtually in the middle of the North Atlantic ocean on a night when I

and a scientific team that included a large, strong post-doctoral researcher named Steve Branstetter were aboard a 140-foot mudboat being buffeted by near gale-force winds. We were trying to set our longline in twelve thousand feet of water to catch sharks. Why would anyone expect to find sharks at such depths, let alone try to capture them? Our mission on this research cruise was to determine how deep sharks live, in order to provide advice to the communications giant AT&T, which at the time was concerned about the danger of shark damage to the first fiber-optic telephone cable system they were planning to deploy across the Atlantic.

The voyage was instigated by the failure of the company's experimental fiber-optic cable system in the Canary Islands a few months before. When that cable was retrieved from fifty-five hundred feet down, shark teeth were found embedded in the plastic coating, and the holes caused by the bites in turn let seawater in and caused the cable to short out. The people at AT&T were surprised because with their standard transoceanic telephone cables they had never had shark bite problems deeper than about fifteen hundred feet. They normally armored their cables with stainless steel mesh down to three thousand feet to protect against damage from sharks and commercial fishing gear. Now, with the evidence that their new fiber-optic system was vulnerable much deeper than that, they wondered exactly *how* deep they would have to provide armoring—a critical question because failure of the system could cost millions of dollars in loss of service and repairs. On the other hand, armoring would add considerable expense to producing and laying the cable. AT&T also wanted to know what manner of beast could be causing the problem. Some months previously at Bell Laboratories in New Jersey, my colleague Guido Dingerkus and I had tried to identify the awl-like tooth fragments to little avail, beyond the fact that they had once belonged to a shark.

"They look a little like crocodile shark teeth," was all Guido could suggest. Even he doubted he was right, but our expedition to the Azores and Canary Islands would supply clues to the mystery.

Why would any shark bite a heavily insulated fiber-optic cable?

The answer lies in basic physics and the extraordinary electrosensory system that sharks possess. Fiber-optic cables utilize light to transmit telephone signals across the ocean, but the signals lose strength unless they are boosted electronically at intervals along the way. An electric wire, which provides signal-boosting power, is packed in the cable alongside the fiber-optic bundles. Even though the cable is insulated, the DC current generates a weak magnetic field that induces an electric field when a shark swims across the cable. This electrical aura can be detected by sharks and other elasmobranchs by way of sensory organs called ampullae of Lorenzini (after their seventeenth-century Italian discoverer, Stefano Lorenzini). Each ampulla consists of a pinhole-sized pore that opens into a jelly-filled canal leading to a grapelike cluster of sensory cells called alveoli, which are buried in a shark's snout and wrapped in nerve endings.

Most of the electrosensory patches are arrayed symmetrically around the shark's mouth, but some are also on top of the snout in sharks that feed in midwater on active prey. Benthic-feeding elasmobranchs such as skates tend to have denser arrays of pores on the undersurface of their heads. Regardless of its layout, the elasmobranch electrosensory system is acutely sensitive, capable of detecting nanovolt (one billionth of a volt per centimeter) electric fields such as those produced by prey organisms and ocean currents. Physiological processes and muscle contractions, such as those controlling gill movements, produce such "bioelectric" fields, which are weak and dissipate quickly in the sea. They are so faint that even sharks can detect them only at distances of a foot or two. The bites on AT&T's deep-sea cable probably were inflicted when a shark swimming close to the bottom passed just above the cable. When the electric field surrounding the cable stimulated the shark's electroreceptors, it triggered a reflexive bite.

The electrical world that sharks and their kin can sense is closed to us, but to them it is a continual source of information, fine-tuning their predatory aim and guiding it, often with astonishing accuracy, in the last moments of a feeding strike. And like so many other biological systems, this one has been honed in different elasmobranch species to suit their particular predatory requirements. Comparative studies in my laboratory, carried out by Bill Raschi, who had worked with me on the hydrodynamics of shark denticles, demonstrated this kind of evolutionary tweaking. Our research subjects were coastal and deep-water skates, which I reasoned might use their electrosensory apparatus in very different ways, given their different hunting environments. What Bill found, in fact, was that coastal creatures like the little skate (*Leucoraja erinacea*) have almost an embarrassment of electrosensory riches: a profusion of pores stud the area around the skate's mouth and can collectively transmit a barrage of separate signals to its brain. The result is a capacity for extremely fine spatial discrimination of the sources of different bioelectric signals—an arrangement that provides exquisite hunting precision to these elasmobranchs, which glide along the bottom sucking up minuscule worms and crustaceans burrowed in the mud. The contrast is keen with large deepwater species like the thorny skate (*Amblyraja radiata*), whose pores are more spread out but connect with more buried alveoli, so incoming signals are picked up simultaneously by more receptors. In effect, as the thorny skate cruises along well above the bottom, its ampullary system amplifies incoming bioelectric signals, and the diameter of the "sensory cone" beneath the skate is large. Thus it can detect prey not only from a greater distance but over a wider area. It's a logical solution for the thorny skate, which feeds on larger prey like crabs and fishes that are sparsely scattered over its deepwater habitat.

One of the most intriguing things about a keen electrical sense is the potential it presents for uses other than hunting—such as, for instance, communications with animals of one's own kind. Indeed, experiments have shown that some stingrays can recognize and orient to other individuals of the same species, using the species' unique bio-electric field as a name tag. Many freshwater bony fishes, including South American knifefishes, actually have specialized electrogenic organs whose signals can be used for communication, and because elasmobranchs are so electrosensitive, it stands to reason that they might also have electrogenic organs geared toward the same use.

Yet such an adaptation has evolved only in skates. The primary reason for this apparent evolutionary oversight could be simply that seawater is a terrible medium for transmitting electrical messages. Because electrical signals dissipate very rapidly in seawater, in order to send or receive them individuals must be virtually next to one another. That is actually the way it works in skates, which have patches of weakly electrogenic tissue at the base of the tail. These organs are larger in males than in females and may be used in social interactions. It's possible that sexual foreplay in skates may involve the equivalent of "sweet nothings" uttered in electrical code and "heard" by the potential mate's ampullary system.

Torpedo rays have taken electrogenesis to the extreme and have evolved large electrogenic organs on the upper body behind the eyes. Capable of producing up to two hundred volts, these organs are weapons used offensively to stun prey and defensively to deter predators. They are built of cells called electroplaques, which are stacked end-to-end; the side surfaces are insulated and the cell columns basically function as a series of electrical batteries. Their power was indelibly demonstrated to me one summer on the docks of the Marine Biological Laboratory in Woods Hole, where a green but cocky summer intern was stationed to meet the trawler *Captain Bill III* and off-load live squid and fishes slated to be used in research projects. Chronically posturing for the benefit of girls passing through en route to the Martha's Vineyard ferry, he had been sparring all summer with the vessel's skipper Henry Clem, a classic old New Englander with a pointed sense of humor. One afternoon after the crew had transferred a load of squid to the young man's cart, they hoisted up a living five-foot torpedo ray, which dangled from the boom hook by a rope looped around its tail. When they swung the ray toward the dock as if to drop it into the cart, Clem shouted "Grab it!" Seconds later the youth was on his backside in a puddle, thrown several feet by the force of the trussed animal's electrical output. It was an experience that almost certainly yielded a new respect for electric rays and for the good captain as well.

At one time, researchers hypothesized that a shark's ampullary system was designed to detect heat or salinity, among other functions, and it wasn't until the 1960s that Dutch behaviorist Ad Kalmijn, then a graduate student, showed its efficacy in detecting bioelectric fields and prey location. Kalmijn also suggested that sharks might use these same organs to detect the Earth's magnetic field—with the navigational potential such a sense could offer for migration. He proposed an indirect mechanism in which a shark's ampullary organs might detect the faint electric fields generated by ocean currents and by the shark's own movement through the Earth's magnetic field. As support for this hypothesis, Kalmijn showed that in a lab setting the round stingray (*Urobatis halleri*) could use an artificially created magnetic field to choose its swimming direction. Working in the Sea of Cortez, Peter Klimley added another intriguing dimension by demonstrating that schools of wild scalloped hammerheads followed local magnetic anomalies in their daily movements to and from a submerged seamount. Yet, while we know that hammerheads have an acutely honed electrosensory system, its possible use in detecting geomagnetic cues for navigation remains to be proven conclusively and in fact an alternate hypothesis may be more plausible.

Many groups of organisms are indeed known to have a geomagnetic sense, and to be capable of differentiating not only north from south (the horizontal component of the field) but also the dip angle, or the vertical component, of the field. As this angle changes with latitude, the animal can use it as a magnetic map. Not one of these creatures, including monarch butterflies, trout, and sea turtles, has ampullary organs, but all can perform astonishing feats of geomagnetic navigation nonetheless. Apparently, their secret lies in sensory cells containing biomagnetite. In rainbow trout, these cells are embedded in the lining of the nasal passages and connect to the trigeminal nerve, which passes signals on to the brain. Sharks, too, have magnetite in their heads, and while little is known about the location or structure of magnetite sensory organs in sharks, I personally will wager that they not only have such structures but use them for navigation. In the living world, natural selection usually favors the simplest solution to a problem. And a sense that can detect geomagnetic cues directly is intuitively more probable than one like the ampullary system, which would have to translate highly variable electrical signals, which are affected by the animal's own movements, into geomagnetic information. It's possible that sharks navigate with both.

At the entrance to the dirt road leading to Sonny Gruber's Bimini laboratory, a weathered plywood sign bears a roughly shark-shaped cutout whose color once must have mimicked a bright Bahamian sky. For years this place has been the focal point for Gruber's research on a resident population of lemon sharks, which has yielded classic data on shark senses and behavior. Although the electroreceptive system is a close-range tool and the final sense a shark uses to orient itself for a feeding strike, farther out—up to hundreds of yards away—two other shark senses, hearing and the "smell" sense or olfaction, appear to be essential in detecting prey. Sonny Gruber has been responsible for several decades of groundbreaking work that established first if, and then how, these senses help shape a shark's hunting behavior. Those studies were the subject of several conversations Bev and I had with him during our visit to watch reef sharks feeding, and had proven to be a fascinating short course in the history of much of what we know about shark senses in general.

One of the earliest investigations of shark hearing was devised in the 1960s by Gruber and the future shark behaviorist Donald Nelson when they were both still in graduate school at the University of Miami. Now, so many years later and despite a lengthy, ultimately successful battle with cancer, in his sixties Sonny remains trim, intense, and irreverent. As Bev's tape recorder clicked on in the Bimini lab's classroom, I found it easy to imagine the young academic who challenged more than a few stereotypes about shark senses.

"Both Don and I were spear fishermen," he began. "In those days there were a lot of sharks, and we noticed that when we were spearfishing, sharks would come in. We didn't quite understand it, because they would arrive from any direction. That meant that they could not be detecting blood, and it couldn't be vision because you can only see so far underwater. So we figured it must be sound, although at the time nobody knew very much about hearing in sharks."

For the most part, only some simple anatomy had been elucidated. Although sharks, like other fishes, have no external ears, they do have a pair of inner ears similar to those of most other vertebrates. In a portion of each inner ear are three semicircular canals used in balance and detecting acceleration, as in humans. There also are three sensory patches in the inner ear where calcium carbonate particles called otoconia lie atop groups of sensory hair cells. When sound waves strike the inner ear, the otoconia jostle and bend the hair cells, inducing a signal that the auditory nerve carries to the shark's brain. Sharks, and only sharks, also have a patch of sensory tissue without otoconia in the lower part of the inner ear. This structure, called the macula neglecta, is now thought to be the main apparatus sharks use to determine the direction from which a sound is coming.

Realizing that sharks might be attracted by sounds, Gruber and Nelson went down to Orange Key with underwater recording equipment and spearfishing gear and tape-recorded sounds made by the fish they would capture.

"Then we went back to the laboratory," explained Sonny, "and analyzed these sounds and created synthetic versions of them with just the low-frequency characteristics. We had no idea where this was all going to lead, but we made up an experimental protocol in which we played fifteen minutes with sound, then fifteen minutes without it. Then we went back out on the water and drifted around playing this sound pattern underwater. We didn't really think it was going to work, but we figured that statistically we might see something. So we put the hydrophone down about forty feet and just hung off the back of the boat and drifted. And it wasn't five minutes before we had the biggest goddam tiger shark you could imagine, just swimming around and around the hydrophone. I'd never seen a tiger shark before except in books, and I was so scared that I jumped out of the water. It was a helluva first observation, and as our work continued, we *never* saw a shark during any of the silent periods, and we *did* see sharks during most of the playback periods. There was no need for statistical analysis."

The two scientists discovered that when they pulsed very low frequency sounds (sounds with a low pitch) below 60 hertz (cycles per second) in a rapid but irregular pattern, the sounds consistently attracted sharks such as bulls, tigers, lemons, and hammerheads. Sharks were less attracted to pulsed higher-frequency sounds and ignored a continuous stream of sound no matter what its frequency was.

Subsequent studies have shown that although sharks can hear relatively high pitched sounds up to 800–1000 hz, their hearing sense is most acute at 80 hz and below. (By way of comparison, the human ear is most sensitive to tones between 1000 and 3000 hz.) A shark's hearing range even extends into the "infrasonic" below 10 hz, allowing them to hear sounds to which we are totally deaf. In fact, a shark's attention may be drawn not only by the struggling sounds of prey but by other low-frequency sounds such as the drumming many bony fishes produce.

Experiments in the open ocean have shown that randomly pulsed low-frequency sounds can attract sharks from as far away as four hundred yards, or about a quarter of a mile. Conversely, abrupt, loud sounds (ten times louder than the usual background noise) caused sharks to flee—a discovery that immediately raised the possibility of using loud, pulsed sound as a shark repellent. Unfortunately, sharks rather quickly get used to abrupt sounds after a while and ignore them. How rapidly this habituation develops appears to be species-specific. In one experiment, silky sharks had to be exposed to such signals six or eight times before they would ignore them, whereas oceanic whitetips would withdraw from the signals only once.

For years, a shark's ability to determine the direction from which a sound was coming was attributed to the lateral line or acoustico-lateralis system—small bundles of sensory cells called neuromasts that are arranged in canals or nestled in pores on the head or body. Today, the system's sensory role in a shark's life is less certain. The most prominent canal, the lateral line, runs along the body midline from behind the head to the base of the tail, and it seems to be mainly a mechanoreceptor detecting water movements next to the skin that could signal the nearby presence of prey, predators, mates, or schooling fishes of the same species. Yet a shark's lateral-line system has many features not found in the lateral lines of bony fishes or amphibians, making its overall function and significance to shark behavior still an open question.

The morning before Bev and I sat down with Sonny, I had spent a few placid hours fly-fishing with Bonefish Ray, one of Bimini's premier fishing guides. When he reached down to grasp my first bonefish of the day, his large hand enclosed a streamlined, opalescent creature with huge eyes. Ray gently unhooked the fish, deftly released it at the side of his wooden skiff, and it streaked across the shallow coral flat. In a minute or two, a pair of baby lemon sharks appeared, probably attracted by the sounds of the bonefish struggling. They meandered past our boat, but when their path crossed that of my now-departed catch, they turned suddenly and swam rapidly away, following the bonefish's track. How could they know where the bonefish had gone? Probably through their keen sense of smell. As the bonefish took flight, pricked by my hook and handled by Ray, it had left a dilute trail of blood, body fluids, and mucus.

Sharks and their relatives have fairly well-developed senses of smell and taste, which together provide the animal with a steady stream of chemosensory information about its world. Like humans, sharks smell using olfactory organs, but in other ways differences outnumber similarities. Sharks do have paired nostrils beneath their snouts in front of the mouth, but the nostrils are not used in breathing. In fact, to call them nostrils is misleading, for unlike human nostrils they do not open into passageways in the shark's head. Each is more like a tunnel, with two openings separated by a fleshy flap. As the shark swims along, water flows into the forward opening, over the olfactory organ—a mass of tissue called a rosette, studded with odor-sensitive chemosensors—and then out the rear. In some less-active species, the volume of the olfactory chamber may fluctuate as the shark's mouth opens and closes during breathing, and this rhythmic pumping action forces water over the sensory cells. The organ itself is pleated with folds that increase the surface area able to receive chemical information, and the sensory cells it houses include a multitude of types. Each one is an olfactory specialist that responds to a particular kind of chemical (as far as we know, mainly different amino acids), allowing extremely detailed chemical information to be transmitted to the shark's brain. In addition, the system's sensitivity to chemical cues is keen. In the laboratory, lemon sharks have been able to detect one part tuna extract in 25 million parts of seawater—the equivalent of ten drops in the volume of an average-sized swimming pool. In other experiments, gray reef sharks and blacktip reef sharks responded to concentrations of grouper extract as low as one part per *billion,* or one drop in a quarter-acre pond six and a half feet deep.

In theory, a relatively simple way to study olfaction in sharks is to implant electrodes into the shark's forebrain where its olfactory nerves enter, and then introduce various chemical stimulants, in specific concentrations, into the shark's olfactory organ. Any brain response to the stimulation will show up on an electroencephalogram, or EEG, produced by a recording device to which the electrodes are connected. The first person to attempt this procedure with sharks was Perry Gilbert, the revered pioneer in shark biology. Gilbert, a product of Dartmouth and Cornell Universities and a professor at Cornell for most of his career, did many of his shark studies at the Lerner Marine Laboratory on North Bimini, a short boat ride from Sonny Gruber's present facility. His subjects for the EEG experiments were several of the surrounding lagoon's lemon sharks, which were not necessarily inclined to cooperate with Gilbert's scheme. That problem was solved with the neurotoxin curare, which, if injected in the proper dose, could temporarily immobilize a shark without disrupting its brain functions. Then the team worked to perfect recording techniques, which they knew would determine both the quality of their results and whether the experiment could be replicated successfully. After weeks of frustrating glitches, Gilbert and his cohorts finally obtained a clean and conclusive EEG—a narrow length of recording paper etched with tracings of the changing electrical activity in a lemon shark's brain as its olfactory organs responded to odorant molecules. In the future, the Bimini lab would see successful recordings of both EEGs and ECGs (electrocardiograms) from free-swimming sharks held in a horseshoe-shaped tank, but with this initial effort the drama wasn't yet finished. As the historic recording played out onto the laboratory floor, one of the men grabbed an empty wastebasket to receive it, knowing that the accumulating ribbon of paper was the team's only hard evidence of a major scientific breakthrough. His choice of receptacle was almost the end of the experiment. As the elated scientists celebrated at the Compleat Angler, a Bimini watering hole made famous by Ernest Hemingway, a thorough cleaning lady added the wastebasket's contents to a load of trash on its way to the town dump. Gilbert's revelatory study of shark EEGs would be published in the elite journal *Science* in 1964, but only after several bemused Bahamians were treated to the sight of three white-coated scientists and their staff frantically combing through fish heads and rotting household trash for the world's first shark EEG.

When a lemon shark detects an appealing odor, it usually turns and swims upstream toward the odor. It can orient by using the current itself (a type of directional movement called rheotaxis). In contrast, a nurse shark will scribe an S-shaped course swinging back and forth through the odor train, following the chemical gradient by turning toward the nostril where the stimulation is the strongest. These two behavioral strategies are how sharks home in on an odor source. Hammerheads, whose nostrils are near the ends of their hammer-shaped heads, really smell in stereo, and although much research remains to be done on the subject, of all sharks hammerheads are thought to be particularly adept at following chemical gradients.

It's a given that sharks use their noses to find food, but there is growing evidence that female sharks also produce pheromones that attract males during the mating season. Pheromones are vital communication molecules in the reproductive lives of many bony fishes, and as we learn more I believe we will find the same is true for sharks because, in nature, chemical communication is the only way to leave messages. In particular, it can help individuals recognize members of their own species, so as not to waste time and energy trying to mate with a partner of the wrong species—a mismatch that is nearly always destined to fail. A pheromone trail secreted by a female can waft through the water or cling to the substrate, thus marking a breeding area that can be detected by appropriate male mates. That kind of message might read, in effect, "Receptive lady here; stick around."

Because of sharks' great innate sensitivity to odors, I believe we will find that this keen olfactory sense shapes their lives in major ways, even though at present we are ignorant about the extent to which they use the language of chemistry to communicate. Likewise, perhaps, with taste. Sharks don't have a tongue, but in its place they have a piece of cartilage covered by skin containing taste buds. Beyond that bare fact, little is known about a shark's taste sense, other than that their taste buds physically resemble those of other vertebrates. A researcher working in the early twentieth century found that the dusky smoothhound reacted, presumably negatively, by jerking its head when the inside of its mouth was swabbed with quinine, a substance we humans perceive as bitter. Apparently no serious work on shark gustation has occurred since. I find it a wonder that those of us who work every day with elasmobranchs do not even know whether sharks perceive the four primary tastes—bitter, salty, sweet, and sour—that inform our own gustatory universe.

After a break for a grilled cheese sandwich lunch in the Bimini lab's "dining room"—a sizable space that accommodates a table for sixteen—we adjourn again to the classroom where noise is limited to the hum of filters cleansing glass aquaria. The room, about ten feet by twenty, is a few paces down a technicolor hallway painted with reef scenes and plastered with photographs of several decades worth of students, visiting researchers, and sharks in a welter of situations and poses. Simply keeping the facility operating and productive in the face of perennial money shortages and equipment failures seems to me in itself to be a monumental achievement. Yet Sonny Gruber apparently draws upon a deep personal well of tenacity and scientific creativity. One of the most singular achievements of his career began with his Ph.D. research on shark vision. It is a subject that animates him to this day, possibly because his discoveries dramatically overturned the long-standing but mythical view of sharks as being, in a sensory way, little more than swimming noses.

"At that time, which was a little over a decade after World War II," Sonny recalls, "there was money from the Office of Naval Research (ONR) to do research on sharks. They reckoned that if we understood the behavior of sharks, and their sensory systems, we could make some progress on the question of shark attacks. I had been working with Don Nelson on this hearing stuff, but then the navy approached my major professor, Warren Wisby, with the question of the color of navy flight suits, some of which were green, others international orange. Pilots were calling the orange ones 'yum-yum yellow' because they seemed to attract sharks. ONR wanted to know if sharks really could see color."

At the time, the scientific literature on shark senses was meager, with even some of the most astute researchers believing that sharks could not see color because they did not have the requisite sensory cells, cones, in the retina. Cones are one of two types of light-sensitive receptors in the retinas of vertebrate eyes. They provide visual acuity and, in some animals, color vision in bright light, while rods provide sensitivity in dim light.

"So I began going to shark-fishing tournaments in search of shark eyes," Sonny recalls, with evident affection for a research strategy that would be largely futile today because tournaments no longer produce sharks in significant numbers. "In the Bayshore tournament in New York, they'd typically bring in twelve hundred sharks in two or three days. Blues, makos, duskies, threshers, seven or eight different species. But 80 to 85 percent were blues. One of my most exciting finds was getting a little great white shark, about fifty-six pounds. We went out to the boat that caught it and got a perfect set of great white shark eyes. I guess I was kind of like a ghoul going around and cutting the eyes out of sharks, but eventually we got most of the carcharhinids. We found that the white shark had the most advanced retina of them all, with a high number of cones relative to rods, among other things."

Gruber's discovery that a shark's retina had cones was huge, scientifically, although it did not necessarily mean that sharks had color vision. Some guitarfish have cones but see the world in shades of gray because their cones lack the requisite color-absorbing pigments.

"So the question was, what do the sharks do with these eyes? Most people said sharks have rudimentary vision, but logically you have to ask yourself why would an animal with rudimentary vision have some of the most sophisticated visual structures in the marine realm? For instance, a typical bony fish eye has no pupil or pupillary movements; their lens is basically pushed out through the opening and they have only limited ability to control illumination on the retina. You look at shark eyes, and at elasmobranchs in general, and they allow a great deal of control. The pupil can form pinhole apertures, for example. And some rays and skates have this window shade that comes down, called a pupillary operculum, with multiple fingers that form multiple apertures. It's a very cool system that shades the retina from excessive bright light from above."

Another conundrum was that if sharks had crude vision, why would they have evolved their third eyelid, the nictitating membrane, to protect the eye? Sharks also have a mirror behind their retina, called the tapetum, which is lined with reflecting crystals of the amino acid guanine. The tapetum evolved to enhance visual sensitivity in low light. Lots of animals have this reflecting surface, which produces the eyeshine we see in a cat or a deer when it is caught at night in an automobile's headlights.

"Sharks go that one degree better," Sonny asserts, "because in daylight they can occlude the tapetum. Unlike a cat, whose eye always shines and could be dazzled in the daytime because there's light flashing around inside it, in bright light a shark extends a black layer of melanin over these reflecting crystals. I mean, this is highly sophisticated! In addition, the reflecting crystals of a shark's tapetum are oriented throughout the eye so that incoming light, which essentially is the image, doesn't bounce around in the eye but stays on the same path coming in and going out." In other words, in dim light a shark's ability to withdraw a melanin curtain from the tapetum doubles image brightness and retains the image in its eye not only as light enters but also as it exits, giving the shark's brain more opportunity to process and interpret what it is "seeing."

For Sonny Gruber the process of determining the surprisingly elaborate structure of the shark eye was only a beginning. "Just thinking logically," he points out, "here's an animal with hyper-sophisticated visual mechanisms. You have to ask why would it bother to evolve all that if it didn't use it? *Then* the question became, how can you find out about how this animal sees?" And the answer at which Gruber arrived was the sort of stimulus-and-response training that Ivan Pavlov used with dogs. To train sharks, Gruber set up a tank in which a lemon shark could poke its head into a Plexiglas bubble and look out of its tank into a laboratory that was equipped with an optical system with a stimulator.

"By pairing a slight electric shock with the stimulus, I trained that shark to blink whenever it saw a stimulus. The training was key because normally sharks never blink in response to visual stimuli—they stare. For a shark, blinking is only mechanical protection. And you've got to remember, this was in a time when people thought that sharks couldn't learn, that they were stupid and bumbling brutes. But when we did the numbers, we found that the shark learned this conditioned nictitating membrane response eighty times faster than a rabbit or a cat. After about ten trials, the shark knew that with a flashing light it was going to get a shock, and it would blink in anticipation of that. With a cat, that takes about eight hundred trials, but the sharks were getting it after ten.

"Once I could ask them questions—if they could see this or that—I pretty much had it made. I did color vision tests, which worked pretty well. Then I built a big maze in which I had sharks swim down an alley with two doors at one end. If they picked the correct door, it would lift up and food would come down to them."

Through the years, then, a picture has emerged of sharks as dynamic animals with a specialized sense of hearing, sensitive olfaction, and excellent vision with color perception and reasonable acuity in day-active species but very high sensitivity in nocturnal species. They have an extraordinary electrosensory system found in only a few other fish groups. But is processing this rich sensory stream, and producing regimented behaviors in response, the sum of the workings of the elasmobranch brain? Are sharks and their cousins basically stupid?

Not necessarily, as Sonny Gruber's lemon sharks had suggested. In fact, elasmobranchs have big brains—relative to body weight, larger than those of many birds and as large as the brains of many mammals. From front to rear, the shark brain encompasses a large forebrain or cerebrum, a midbrain, a cerebellum, and a hindbrain, which merges with the spinal cord. Most of these parts are concerned with making sense of a shark's sensory environment. The hindbrain receives cranial nerves that bring input from the auditory, lateral line, and electrosensory systems, the cerebellum seems to be where muscle movements are coordinated, and the midbrain is home to the optic lobes, which integrate visual information. The forebrain includes a region containing the hypothalamus and pituitary gland, a mass of tissue that is the master endocrine control center in vertebrates. As such, it is the place where chemical messages (such as readiness for mating) carried by hormones are integrated with operations of a shark's nervous system. The forebrain also includes the olfactory bulbs, where incoming chemosensory information is processed. But contradicting a long-held assertion that managing olfaction was the principal role of the shark forebrain, we now know that only about 10 percent of the forebrain is devoted to that task; the other 90 percent, it turns out, is devoted to learning, memory, and vision, as it is in higher vertebrates like birds and mammals.

Not all elasmobranchs have big, complex brains. In spiny dogfish (the standard subjects of undergraduate comparative anatomy labs), angel sharks, and sixgill sharks, all squalomorphs, the brain's organization has remained fairly primitive. Some batoids, such as the skates, also have structurally simple brains. But others, such as stingrays and eagle rays, which are much more active and can execute complex pelagic movements, have large cerebrums and highly convoluted cerebellums. The same holds true for large, active galeomorph sharks like mackerel and requiem sharks—great whites, makos, blues, tiger sharks, bulls, and lemons, among others. Sandy Moss, a shark researcher who has been my lifelong friend, expressed this link between shark lifestyle and brain power when he wrote, "To be active requires an enhanced sensory picture of the environment . . . and a greater degree of muscular coordination. . . . More sensory input with heightened decision-making obligations demand a more complex and larger brain."

Sharks that have risen to the intellectual occasion, so to speak, display an intellect that most people probably wouldn't credit to a fish. For example, they can be trained to perform a host of tasks that in nature would have no relevance to them, such as retrieving a floating hoop or the maze tests in which Sonny Gruber's lemon sharks performed so well. This latter sort of training, in which sharks learned by trial and error to find the food door, is an example of operant conditioning. Eugenie Clark, the grande dame of shark research, did much of the initial work on operant conditioning in sharks, training adult lemon sharks to push a target that rang a bell and then to swim to another location to be rewarded with food. Famous for her articles in *National Geographic* magazine, Clark became the founding director of the old Cape Haze Marine Laboratory in Florida, an early center for lab experiments with sharks, which would eventually become the Mote Marine Laboratory and later be directed by Perry Gilbert. It was upon Gilbert's description of the overall architecture of the shark eye that Sonny Gruber would base his own studies.

At the Lerner lab, with funding from the Office of Naval Research, Gilbert set up large shark holding pens to investigate a range of behaviors of sharks and stingrays. In one famous study, southern stingrays learned to swim up a ramp to be fed by a human trainer, scooting themselves up so far that they were half out of the water.

Sandy Moss spent time at the Lerner lab during his graduate school stint at Cornell. Once when I asked him what it was like to work with Perry Gilbert at Bimini in the days when research on shark behavior was just beginning, he recounted a story that was revelatory about both man and beast. "There were several large lemon sharks swimming around in the shark pen," Sandy recalled, "and one morning when Perry walked out on the catwalk to get a better look, he slipped on the dew-soaked planking and fell in. I never, ever saw a person levitate so quickly. It wasn't two seconds before he was hanging by all fours from the undercarriage of the catwalk, dripping and yelling for help. The sharks, meanwhile, were huddled at the far end of the pen, and I think they were more frightened than Perry was."

The threads of shark sensory and mental capacities are slowly weaving together into an unexpectedly rich tapestry, particularly as new behavioral studies confirm that many sharks have complex social and reproductive behaviors. A nurse shark's sex life, its courtship details so delicately and thoroughly revealed by Wes Pratt and Jeff Carrier, is just one example. And just as we have discovered that reproductive behavior in elasmobranchs is more complicated than anyone originally thought, so too are other kinds of social interactions. Many species of sharks and rays aggregate, at least seasonally, and individuals within these groups may form social hierarchies, similar to pecking orders in birds, with the largest females being dominant. Scalloped hammerheads aggregate seasonally in the Straits of Florida and at offshore seamounts in the Sea of Cortez (and probably other places as well). In the Sea of Cortez aggregation, Pete Klimley found that the larger females occupied preferred positions toward the center of the group. In the related bonnethead, a small species, studies by Art Myrberg and Sonny Gruber at the University of Miami uncovered a clear size-dependent dominance hierarchy among females, but also found that males usually had dominance over females, regardless of size. This pattern is common in social groups of many other animals, from bony fishes to birds and mammals, and has been attributed to a "testosterone factor"; that is, males in general tend to be more aggressive than females. We have learned that dominance hierarchies in sharks also extend beyond single species. Oceanic whitetips, for instance, are dominant over silky sharks, and gray reef sharks have dominance over reef whitetips.

Years ago Don Nelson broke new ground by demonstrating in sharks the stress-related social interaction known as agonistic behavior. Diving with gray reef sharks in the Pacific, he noted a predictable exaggerated swimming display when an individual was approached too closely either by a shark of its own species or by a diver. The displays were often followed by a charge and then a bite if the encroaching individual failed to withdraw, and some shark attacks on humans indeed may be triggered this way. Social hierarchies that are maintained in part by agonistic displays help animals avoid potentially fatal injury that could result from fighting. This protective function is particularly relevant in the lives of animals like sharks, which have such formidable dentition.

Understanding shark behavior will be the work of many professional lifetimes. Sometimes the insights come when a shard of information suddenly falls into place. Several days after the raging storm that had nearly washed me off the heaving deck of the *Pierce* in 1986, the ship's big winch was humming and rumbling in the background as the braided blue-and-white longline was hauled up from a mile below the ocean's surface. I stood out on the steel-grated "hero" platform removing the dripping gangions one by one as they emerged from the deep and approached the block above my head. There were sharks— lots of squaloids, mostly yard-long black Portuguese sharks with their big green eyes reflected in the bright sunlight. Then a different fellow appeared, a bit larger with different fins and a shorter snout, its face looking for all the world like Steven Spielberg's E.T., except for the fact that it had huge, nasty-looking teeth. Those in the lower jaw were broad, flat, and curved with razor edges, while the upper teeth each had three wickedly curving, pointed awl-like cusps. It was a kitefin shark (*Dalatias licha*), a much larger relative of the dwarf cookiecutters infamous for their habit of scooping balls of flesh from large tunas, swordfishes, and whales. (True to form, this shark would be found to have a neat ball of whale blubber in its stomach.) When I examined its teeth closely, I realized that the cusps on the upper teeth were very similar to the broken tips of shark teeth recovered from the AT&T cable retrieved from that very place a few months before. It was, finally, the answer to the fiber-optic cable mystery: Guido and I had been looking in the wrong taxonomic bin for the villain. Seeing rather substantial individual curved teeth extracted from the cable, we had assumed that they originated as simple teeth from the culprit shark, and so were looking for an animal with that sort of dentition. I had not considered the kitefin because I had never seen one in the flesh, and didn't realize how imposing their tricuspid uppers were. I thought then about the kitefins and black Portuguese sharks living a mile below in the dark, and how little we know about their behavior, which in one way or another is a response to the sensory information these sharks process. When you come right down to it, we are only now beginning to appreciate the complexity of the sensory systems and behavior of shallow-water sharks that we can observe along a coast or in a laboratory. Will we ever know anything about behavior in these denizens of the barely accessible deep? At least some of us are trying.

6 *Shark Worlds*

One August evening in 1999, Dean Grubbs must have observed the heat lightning in the dark western sky long before the thunder squall hit. Only a few tens of miles away as the crow flies, Bev and I were at home on our deck eating a late supper. At first the fresh breeze was a relief from the hot muggy air that had lain over Chesapeake Bay for two days and nights. But as the wind continued to build, I knew that it must be blowing the tops off surging whitecaps where Dean was, and I could picture him struggling to prevent the little twenty-four-foot Wellcraft from swamping. Sudden summer storms in the Bay have taken down much larger vessels. However, this system scooted along to the east and stars appeared overhead. Dean later reported that as the heavy seas relaxed to a choppy swell three relieved graduate students appeared from the vessel's small cabin while he placed a hydrophone over the side and slipped on his earphones. "The little bugger was still in range," he would tell me cheerily the following day, referring to a tagged baby sandbar shark. "We tracked that critter for more than two days."

In the course of the summer Dean would discover that in a single night these young sharks—barely as long as a man's forearm—may swim all the way across murky Chesapeake Bay, some twenty miles, and ten miles north or south, moving back and forth with the rolling tide. In the course of twenty-four hours, some baby sandbars carve out an activity space of more than a hundred square miles while never leaving the Bay.

Technically, an "activity space" is the area in which an animal spends the bulk of its time during a given period. You can talk about activity space where sharks are concerned—ecologists do—but what you really are talking about is the shark's world at a given moment in time. And if you think about it, the borders of that world delimit some of the simplest and most important facts about a shark, or any living thing—namely, where it is and the possibilities of what it can do there. Those boundaries determine, for instance, which creatures the shark will encounter as prey, predators, or competitors on any given day, or in a given season, or in a particular stage of its life. In short, a shark's world is a portrait of its place in nature—and for the most part that is still one of the most closely held secrets of shark existence.

My grandparents all were immigrants with little leisure for pursuits like fishing, but my father and mother loved the Jersey shore. In what I remember as shimmering summers of my boyhood, although we knew sharks might be swimming beyond the breakers, the routines of their lives were mysteries. There also were no detectives on the case. Back then, when scientific research on sharks was limited mostly to enumerating body parts, the face of the deep was essentially an unpenetrated barrier, the sea below it an environment hostile to human observers. All that anybody knew about the comings, goings, and doings of sharks was pieced together from chance local encounters (not always pleasant) with divers or swimmers, occasional sightings at sea, and evidence of the seasonal whereabouts of certain sharks when they turned up dead in the holds of fishing boats. In part, what has changed this state of ignorance is technology, ranging from tools as simple as fishing rods to ones as sophisticated as satellite transmitters that can be deployed for as long as a year, archiving oceanographic data all the while. And in part the change has come from the decision to ask the necessary questions, however and wherever possible.

One question has been whether a shark's world changes as the shark passes from infancy to adulthood. This was the object of Dean Grubbs's tagging of baby sandbars. Dean would catch his tracking subjects by rod and reel (a method that attracted fellow graduate students to volunteer for two days on a very small boat in the largest estuary in the United States). He could distinguish newborns from older one- and two-year-olds not only by their comparatively puny size but also by a small slit or scar located on each animal's snow-white underside, between the pectoral fins. This slit, analogous to a mammal's navel, is the place where the umbilical cord connected the embryonic shark to its yolk sac placenta. Once Dean had a tracking subject in hand, he would measure it, note its sex (claspers or no), then punch a small hole in the first dorsal fin. Into this hole he would insert a short bridle made of monofilament fishing line and soft surgical tubing. The transmitter, a simple device about the size of a roll of breath mints, trailed from the bridle.

After releasing an instrumented shark, Dean and his crew would track it at a distance of a hundred to two hundred yards—close enough to maintain reliable contact but not so close as to frighten the little creature and alter its normal behavior. The transmitters emitted pulses at frequencies well above the shark's range of hearing, and they were designed to change pulse intervals with depth so that Dean could tell how deep the shark was swimming. Using this method he discovered that these little sharks, once believed to hug the safety of the bottom, in fact spent more than half their time swimming up in the water column, staying in deeper channels during the day and moving into shallow water at night—even, at times, coming to the surface.

. . .

Baby sandbar sharks are considerably more difficult to monitor than the little lemons once tracked in Bimini by John Morrissey, now a professor at Hofstra University. For his Ph.D., Morrissey studied the lemons' behavior with Sonny Gruber. The shark equivalent of couch potatoes, they stayed within a home range of roughly 150 acres. Those sharks, none more than two and a half feet long, preferred to hang out on shallow sand flats where, in the dim light of dawn and dusk, they would patrol the shadowed edges of mangroves. Unlike sandbars, which are obligate ram ventilators and therefore constantly active, lemon sharks often rest on the bottom. Morrissey's animals were so sedentary that he was able to track their local travels by setting out an array of computerized underwater receivers that would record whenever a shark would come within its two-hundred- to three-hundred-yard range; the setup was a precursor to the one used by Jeff Carrier and Wes Pratt in their nurse shark studies. As lemon sharks grow older and larger, they begin exploring deeper water and expand their home range a little. By the time they approach adult size, at seven and a half feet, they move out to the reef edges and range over thirty-five to forty square miles. Some other shallow-water tropical sharks also live their lives within what amounts to, in terms of area, a large city park. For instance, adult gray reef sharks have home ranges of less than two square miles, and juvenile hammerheads in Kaneohe Bay in Hawaii range over less than half a square mile. Their parents, by contrast, may migrate hundreds of miles.

Epic migrations—of caribou and Monarch butterflies, of birds like the Arctic tern and golden plover—have always captured human imagination. But try to really visualize the Arctic tern's eleven-thousand-mile flight from the Arctic Circle to Antarctic realms, or the bobolink's even more demanding fourteen-thousand-mile flight from a summer nest in North America to its winter home in southern Argentina, and after a while the mind has to capitulate. We humans may sometimes be nomads, but we are not natural migrators. For animals that are, including many sharks, their journeys are instinctual and driven in some measure by sheer necessity.

A tropical sea, for instance, holds its bathtublike warmth year-round, but other parts of the ocean are places of huge environmental extremes. A thermometer immersed in the Chesapeake system, for example, registers in the mid-eighties Fahrenheit in July but six months later dips to near-freezing. While native tropical sharks like lemons and reef sharks may spend their lives gliding through the same stretches of azure ocean, the sharks of temperate coasts must literally swim for their lives each autumn. In the space of a few weeks at summer's close, their world changes thermally in a way that can kill them if they don't get out. Thus, sharks such as duskies, sand tigers, and the sharpnose form a phalanx of travelers, embarking on what will be long and strenuous migrations.

Even Dean Grubbs's baby sandbars demonstrate this flight for survival. When the first cool winds of autumn blow and the water temperature begins to drop around late September, they leave behind the relative safety of their estuarine nursery grounds, swim past the Virginia capes, and head south along the beach to Cape Hatteras. There they seek out the edge of the Gulf Stream, that ever-balmy river in the sea that brings the tropics to these midlatitudes even in the dead of winter. The young sharks will spend the entire winter off North Carolina, where they can shelter offshore at the edge of the stream as winter's grip cools inshore waters. We know this because in my laboratory Dean and now others have been tagging these baby sandbars for years. Each tag bears VIMS's address and telephone number, and in winter, when commercial long-liners off North Carolina hook a tagged animal, they retrieve the tags and sometimes mail them in.

For a long time, tagging depended heavily on luck and the kindness of strangers, and for a long time nobody bothered to try it as a serious method for exploring the worlds of sharks. It wasn't until 1963, when my energetic and charismatic friend Jack Casey rallied scientists and fishers to the cause, that it began to be used as an effective scientific tool. Casey's brainchild was the National Marine Fisheries Service

(NMFS) Cooperative Shark Tagging Program, or CSTP, based in Narragansett, Rhode Island. Since then the number of volunteer CSTP taggers has grown from an initial core of 150 to more than 6,500, spread over the Atlantic and Gulf coasts of the United States and Europe. For larger sharks they use dart tags, which trail a Plexiglas capsule containing a vinyl note bearing return instructions in five languages. This multinational effort has yielded a virtual encyclopedia on how fast some sharks grow (because some are caught repeatedly), on the geographic borders of different populations, and on their migratory habits. By 1993 the CSTP had tagged more than 100,000 sharks representing thirty-three species, of which more than 4,500 animals encompassing twenty-nine species have been recaptured at least once.

More than 15,000 of these sharks have been sandbars, including the individual shark with the record for the longest time at large. In June of 1965, an NMFS biologist named Chuck Stillwell gillnetted and tagged an adolescent sandbar in the sound behind Virginia's wild and remote Eastern Shore barrier islands. The animal was next seen twenty-eight years later when it was caught by a commercial longliner working off Daytona Beach, Florida.

Probably because so many of them have been tagged, sandbars have become the poster sharks for the patterns that shape the worlds of migratory sharks. For instance, larger animals, and larger species, generally cover more distance or have more extensive ranges. In a path shaped roughly like an inverted question mark, adult sandbars may trek all the way from Chesapeake Bay to the Gulf of Mexico in winter and maybe even as far west as Mexico's Yucatán coast. From the place where it was tagged to the point of its recapture, one CSTP sandbar traveled 2,346 miles—a sandbar record—and the animal's actual swimming distance must have been much longer.

When sandbar sharks are young they return to Chesapeake Bay each summer, but like the world of a child, theirs slowly edges outward as they get older. They begin to frequent shallow coastal areas, abandoning the Bay altogether by around age five. A few years later, at about age eight—sandbar teenagehood—variations related to sex show up. The females still spend their annual summer stint north of

Cape Hatteras, but males leave to make their home in the south for the rest of their lives. When a female matures sexually several years later, she also will make one last adjustment to her migratory behavior. In more than thirty years of shark fishing off Virginia, every mature female sandbar shark I have seen had recently pupped or was carrying full-term pups in her uterus. Sandbar females have about a nine-month gestation period but a two-year ovarian cycle, with a resting year between pregnancies. That means that a female in her resting year stays in the south, and does not make the long move north that summer.

When winter chases Virginia's subtropical sharks south, they are replaced by the spiny dogfish. Before becoming overfished, these cold-water sharks showed up off my doorstep by the millions, spending the winter off Virginia and North Carolina and then heading northward in spring to summer in the Gulf of Maine and off Nova Scotia. Those amazing dogfish schools, sometimes numbering in the tens of thousands, were usually segregated by size and sex. Females grow larger than males, and larger females school together, usually separate from smaller females and males. This predictable behavior made it easy for commercial gillnetters in the 1990s to target adult females, most of them pregnant, for European markets, which like their dogfish big. The result has been the loss of mature females and, accordingly, a subsequent dearth of baby dogfish. We now have a population that can no longer replenish itself. This phenomenon, known as recruitment failure, is a formula for the complete collapse of the spiny dogfish population in the northwest Atlantic.

Sharks that navigate along coasts inhabit a band of sea that varies in length from hundreds to a few thousand miles, more or less following the edges of the Earth's great land masses. The breadth of their world is limited by the shore on the one hand and on the other by water that is deeper than about 180 meters, or 600 feet. Beyond that depth the world of coastal sharks ends and that of open-ocean species—the true long-distance champions—begins. Among these marathoners, the blue shark holds the CSTP record; one snared by a recreational fisher off Long Island, New York, was recaptured less than eighteen months later by a long-liner 560 miles east of Natal, Brazil. It had completed a straight-line journey of around 4,900 miles; we can only guess at the actual distance it covered following currents, avoiding islands, and so forth. Blue sharks are remarkable nomads, moving through the North Atlantic in a clockwise path that takes them in summer up onto rich feeding areas over the continental shelf off Long Island and southern New England. Then, in autumn, they head eastward into the oceanic realm, traveling with the Gulf Stream as far as the eastern Atlantic. Some may reach the Azores, Spain, even Africa, or venture south to the Caribbean, Venezuela, and Brazil. Because blue sharks prefer cooler water, when they arrive in the tropics they submerge, finding a refuge hundreds of feet down in the twilight zone of the thermocline.

A similar pattern holds in the Pacific, where Japanese researchers have found blue sharks traversing the entire North Pacific Gyre. Within the gyre's vast compass, the blues favor different areas at different ages and during different seasons. Some, for instance, are the reserves of females about to give birth, whereas others are used mostly by females outside the pupping season or by males.

Sharks routinely remind us how much there still is to know about them. Around the time that tagging was still new and when scientists really had no clue that blue-water sharks like blues and makos periodically covered hundreds or thousands of miles of ocean to assemble in great coastal crowds, Shelley Applegate and I decided to set some exploratory longline off the southern California island of Catalina. This was before Shelley's departure to the fossil fields of El Cién; at the time he was working in the Vertebrate Paleontology Department at the Los Angeles County Museum. Our research vessel was a borrowed and impeccable twenty-six-foot cabin cruiser normally used by its owner, a museum benefactor, to tend a much grander sailing yacht. I was still in graduate school at Harvard and was spending the summer taking courses at Hopkins Marine Station in Pacific Grove. The night before our outing we rendezvoused with Leonard Bessom, a preparator at the museum and jack of all trades, tall, and wiry with a gray crew cut. He could have doubled for actor Lee Marvin were it not for a conspicuous limp from a leg shattered in a motorcycle accident.

The three of us arrived at the exclusive Newport Yacht Club before daybreak, jammed into a museum pickup truck loaded with longline gear and boxes of frozen mackerel. We met the boat's owner and his skipper, loaded our bait and gear on board, cast off the lines, and headed west out of the harbor just as the horizon was beginning to lighten behind us. Once offshore, the little boat began to dance as the breeze studded the sea with whitecaps and the owner proudly displayed a magnum pistol he had brought along as shark-killer. In fact it was the ideal instrument for shooting me in the back of the head as I hauled back the line while the owner, wobbling on the flying bridge above, took aim in a rolling sea. Sharks brought up to a vessel usually are killed by a quick blow to the top of the head with a "priest"—a version of the short club that anglers use for the same purpose.

As the dawn opened into a glorious sunny day, Catalina appeared like a camel's hump rising on the horizon. After baiting and setting about a mile and a half of longline, each hook on an eighteen-foot gangion (dropper), we cut the engine and drifted while the line fished, suspended from inner tubes placed at twenty-hook intervals. The boat's layout made it impossible to haul the line back from the bow, the safest, driest method, and after four hours we began to haul back stern-first into the sea. By hand, I pulled the line in over the gunwale while the captain backed the boat down the line, trying to keep it out of the boat's propeller. Surprisingly, there was a blue shark on the very first hook, a small fellow about six feet long with a snow-white belly and a back the color of the bluest ocean. To the owner's disappointment it was not of sufficient size to warrant a bullet, so Leonard gaffed it, Shelley dispatched it with the priest, and together they lifted the animal over the rail and into the cockpit. Then another blue appeared on the next hook, I yelled up to the captain, and so it went: a blue shark came up on nearly every hook with an occasional little mako thrown in. I had never seen so many sharks come up on a longline, and to this day never have seen such abundance again. A good day long-lining is a day when a hundred hooks bring up five sharks, or ten at most.

Yet sharks were mounding behind me like cordwood. At the fiftieth hook, when a boisterous blue surged under the boat, the skipper failed to throw the engine out of gear in time and the dropper line whipped around the propeller. Jamming a knife between his teeth and oblivious to his disability, Leonard plunged under the boat and cut the thrashing shark free. From then on the haulback continued, yielding a total of eighty-four blue sharks and twelve makos on a set of 112 hooks. While sharks piled up in the cockpit oozing blood and slime, the boat's trigger-happy owner and appalled captain became increasingly disenchanted with shark fishing. But Shelley and Leonard and I were elated. When we arrived at the dock Leonard found a sail cart; we loaded the sharks onto it and wheeled them up a ramp to the parking lot where Shelley had the museum pickup waiting. It took three trips to move our shark trove down the dock and up the ramp, all trailing crimson gurry.

I would spend the next three days rubber-booted and shirtless on the roof of the Los Angeles County Museum, under a broiling sun and without the benefit of official sanction, measuring and dissecting those sharks. I examined ninety-six sets of shark gonads and sliced open ninety-six stomachs to record their contents, in the evenings removing carcasses by way of a little-used freight elevator convenient to the museum's garbage bins. I heard later that some of Shelley's coworkers noted a strong odor of ammonia wafting through the premises, and now, so many years later, I must confess to being responsible for that inconvenience. But those sharks we sacrificed constituted a revelation. Not only were their sheer numbers startling, and the first scientific evidence of very large gatherings of blue sharks off southern California, they also provided some of the first reliable information on the sizes and sex ratios of blue and mako sharks there, as well as on the prey they capture and their reproductive biology. It's the kind of knowledge that is key to getting a grasp on the worlds in which these species live. Conservation—the "wise use" of sharks that is such an urgent need today—is impossible without it. Then as now, we hoped that the deaths of those ninety-six animals might become a lifeline for whole populations, tens of thousands of blues and makos who in a few years would find themselves on a collision course with our own kind.

Seven hundred miles southeast of Catalina, where the glittering Sea of Cortez splits Baja California from mainland Mexico, another shark enigma has begun to be illuminated only in the last few years. In the space of a couple of autumn months those waters swell with whale sharks, living, spotted shoals of sharks the members of which average thirty to forty feet long and weigh in the neighborhood of twelve to fifteen tons apiece. It is a whale shark convention, the attendees drawn from god-knows-where, feeding on a concomitant smorgasbord of zooplankton. A few weeks later, as the weather and water cool, the throngs of the sea's largest fish break up as suddenly as they formed, and one by one the immense sharks disappear.

Where in the deep blue sea do they come from—and where do they go? In the mid-1980s it became possible to address this question using radio transmitters that loft signals to Argos satellites—a technology that can be employed with whale sharks because they spend so much time at the surface. (Radio waves disperse too rapidly in seawater to be effective with submerged animals.) Two enterprising shark biologists, Scott Eckert and Brent Stewart, designed buoyant, foot-long, hydrodynamically shaped transmitters attached to tethers of heavy monofilament or stainless steel ten to twenty feet in length. Each tether was equipped with a harpoonlike point. Armed with a ten-foot spear pole or a pneumatic spear gun, the two men would approach an unsuspecting candidate in a small boat, or sometimes simply swim up to it, and implant the apparatus next to the first dorsal fin. Once a whale shark was trailing a transmitter, radio signals about the animal's location, its recent dives, and the water temperature were beamed to the satellites and then downloaded and forwarded to a land-based processing center.

The scheme worked beyond Eckert and Stewart's wildest dreams. They learned, for example, that while the whale sharks spent more than 80 percent of their time within thirty feet of the surface, sometimes the huge animals dove as deep as eight hundred feet. They found that the sharks lingered in warm places, but also spent time below the surface in chilly water of 50° F or less. These tropical sharks can be so flexible about their thermal surroundings not because they can thermoregulate, but simply by virtue of their huge bodies. A phenomenon known as thermal inertia applies to whale sharks. Massive and warmed by basking at the sea surface, a whale shark descending to colder depths cools only by slow degrees because the volume of its body is so huge compared to its surface area, through which heat is lost.

Scott and Brent were able to track a handful of whale sharks for more than three months. Eventually the approach of winter sent every one of those great beasts packing out into the Pacific. The record-setter, tracked for nearly three years, angled southwest first, then directly west, swimming past Hawaii to Micronesia where the transmitter's battery finally failed. At that point, however, the animal had journeyed 8,080 miles—an elasmobranch record. By and large its course seemed shaped by features of its ocean universe that correlate with food, especially the upwelling that in places fuels the bounty of plankton.

As a matter of sheer survival, every wild animal's existence is molded by where its food is. At Ningaloo reef off western Australia, during the spawning season for reef corals, gaggles of young whale sharks materialize out of the open ocean to gorge on a brief, rich banquet of coral eggs. The megamouth shark—another large, much rarer, plankton eater—migrates vertically twice a day on a schedule set by changing levels of daylight. At sunrise, one megamouth tracked sonically dove from its starting depth of 65 feet down to 330 feet, then at sunset returned to the shallower water. This cueing on light levels precisely follows the same habit in zooplankton, the mainstay of a megamouth's diet.

. . .

In conjuring up the worlds of sharks, you must come eventually to the Farallon Islands—a three-hundred-foot-high pile of windswept rocks protruding from the great swells of the Pacific Ocean twenty miles west of San Francisco. There, a great amalgam of migratory birds pauses to rest in the fall of the year before venturing farther south. In the same season, great white sharks arrive, too, on the trail of easy pickings represented by succulent young elephant seals and the throngs of California sea lions that abound around the islands. Migrating along with the birds and sharks for many years have been the ornithologist Peter Pyle and ichthyologists like Pete Klimley and John McCosker. While Pyle mostly documents the birds, the shark biologists have focused on the fundamentals of *C. carcharias*.

Klimley is known for his observations of white shark behavior, including the sharks' strategy of hunting in the Farallones inside in a zone extending around the islands from about thirty yards to five hundred yards out. (Divers take note.) And like the biologists who work with humpback whales, he also figured out that if you've seen one great white you haven't seen them all. Working with Scot Anderson, who would later accompany Ken Goldman to Alaska, Klimley discovered that careful photography could pinpoint visible differences among particular sharks, including variations in body color and the shapes of their dorsal and caudal fins. The visual ID made it possible to tell one white shark from another. Between 1988 and 1992 the two men identified eighteen individuals and determined that a coterie of nine to fourteen white sharks hunted around the Farallones in the fall. Some of them stayed as long as ten days, and three of the great whites returned at the same time several years in a row. More recently Anderson and Pyle have found that while *male* white sharks appear every year, the ladies come only every other. We don't yet know the meaning of this rhythm; it may be part and parcel of a female white shark's two-year reproductive cycle.

In the early 1990s, before Ken Goldman began working with

salmon sharks in Prince William Sound, he, too, came to the Farallones, lured in part by John McCosker's pioneering research on the mechanics of how white sharks take their prey. Scot Anderson joined in again, and their method became a practice session for the bait-and-swallow technique they would later employ with salmon sharks. If you have not been there, it is difficult to imagine the inhospitality of the Farallones, beautiful as they are. The islands' rock shores and sheer cliffs preclude easy, safe landing of any craft that can be used for shark tracking. Ken and Scot's vessel was an eighteen-foot Boston Whaler suspended from the island cliffs by davits and lowered into the surging sea by block-and-wire winch—a tricky operation even when conditions are superb. High winds, storms, and fog all routinely made conditions bordering on miserable and severely limited the men's ability to observe shark kills from the island. However, when weather permitted and a diaphanous, reddish cloud of blood and a distant flock of seagulls signaled a white-shark seal kill, they would take a bearing on the location, dash to the Whaler, lower themselves into the sea, and as fast as possible motor out to the area with a hunk of frozen blubber—all the while maneuvering along rocky shoals just beyond the surf zone. They then would insert an ultrasonic transmitter into the blubber, toss it into the water, and wait.

Generally the two scientists didn't have to wait long. After they shut off the outboard engine so they could drift with the kill, white sharks frequently would be attracted to their little vessel, circling it and sometimes mouthing the engine's metal lower unit, probably drawn by a weak electric field around it. After feeding a transmitter-laced piece of blubber to a curious great white, Ken and Scot would follow along behind it as closely as possible, tracing its movements around the island. Because of the dangerous environment, each evening they had to return to the island to wait for early morning when, with luck, they might relocate their study subject. Though cumbersome, this system worked often enough that Goldman and Anderson would eventually be able to delimit white shark daily activity spaces around the island: areas that ranged from relatively small—less than a square mile—to more than three square miles. The variation is scientifically interesting for several reasons, including an intriguing puzzle. It's a rough general rule in nature that older, larger animals roam larger hunting ranges than younger, smaller ones do. Yet in the Farallones the older great white sharks tend to patrol *smaller* specific areas than the younger sharks, who seem to wander more or less at random. One hypothesis is that more-experienced great whites develop favorite hunting places, honey holes where the food-finding is dependably good.

Until a few years ago white sharks were thought to be coastal vagabonds, moving with the seasons from one pinniped cafeteria to another. Recently, though, two sophisticated lines of detective work have raised the possibility that some may forsake their coastal haunts and, like the whale sharks, embark on prolonged oceanic excursions. A key piece of evidence is white shark mtDNA (genetic material in cell structures called mitochondria), which, unlike the rest of their DNA, animals inherit only from their mothers. Geneticists looking at the mtDNA of white sharks off South Africa, Australia, and New Zealand—the DNA fingerprints of generations of white shark mothers—found a clear genetic split. The breeding females off South Africa were one genetic strain, those of Australia and New Zealand another. The real surprise, though, came when the nuclear DNA, with its 50 percent contribution from males, was examined. It was roughly identical in all three populations. In short, the same males were impregnating female white sharks along the coasts of two continents. A reasonable conclusion is that male and female white sharks have, in a manner of speaking, different ocean worlds. Females may spend their lives within a limited coastal region, while some males— and perhaps many—cross entire oceans. Reaching a coast, those males breed with females where they encounter them, leaving behind the genetic signs of their passing.

Bolstering this hypothesis is new data from a hybrid instrument, the PSAT (pop-up satellite archival tag), which can gather and hold oceanographic information and then pop to the surface after a predetermined time to download its data to a satellite. This technology has revealed that some male white sharks that summer off California trace a late autumn course out into the open Pacific, cruising over the deep ocean for several months. One swam 2,360 miles to the west coast of the Hawaiian island of Kahoolawe. White shark sightings in Hawaii are rare, but this animal spent at least four months of its winter vacation there. The other sharks all made for the subtropical eastern Pacific, spending part of their time as deep as sixteen hundred feet! This kind of discovery spawns questions. What are white sharks doing out in the middle of the eastern Pacific Ocean, where nobody ever guessed they might be? What do those four-ton animals find there to eat? Tunas or spinner dolphins or sea turtles? For now, no one has a clue.

Like most human beings, I move through a world governed largely— far too much, I often think—by time measured by clocks and deadlines, with spaces bounded by property lines and fences. Sharks and their relatives, we are now beginning to grasp, inhabit worlds shaped by patterns of time and space that are as diverse as elasmobranchs themselves. For some, the cadence of a day's activity may unfold within the confines of a home range the size of an average shopping mall, while others meander over a hundred square miles during the same twenty-four hours. As a shark grows, so, usually, does the geographical extent of its daily routine and often, if it is a migrator, the distance it will travel. Species adapted to tropical coasts tend to be faithful to their thermally constant habitat, while the coastal sharks in temperate seas follow their food, or seek it out, in a seasonal exodus spurred by sometimes-huge fluctuations in water temperature. The large, long-distance migrators may navigate over entire ocean basins during the course of a year, whereas small benthic forms hold tight in an area the size of a baseball field.

Today a child who looks seaward from the shore gazes on a whole universe of shark worlds that technology and ingenuity are helping us know. Studies of deep-sea species are beginning, and scientists are even finding ways to tag and track sharks in such hostile environments as the ice-covered Arctic.

Still, too many vital pieces of the puzzle are missing—things such as where species like great white sharks, and many others, mate and bear their pups, and where those young gain their first footholds in life. Things such as the borders of migration corridors used by animals like blues and makos and even whale sharks, and the boundaries of sharks' ocean gathering places, especially in international waters where fisheries now are removing many shark species from the sea at a breathtaking pace. Things that might allow those who come after us to truly understand the worlds of sharks in new and enlightening ways.

7 The Carnivore Café

Nago, Okinawa, Japan
January 2000

The creature's approach from below is so slow, so languid—at first I see only spots, then a moment later its huge body. This whale shark isn't here by chance; it and another are captives and have learned that people in boats, like the little aquarium vessel I am on, come to feed them. Confined by a net roughly two hundred feet in diameter in the middle of Nago city harbor, the sharks are conditioned to respond to the slap of a white plastic bucket on the water. Loaded with frozen krill, this gallon-sized dinner bell is attached to a long pole wielded by an aquarium curator. He slaps it on the water once, then again, and spots surge upward so fast that I have to force myself to stay put. Then just as the bucket inverts, what looks like the mouth of a giant tadpole gapes open below the water's surface and several thousand krill swirl into it as if they had been flushed down a toilet.

It is difficult to think of an animal whose feeding biology fascinates and frightens the human race as much as a shark's. In our imagination, conflicting images jostle for primacy, cruel feeding frenzies rubbing shoulders with visions of hunters sculpted so perfectly for their natural role in the ocean—the fearful symmetry of the apex predator. In fact, though, what sharks eat, and why, is a story built on a modest assortment of feeding strategies, curious jaw mechanics, a smorgasbord of tooth shapes and sizes, and hunting prowess wired with precision to powerful sensory systems—it is a tale, in short, of finely matched form and function.

Every animal is born, lives, and dies with a genetically programmed feeding strategy, and every animal's feeding strategy is accumulated evolutionary wisdom. It is the sum of adaptations—teeth, jaws, senses, behaviors—that, in a given moment in time, allow a given animal of a particular species to obtain the nutritional essentials that keep it alive long enough to produce a new generation. And every feeding strategy is the outcome of eons of evolutionary negotiation—give up this, get that, and survive.

As ancient elasmobranchs were diversifying and spreading through the aquatic world, natural selection found ways to reduce competition for available food by dividing up the means by which food could be captured. Dick Lund, the shark fossil maestro, has figured that even 320 million years ago sharks already had a slew of feeding strategies, based on the incredible array of jaws and tooth types and body shapes unearthed at Bear Gulch. Then as now, it behooves competing animals to partition the limited food resources so that all can get enough to survive, and so, indirectly, the adaptations that come together in a feeding strategy are born.

Modern sharks capture prey in four basic ways: by ram feeding, through suction, by biting their quarry, or by filtering it from the sea. Many use a combination of strategies. Ram feeding, analogous to ram ventilation, is the simplest: the shark simply swims up to its prey with an open, gaping maw and engulfs it. The shark's closing jaw may shear off pieces of the prey's body, making it small enough to be swallowed. A cruising sandbar shark can swoop down on an unsuspecting flounder half-buried in sand and scoop it up in a single fluid motion.

By contrast, suction feeders like the nurse shark, which suck in prey like vacuum cleaners, have a small, almost pursed, gape. The suction develops as its jaw and pharyngeal cartilages move in ways that expand the volume of the mouth and throat. And as with a vacuum cleaner hose, the small mouth opening relative to the expanded mouth volume both pumps up the suction and makes it more precise. All of these changes take place incredibly rapidly. At the University of South Florida, shark researcher Philip Motta, one of the world's experts on the details of shark feeding mechanisms, has clocked the nurse shark's "bite sequence" at one-tenth of a second.

A bite-feeder like a great white or a bull shark uses its formidable jaw and teeth to separate a chunk of flesh from its large prey. When a bull shark attacks a dolphin it first mounts a burst of speed—the feeding rush. In the fleeting moments before contact, its pectoral fins tamp down, in effect pushing the shark's snout upward like the nose of a jet. Next, muscles behind the head contract, lifting it more, then muscles under the snout follow suit and pull the open jaws forward. All of this happens in the space of an instant. Most sharks have their impaling teeth in the lower jaw, so the lower teeth enter the prey first, spearing it like a clod on a pitchfork. Now the upper jaw snaps down while the shark's upper body begins to thrash from side to side. As the head goes, so go the teeth, which simultaneously bear down on and saw through the victim's flesh. The retrograde angle of a shark's teeth, directed back toward the animal's gullet, increases the likelihood that struggling prey will not be able to escape.

Cookiecutter sharks, which have impaling teeth in the upper jaw and a handsawlike band on the bottom, present a variation on this theme. They bite with a simultaneous dig-and-twist motion, the way a soda jerk wields an ice-cream scoop. Like mosquitoes, they have mastered a hit-and-run technique that lands them somewhere along the spectrum between parasite and predator: their prey lose a scoop of flesh but live, perhaps to serve up another meal later on.

The ancestors of whale sharks, basking sharks, and megamouth sharks, and of their cousins the manta rays, took separate evolutionary paths that converged at structures suited for filtering seawater of its plankton. The whale shark is a case in point. As the largest fish in the sea, it is the sluggish piscine equivalent of a double tractor-trailer. But to satisfy the metabolic demands of such a huge body, a whale shark relies not on hunting down prey it can rip apart with rapier teeth, but on sucking in and sieving the tiniest animals from the ocean. As the shark opens its cavernous mouth, the expanding maw literally sucks water in. Dense gill rakers like fine brush bristles pack the rear of the shark's pharyngeal cavity and strain food from the water rushing in. After being relieved of its food load, the water streams onward across the whale shark's gills and exits, while a thick soup of food items flushes down its gullet.

Whale sharks do have teeth, hundreds of them aligned in rows, but they are tiny and pretty much useless for feeding or anything else. The reduced teeth are just one of the trade-offs that have occurred as selection pressures—including predators and limited food resources—impinged on *Rhincodon's* evolutionary journey. In response to such pressures, whale sharks grew large and evolved an economical feeding strategy based on powerful suction and filtering instead of fast-paced hunting of large prey. As with whales, size deters predators (except *Homo sapiens*). And specializing in the harvest of small swimming animals, a cornucopia of creatures that exist near the base of the marine biomass pyramid, ensures that there will virtually always be adequate food available. Basking and megamouth sharks followed a similar though not identical path. They ram feed, forcing food morsels onto their brushlike gill rakers as they swim open-mouthed through the water. Ram feeding also is a way of life for the manta ray, its mouth flaring open in front of a starship silhouette.

Many sharks use a combination of ram, bite, and suction feeding, and may change their diet and dominant feeding mode as they grow. Younger makos feed on bony fishes (as most sharks do), with the occasional invertebrate added to the mix; in general about 85 percent of makos' diet consists of bony fish and squid. The larger a mako becomes, the larger the prey it can and does pursue. This sort of change, in which the diet of an animal alters as the animal grows, is called an ontogenetic, or "after the beginning," dietary shift. Applied to makos, the shift's outcome can be striking: once a mako reaches a weight above three hundred pounds, it may take adult swordfish that are as large or larger than the shark itself. On the east coast of the United States, bluefish in the ten- to fifteen-pound range are another favorite. Writing in 1989, Chuck Stillwell, the National Marine Fisheries Service biologist, noted that makos then consumed more than 7 percent of all the bluefish in the coastal ocean from southern New England to Cape Hatteras, North Carolina. Some commercial fishers accuse makos and other sharks of what amounts to theft, making meals of the fishery resource that the fisher hopes to catch and sell for a profit.

Lots of sharks will feed on other elasmobranchs when the opportunity presents itself, and for some doing so has evolved into a true feeding specialization. For example, the great hammerhead shark preferentially pursues stingrays, and when a great hammerhead is caught, there is often a prickly handful of stingray spines embedded in its mouth. (One popular shark book has a picture of a hammerhead whose head and jaws bristle with some ninety-three spines and spine fragments.)

Alone, or studded in bleached jaws displayed on a shelf, the shark tooth encapsulates the uneasy relationship between sharks and people. Yet there are striking resemblances between a shark's teeth and the teeth you brush every morning. They have a pulp cavity, tunnels that house blood vessels, and a hard enamel covering. Examine representative teeth from, say, twenty different modern shark species, and you'll find the same components. On the other hand, in its details elasmobranch dentition is so structurally variable that some experts can identify a shark species by examining a single tooth, or even a fragment of one. This is because the teeth of each species possess a distinct constellation of size, shape (such as pointy, blunt, flattened, triangular), symmetry, and assorted cusps and projections. Because a shark's teeth get bigger as it does, you can roughly estimate a shark's size from its teeth. And in some cases, in a single species the distinctions between male and female teeth are so clear that a tooth reveals its former owner's sex as well. Analyze the physical characteristics of a particular elasmobranch's teeth and you'll also know a good deal about its eating habits—whether it is adapted for capturing the wide variety of prey opportunity provides, or whether its teeth are those of a specialist.

Compare, for instance, the teeth of the great white and the tiger shark. Each of the great white's teeth sport an imposing, razor-sharp, triangular cusp with serrated edges. Such an object is the perfect implement for slicing away chunks of flesh from seals, whales, and other large, rather squishy prey. (It's arguably no coincidence that early human toolmakers fashioned just such tools from stone.) Tiger sharks, on the other hand, have more rounded, serrated teeth with a broader cutting surface, a configuration that can saw through the hard shells of sea turtles as the tiger shark shakes its head. If a great white were to attack a hard-shelled sea turtle, the points of its teeth would more likely break off. Scores of other tooth/feeding variations are known. Like some other members of the great, rapier-toothed order of lamnid sharks, sand tigers have long, narrow teeth arrayed in phalanxes that point backward into the mouth. Aligned this way, they are not as well adapted for slicing away pieces of a prey animal, but they do present a superb apparatus for seizing and holding on to slippery, struggling fishes that often are destined to be swallowed whole. The blunt, flattened teeth of an eagle ray are tools for crushing, and their owners glean a living mostly by pulverizing mollusks, adeptly rejecting the broken shells. A recitation of the varieties of tooth specializations could go on, roughly equaling the approximately one thousand known species of living sharks and rays.

. . .

Predators like sharks depend on their teeth to make their living, and predation may involve violent interactions with prey organisms that do not particularly wish to become a meal. Thus teeth may be broken or lost. In predators that have to get through their adult lives with a single set of natural teeth, wear or disease can leave them without the tools of their trade; I once saw a toothless lion in an African game park, doomed to a slow death by starvation. Sharks, though, never face this predicament because they replace their teeth constantly throughout life.

The elasmobranch tooth factory operates the way armies once did on the field of battle, by lining up soldiers—in this case, teeth—one behind the other in organized files. In the front rank is a row of mature teeth. Arrayed behind this outer row are a few rows of smaller, still-maturing teeth, and still more tooth buds are hidden under a membrane that sweeps around the inside of each jaw carti-lage. In effect, every tooth on the firing line has a file of backups ready to move forward if the tooth is lost. A developing tooth bud gradually moves forward from its origin, migrating from the base of the jaw toward the crest as it grows. As a bud departs the groove where it arose, another bud takes its place ad infinitum. In the course of a nat-ural life span, a shark may manufacture tens of thousands of tooth buds and lose and replace tens of thousands of teeth.

If a lifelong conveyor belt of replacement teeth is a major charac-teristic that helps distinguish sharks from other fishes, another is the structure and functioning of shark jaws. Front to back, they are short compared to the jaws of bony fishes, and in nearly all species the jaws are underslung, sitting some distance back from the tip of the shark's snout. Until a shark opens its mouth, it looks like a chinless wonder with a serious overbite. But shark jaws have biomechanical features that enable them to thrust forward, bringing along the serried ranks of teeth, and to engage prey with an extremely powerful bite. The jaws of modern sharks are protrusible in this way because they are not rigidly connected to the chondrocranium, the calcified cartilage framework of the shark's head. Instead, the jaws are cantilevered, braced against a rectangle of cartilage located behind a shark's eyes and anchored there by muscles and ligaments attached to the chondrocranium. In skates and rays these parts are arranged in a way that makes the upper jaws extravagantly mobile: they can be extended like claws to suck up clams or other prey animals living on or near the ocean floor where those elasmobranchs feed.

For a solid 250 million years sharks had long, alligatorlike jaws situated at the end of the snout. The upper jaw was more or less stationary because it was rigidly secured to the underlying cartilage. It is a configuration that limits the jaws' range of motion to "open" and "close" with a bit of side-to-side wiggle, and most vertebrate jaws, including the human jaw, still are constructed this way. A predator can hunt with jaws like that, but perhaps not as efficiently as it could if its jaws became adapted for greater strength and more flexibility—which is exactly what happened to elasmobranchs. Over time, elasmobranch jaws acquired more mobile ligature with the cartilage of the head, and they became shorter from hinge to tip. A suite of strong muscles and muscle groups evolved to operate them, increasing the force the jaws could exert and allowing changes in the volume of the inside of the mouth so suction could be generated. Together, these adjustments to the elasmobranch body plan carved out a whole new ecological role for the group. Short, underslung, protrusible, and exceedingly powerful jaws, armed with teeth designed for grasping, piercing, and slicing, opened up a smorgasbord of prey choices for sharks, helping to propel them to the top of the predatory heap. Small prey could be captured more efficiently and still be eaten whole, but larger animals also could be attacked and held long enough to be torn apart. Chunk by chunk, the whole of a large animal could be consumed. There are exceptions to and permutations of this scenario, of course; for instance, the broad mouth of a whale shark is located front and center, at the equally broad terminus of its snout, and a frilled shark's jaws still are long and relatively immobile, like those of its ancient progenitors. But the vast majority of living shark species have protrusible jaws imbued with the capacity to generate tremendous force.

In the late 1960s and early 1970s, Perry Gilbert and several of his coworkers at Mote Marine Laboratory in Sarasota, Florida, measured the bite force of tiger, lemon, dusky, and silky sharks, using a gnatho-dynamometer—a "jaw-power meter." The number they arrived at for these species was three metric tons per square millimeter, which works out to be roughly 42,674 pounds per square inch of tooth surface applied. By comparison, an adult human can bite down at a healthy 30,000 pounds per square inch—although with blunt teeth that cause a good deal less damage. No one has ever measured the bite force of a really big shark, such as a great white.

On a July afternoon in 1961, when I was long-lining off New Jersey with Jack Casey aboard the *Cape May,* I opened up the stomach of a twelve-foot tiger shark—back then, the mid-Atlantic Bight was full of big sharks—and burned my hands in the shark's caustic stomach acid. (Green and eager, I hadn't yet figured out that I should be wearing rubber gloves.) But while the gastric fluid could make easy work of digesting my flesh, it hadn't yet made a dent in the shark's stomach contents—a five-gallon steel bucket, with a load of garbage still in it.

Tales abound of weird things in shark stomachs. Along with scraps of fish and invertebrates, dissected shark innards have yielded up license plates, carcasses of dogs, birds, and horses, and sides of rotten beef jettisoned by cruise ships. The navy occasionally finds evidence of shark bites on its submarines. Tiger and bull sharks apparently are willing to scavenge just about anything that ends up in the ocean—shoes, a roll of tar paper, and a famously reported suit of armor. Yet the vast majority of sharks stick to the living prey for which their dentition and foraging behaviors are adapted, following age-old patterns from the time before the ocean was shared with humans and used by humans as a dump.

Regardless of how finicky most elasmobranchs may be, sharks are often thought of as insatiable—a misconception that biologists have begun to erase through studies of both wild and captive animals. As it turns out, pound for pound, wild sharks eat much less and less often than other carnivorous fishes. Exactly how much and how often a shark will eat in a given period is related in part to how much food is required to sustain its activities. On an average day, an indolent, slow-growing shark like the sandbar eats the rough equivalent of a single McDonald's hamburger. Nibbling through life, taking a smattering of smaller fishes and other prey, a sandbar shark may spend twelve to fourteen years gaining a measly hundred pounds. (Older sandbars—rare nowadays, due to intense fishing pressure—may attain weights in excess of two hundred pounds.) At the other extreme, the swift, fast-growing, warm-bodied mako may eat enough fish to equal twelve to fifteen times its body weight in a year. Lemon sharks prey on fishes and crabs, and a lemon shark typically consumes enough during each feeding period to equal 1–2 percent of its body weight, a percentage that seems to hold for a great many shark species. On average, lemon sharks actively hunt in stretches of eleven hours, then more or less abstain for the next thirty hours. Once again, in its general outlines, this short feeding/longer nonfeeding pattern seems to be the norm in the elasmobranch world. Based on limited studies, some researchers believe that great white sharks actively hunt their usual large, pin-niped quarry only about once a month.

It is true enough that a shark in feeding mode is constantly prowling for food. Once fed, however, like a sated diner leaving the table, it settles back while its gastrointestinal tract takes on the arduous task of extracting nutrients from a large meal, absorbing those that must nourish the shark until it is time once again to go in search of a meal. The rather short human gut typically takes three to four hours to process each of a person's daily meals. All meat-eating animals, including sharks, have a similarly short gut (at least compared to the long, multiple-stomached ones of vegetarian species such as deer and cattle). But as readers will know by now, almost nothing about sharks is as simple as it appears on the surface. Basically, and unlike most bony fishes, sharks have a primitive, conservative gut, one whose structure hasn't changed for a very long time. Getting food from a shark's mouth to its inevitable exit, culling essential nutrients along the way, is a process that literally has a twist: elasmobranchs are on an exceedingly short list of modern aquatic vertebrates whose intestine still includes an ancient feature: inside the intestine there is a series of folds, called the spiral valve, in the contour of a corkscrew.

For sharks, the usefulness of a spiral valve probably springs from the confluence of factors related to its lifestyle. Consider, for instance, two central issues for a highly active aquatic carnivore—processing food efficiently to extract needed energy and nutrients, and maximizing one's sleek, hydrodynamically efficient body shape. Twirling through a shark's intestine, the spiral valve saves space while adding to the gut area where nutrients can be absorbed. (Many other vertebrates have a bulky, coiled, and folded intestine that packs into the abdominal cavity.) The spiral valve's ample absorptive surface also comes without increasing the amount of room the shark body has to allot to the intestine. In some species the arrangement entails only a few, fleshy twirls, but in others it is elaborate: the spiral valve of a basking shark houses more than fifty turns of the "screw."

Another curious attribute of the shark digestive system is the ability sharks have to evert their stomach so that its contents come tumbling or gushing back out. Sometimes the eversion is so violent that the stomach follows along and ends up outside the shark's mouth as well. How the stomach responds to being turned inside out, especially if it also transits a mouth full of razor-sharp teeth, isn't really understood; eversion is probably rare in nature, a response to overwhelming stress. More often, a stressed shark will simply vomit up things that haven't been, or can't be, digested. In a gruesome, recent incident, a great white shark killed and consumed an Australian diver, regurgitating the man's torso when the shark was briefly captured the next day. Had the shark not been detained, with such a huge meal in its stomach it presumably might not have hunted again for weeks.

Sharks digest their meals slowly, the way a picky eater cleans a plate. Assuming the stomach contents are digestible in the first place—that is, not something like a garbage bucket—it can take at least twenty-four to thirty-six hours, and sometimes hours or days longer, for food to make its way through a shark. First, enzymes and a powerful acid soup in the animal's stomach start the process of breaking ingested chunks into pieces small enough to enter the intestine, where the spiral valve and another suite of chemicals await. Corkscrewing their way to the end of the shark's intestine, the contents of the spiral valve are gradually relieved of nutrients that can maintain the shark's body and fuel its metabolic fire.

Not much is known about how sharks metabolize their food, in part because it's hard to ensure the reliability of research done on captive animals. We have clues, though, that a shark's metabolic fire burns with remarkable efficiency. It takes oxygen to make use of food energy to power muscles and other bodily functions, so an animal's metabolic efficiency is measured in terms of the amount of oxygen it burns relative to the number of kilocalories it uses to sustain its normal life (one kcal equals one human dietary calorie). And every study that has ever been done on shark metabolism has shown that, pound for pound, sharks burn less oxygen to extract the energy for comparable activities than bony fishes do. Compared to a bony fish with a similar lifestyle, a shark may need to take in less food per unit of time because it somehow is more adept at extracting energy from what it does eat. In sharks that warm their blood by way of retes (again, including the great white and the mako), the operation apparently gets a boost from the network of blood vessels juxtaposed to the gut and liver, warming them enough to maximize the activity of digestive enzymes.

Beyond the arcane details of metabolism, there are a good many other things we would like to know about how and what sharks do and don't eat, about behaviors that are still black boxes, about the triggers that send some kinds of sharks in pursuit of humans as if they were natural prey. Standing on a boat in Nago harbor, even a captive whale shark sucking down a bucket load of krill seems in a way unfathomable—a massive, powerful animal that poses no threat, another of the paradoxes of the universe of sharks.

8 *Shark Eats Man*

It's 10:37 at night when the phone on my bedside table rings yet again, its shrill trill jolting me out of exhausted sleep. The voice on the line, a reporter from the *Richmond Times-Dispatch,* quickly apologizes for the late call before launching a barrage of questions—more or less identical to questions I have been fielding for two solid days. In the previous forty-eight hours of this Labor Day weekend, sharks have fatally attacked two people, a ten-year-old boy in the surf off Virginia Beach about an hour from my home, and a young Russian wading with his girlfriend off Cape Hatteras, 130 miles to the south. The attacks occurred at dusk, around six o'clock. The man bled to death after the shark took his lower right leg; his girlfriend lost a foot and suffered other injuries but survived. One result of the horrific incidents has been a media feeding frenzy. Every major news organization in the United States, and scores of others, have called for interviews, opinions, anything. One editor at a television station has even telephoned to ask for my speculation about a viewer's home video, shot months earlier, that purports to show what could be a shark's fin where children are playing in the shallows. As they say in the news business, if it bleeds it leads.

Among other things, the reporters and talk show hosts almost uniformly have wanted to know if a rogue shark has begun to hunt people—something, I reply, that happens only in Hollywood—and what kind of shark has been doing the killing. Since the first attack there has been some confusion about the latter question, because several species of large sharks frequent the waters off Virginia and North Carolina in the summer months. This inexpressibly sad night, however, I finally know the answer, at least for the first attack. The Virginia Beach perpetrator had been a bull shark a little over nine feet long and weighing in the range of four hundred pounds. I had been able to calculate its size because a few hours earlier I had examined autopsy photographs of the boy's wounds in a Virginia Beach police station. Before that, at the request of the child's father, I had met with the distraught family, including two young brothers who had watched the attack unfold. From the bite pattern, I knew we were dealing with a very large carcharhinid, of which two species visit Virginia waters— the bull shark and dusky shark. Examining detailed illustrations of various sharks, the little boys didn't hesitate. They identified the bull, with its sturdy build and snub nose. The attack occurred during a surfing outing, the shark lunging for the boy's left thigh as his father frantically tried to pull him from the waist-high water to the relative safety of a surfboard. The cavernous bite, nearly a foot in diameter, had ripped open the child's femoral artery, leading to a rapid catastrophic loss of blood. The entire encounter lasted only moments, and the family hoped, as did I, that knowing more about the attacking shark could help frame their grief with something that at least might be understood.

Months before the Labor Day shark attacks, Bev and I paid a call on George Burgess at the Florida Museum of Natural History at the University of Florida in Gainesville. A friend of more than twenty years,

Burgess is director of the International Shark Attack File, or ISAF. It might be thought of as Shark Attack Central, and although he didn't know it at the time, the ISAF was in for a long summer. In early July a bull shark would take off a boy's arm at the Fort Pickens area of Florida's Gulf Islands National Seashore near Pensacola, and that incident would be followed by the usual spate of shark bites to Florida surfers. Then would come the Virginia and North Carolina tragedies. Our visit was designed to augment my education, for I knew little about the detailed workings of the ISAF. In the universe in which most shark researchers spend their time, there isn't much scientifically noteworthy about sharks' occasional attempts to feed on humans. My professional concern usually focuses on the millions of sharks humans kill every year for food, trophy jaws, and worthless anticancer pills.

Established in 1958 at the Smithsonian Institution, the ISAF has been maintained by George Burgess since 1988 and is operated jointly by the Florida Museum of Natural History and the American Elasmobranch Society. Its records—replete with medical and autopsy reports, and victim or rescuer interviews—fill several large tan filing cabinets in an overstuffed warren of cubicles leading to a corridor the walls of which are decorated with dozens of immaculately cleaned shark jaws. The lineup includes the dentition of the thirty species commonly associated with attacks, such as great whites, bull and tiger sharks, sand tigers, makos, several reef sharks, smooth and great hammerheads, and even the porbeagle. A knowledge of variations in shark teeth is useful for determining the species involved in an incident. These days, maintaining and updating the ISAF is a full-throttle operation, because confirmed reports of shark attacks are increasing all over the world.

An eyewitness description of a shark attack was first committed to paper in 1580 by a horrified Spanish seaman whose fellow sailor had fallen overboard. Clutching a wooden block tied to a rope, the man in the water was being reeled in when "there appeared from below the surface of the sea a large monster called Tiburon that . . . tore him to pieces." That report was the beginning of a lot of bad press for sharks.

In the four-hundred-plus years since, they have been accused in thousands of injuries and disappearances, although only about twenty-two hundred shark attacks on humans have been confirmed—the count rising in the twentieth century as more people began spending more time in shark habitat.

In a typical year, Burgess's team registers about seventy-five confirmed reports of shark attacks, amassing myriad details: the exact location, time of day, and distance from shore; the victim's age, sex, apparel, and activity at the time; whether other people were in the vicinity; whether the shark made contact before its strike, and so on. The list of blanks Burgess tries to fill in totals more than two hundred categories of data, including arcane but potentially useful information such as whether the victim was wearing shiny jewelry or buckles, or had recently urinated. One object of this fact-gathering and -sifting is to maintain the statistical archive that continues to confirm how rarely sharks harm people, compared to injuries from sources such as dogs, cats, insects, lightning, and encounters with power tools and even plumbing. (According to one slice of ISAF data, in 1996 nearly forty-four thousand people in the United States were injured during interactions with toilets, while no more than eighteen were hurt by a shark.) It also feeds the ISAF web site, which has become a staple source of information for journalists, schoolchildren writing term papers, physicians treating bite victims, and lawyers pressing lawsuits on behalf of shark attack victims. The statistics also illuminate factors that contribute to or increase the likelihood of a shark attack, or vice versa.

After guiding a quick tour around his domain, George Burgess has scrunched his broad-shouldered frame into a small wooden armchair in the book-lined cul-de-sac that serves as his office. In response to a question, the earnest, bespectacled biologist has begun to outline the current state of knowledge and speculation about shark attacks on humans.

"In my view, shark attacks on humans are an asterisk in the book of science about sharks," he says with a shrug. "There are so few incidents compared to the millions of people who go in the water in any given year. Of those few attacks, most are unprovoked. Why? Certainly not because sharks are out to get people. Probably 95 to 98 percent of attacks are feeding-related—a shark simply using its jaws and teeth the way they were meant to be used.

"The most common are the mistaken-identity attacks, most of which we call hit-and-run attacks. Predators make mistakes all the time. With sharks, mistakes happen when something like a splash—maybe your hand or foot while you're swimming in the surf—draws a shark's attention because that's what its natural prey does. When the shark goes after it, it discovers that the 'prey' was bigger than it expected. The foot it has grabbed is attached to a large animal, which the shark doesn't want to mess with, or it doesn't taste like mullet. So it backs off and swims away."

The science of shark feeding behavior provides keys to help us understand such attacks. It's the long sensory response sequence that transforms a cruising shark into a curious one, and a curious, investigating shark into a focused hunter. Beginning with vibrations or sounds generated perhaps hundreds of meters away and detected by a shark's acutely sensitive hearing structures, it's the steady arrival of information about prey in the form of odors, and visual and electrical cues. Such innate sensory responses by sharks—which evolved long before humans were ever on the scene—are at the heart of hundreds of attacks documented in manila folders in the ISAF's file cabinets.

Sharks are most likely to mount hit-and-run attacks when environmental conditions encourage errors, such as when the water is murky or the light is low—early morning or dusk. The presence of normal shark prey in the area, which the shark may already be hunting, compounds the risk. Those are the times and conditions, says Burgess, when understanding the kinds of miscalculations a shark can make might encourage a swimmer or surfer to steer clear of the ocean.

"The second sort of attack," Burgess continues, "is also a natural feeding behavior. We subdivide it into two groups because there are two distinct patterns: bump-and-bite and sneak attacks. In bump-and-bite, the shark makes contact with the victim prior to the attack, then circles around and comes in and does the deed. It's probably trying to get an impression of the size and strength of the prey before it attacks. In a sneak attack there's no warning at all." Like a cat stalking a bird, a shark's stealth attack is the culmination of a barrage of sensory signals that its brain interprets as clear signs of a prey animal. The powerful rush "out of nowhere" typically comes from below and behind or to the side. In roughly two-thirds of reported great white shark attacks on humans, for example, the victim had no inkling a shark was anywhere in the vicinity.

By contrast, when the feedback to the shark's brain from an investigatory bump doesn't pass the "suitable prey item" test, it's possible, even probable, that the shark will retreat and move on. Statistics on post-bump events are meager, in part because people who only get bumped may not report the incident, or may not realize that the bump came from a shark. ISAF files are full of cases where attack victims were bumped but didn't grasp in those first moments that a shark was sizing them up.

Bull sharks, great whites, and tiger sharks are masters of the sneak attack and the bump-and-bite. Both patterns commonly include repeat attacks, causing severe damage or death. A few months before our visit Burgess had been called upon to examine the body of a Florida man who had been struck by a bull shark within moments of diving off the dock behind his house. Like the incidents at Virginia Beach, Cape Hatteras, and Fort Pickens, the attack was almost certainly a lethal coincidence; the shark likely was hunting schooling mullet seen near the dock when the victim plunged into the water. In a single bite, its powerful jaws closed around the man's midsection. Although the victim was otherwise left intact, the bite caused multiple and mortal injuries. The ISAF also documents attacks by great whites and tiger sharks in which an initial, surprise lunge tears off a limb or chunk of flesh. Surviving such an encounter requires not only emergency medical attention but a large measure of luck.

. . .

White sharks may well be responsible for most fatal attacks on humans and have garnered the majority of the attention. Researchers who have spent time studying the natural feeding behavior of great white sharks have proposed a couple of different hypotheses to explain some peculiar variations in their attacks. Roughly 57 percent of those attacks documented in the ISAF involved just a single, violent bite, and in about 70 percent of cases the shark seemingly rejected its victim, disappearing from the scene as suddenly as it came. Common targets have been humans, penguins, pelicans, and sea otters. (An otter may simply have its head bitten off as it basks belly-up at the sea surface.) Another great white attack pattern, though, is a succession of bites, with the prey briefly released after each one. In still other instances a great white shark may "carry" its intended meal, swimming off with it firmly clenched in the shark's massive jaws, like a dog with a bone.

Researchers have proposed varying explanations for these observations. John McCosker has suggested that great whites habitually "bite-and-spit" their prey, inflicting a devastating first bite and then briefly releasing the animal. After the victim goes into shock or begins to die from blood loss, the shark returns to finish its meal. Alternatively, Peter Klimley and his coworkers have proposed that the carrying behavior is more the norm, although in that scenario, too, the shark waits until its quarry has bled to death before releasing the corpse and eating it. Klimley has postulated that the shark may reject its catch sooner if the initial strike somehow signals that the prey isn't palatable—for instance, he has speculated, if it doesn't have enough body fat to make the effort worthwhile. It has also been pointed out that sharks can't get oxygen unless water is flowing through their mouth and over their gills. Swallowing a mouthful before returning for another could simply be a way to keep on breathing.

George Burgess offers some other plausible interpretations, beginning with the observation that every predator misses its mark some of the time. Plus, he notes, sharks in general "are going to go after prey items that present the least chance of personal damage. That's why, I think, the white sharks do what they do. Their typical prey, seals and sea lions, have big teeth and big claws. . . . It makes sense to try to do some serious damage, then wait until your quarry can't put up resistance anymore." As for the fact that many human targets of great whites are released after the first bite, Burgess says: "Humans are novelties in the shark's world, so they might be treated more cautiously when it comes to secondary attack behavior. Besides, when you or I become the prey item that gets bitten and spit out, we try to get out of the water. We often have other people nearby, and we've certainly got more brain power than a sea lion. When we can, we get on our surfboard or into the boat and get away before the shark comes back to finish us off. I question the body-fat hypothesis because there are plenty of cases of people being consumed entirely by a white shark when they couldn't get away."

In fact, the pages of books on shark attacks are liberally sprinkled with stories of people who couldn't get away, either because the initial bite was so severe or because there was no place to go. High-profile cases have occurred after air and sea disasters, such as the infamous sinking of the USS *Indianapolis* in the Pacific by Japanese torpedoes on July 30, 1945, when numbers of people (and corpses) have been suddenly dumped into the sea, essentially ringing a dinner bell for large open-ocean sharks such as blues, makos, and oceanic whitetips. *Indianapolis* survivors reported frequent bump-and-bite sequences that victims were helpless to escape before the shark's final rush. In all, some sixty to eighty sailors were attacked as prey and killed over a period of several days, or were eaten after they died of exposure.

Earlier in the sultry afternoon, clad in shorts, sandals, and a short-sleeved button-down dress shirt, Burgess had led me and Bev along the banks of a small lake on the University of Florida campus where on most days one can see alligators. He knows I am fond of reptiles in general and of gators in particular. This spring day, though, only a few ducks and egrets appeared, and the only reptiles we saw were sketches on signs saying, in effect, please don't feed the alligators. Back in his office, our conversation turned to other elusive but ever present creatures, the sharks that swim off eastern Florida, where it might make sense to have signs saying "Please don't feed the sharks." Most years, the swath of coastal ocean from Fernandina Beach at Florida's northeastern terminus to the Florida Keys achieves dubious distinction as the area where most of the world's shark attacks occur. The reason is the confluence there of conditions ripe for encounter between sharks and people.

In 1974, writing what would become a classic early analysis of shark attacks, biologist H. David Baldridge noted dryly that "sharks attack people in essentially every location where it is possible to get a man and a shark together." Along the Atlantic coast of Florida and virtually every other coastline where humans enter the water, people have sporadically been bumped, bitten, maimed, and occasionally killed by sharks. Incidents also occur occasionally in rivers from the Ganges and Tigris to the Hudson and Mississippi, and in hospitable lakes such as Lake Nicaragua and Guatemala's Lake Izabal, where bull sharks forage for food.

As Baldridge observed, the main prerequisite for a shark encounter is the simple combination of natural shark habitat and humans in the water. These days in certain areas knowledgeable divers accept that they're entering the sharks' domain and that vigilance is part of the gig. It's what George Burgess called the sharks-plus-people equation, which invariably equals risk, even if the risk is small. Most places in Florida are within an hour of a beach, and people who live or visit there use the ocean in just about every way imaginable, from surfing, kayaking, and diving, to fishing, swimming, and wading. Each spring, during a weeklong onslaught of humans off the Sunshine State's Volusia County that coincides with spring break, there is a predictable rash of shark bite incidents. George Burgess knows that during this period his phone will ring off the hook. I know from my own research that, globally, shark stocks overall have declined in recent years by about 70 percent, mostly due to overfishing and practices such as finning. Even so, says Burgess, in Florida the sharks-plus-people equation has been increasingly skewed in favor of *more* attacks just by the steady rise in the number of people using the ocean for recreation.

Listening to George, it occurs to me that, more or less, sharks are the last large carnivores that we humans have not yet tamed. Even in this twenty-first century, much of the ocean is wilderness, as the Earth's great forests and grasslands once were. Lions, tigers, and bears—the great terrestrial carnivores that could prey on humans—have for the most part been subdued by technologies from bows and arrows to high-powered rifles, and their depleted habitats largely destroyed. Because sharks live in the aquatic realm where we cannot so easily pursue them, they've been able to hold their own a bit longer—at least until recently, when longlines and gill nets have become the oceangoing equivalents of gunpowder and subdivisions.

Florida is a dramatic example of the shift in the sharks-plus-people equation, but the shift has occurred in other locales as well. For example, shark attacks used to be rare along the coast of Brazil. ISAF statistics, which are garnered through a global network of cooperating scientists and organizations, confirm how the situation has altered. Especially in the Recife area, surfing took off in the late 1980s. In an eloquently simple chart on the ISAF web site, the boom is juxtaposed with numbers showing that more than half of all known attacks in Brazil have occurred since 1990. Predictably, the sharks involved are mainly large coastals such as tiger sharks and bulls, and the increase in attacks includes a notable rise in the number of fatalities.

Tourism has fueled the geographical shift in shark attack incidents, with certain areas becoming hot spots as people have the ability to travel more and flood the water for recreational pursuits. Hawaii has always been a prolific source of shark attack reports, but now, in once remote places like Réunion island off Madagascar and alluring Indo-Pacific destinations such as Fiji and Pulau, tourists are snorkeling, windsurfing, and diving their way directly into the age-old coastal haunts of tropical shark species. George Burgess notes that local tourism officials understandably don't like to advertise the changing environment off their coastal paradises. But, he says, "It's simply a function of people intruding into areas where sharks have always been but people haven't. Common sense kept the local people away. They knew better."

Other changes are shifts in the scope, character, and style of human activities. Burgess observes, "Things like windsurfing and ocean kayaking, which were relatively rare in most places a couple of decades ago, have exploded in popularity. Clothing has changed. And one of the biggest changes is the demographics of who goes into the water. When David Baldridge did his analysis, shark attack was essentially a young-white-male phenomenon. Now, more and more females are engaged in active aquatic recreation, and so females are being attacked more. They've become equal-opportunity shark attack victims."

As George rattles off the changing terms of the modern shark-human equation, I think of a notorious incident he told us about in which a young woman crew member on an oceanographic research vessel took a swim in the sea off Easter Island. That afternoon she lost a leg, torn off at the hip in a stealth attack by a great white shark. Her life was saved because the ship's staff and researchers included people with training in emergency medicine, and the U.S. Air Force flew her to a hospital in Panama where doctors were standing by to treat the grievous wound. All over the world, female swimmers, divers, surfers, anglers, and kayakers are not so fortunate, and they are having the same fateful encounters with sharks that their male counterparts have had for centuries.

Regardless of their sex, humans also have extended the opportunities for sharks to feed on them by taking advantage of technological advances such as wet suits, which came into general use in the late 1950s and allow people to spend more time in colder water than they ever could with just fins and a snorkel or air tank. An enduring myth assures divers and surfers that sharks attack only in water warmer than about 68° F. Years of speculation that fueled the myth didn't consider the fact that humans aren't physiologically adapted to spend time in water much colder than that, so until recently, few did so. Ever since we've had neoprene to keep ourselves warm in cold water, more people have taken to the sea in places like the coast of

California, and as ISAF records attest, shark attacks in those places have increased.

Other factors also may be at work. More than half the known attacks by great white sharks have occurred along the Pacific coast of the United States, with most of those off California hot spots such as the Farallon Islands west of San Francisco. There, and in the western North Atlantic, another people-driven adjustment in the ecological status quo has occurred. Increased legal protection of marine mammals from human hunters has put more of the great white's natural food on the table, and its numbers probably are increasing as a result. Bob Hueter, director of Mote Marine Laboratory's Shark Center, has studied shark abundance in coastal nursery areas for several years. He believes that bull shark populations in the Gulf of Mexico may be rebounding to historically more normal levels more rapidly than other species decimated by the overfishing that occurred in the 1980s and early 1990s. The reason why could be their ability to survive in low-salinity or even freshwater habitats; spending much more time in such places than most other sharks do, bull sharks may have inadvertently found a refuge from the fisheries that operated mostly in the coastal ocean. (Also, bull sharks are not targeted by fisheries because their meat and fins are not considered desirable.) Conversely, George Burgess has seen no increase in bull sharks in the offshore commercial longline catches, which he monitors. Of course, the first sign that a stock is recovering from overfishing would be an increase in the number of young sharks in nursery areas.

One effect of the increasing human preoccupation with shark attacks has been more research on the biology and predatory behavior of these powerful carnivores. We have learned, for example, that great whites, like most other large sharks, don't feed according to a set schedule but rather whenever the opportunity presents itself. Unlike many other sharks, however, they are effective daytime hunters, with the ability to see sharply and in color. Experiments also support the commonsense supposition that great whites are visually attracted to

roughly oval shapes and silhouettes—say, surfboards and sea kayaks—
that resemble sea lions and other pinnipeds they prey on naturally.
There's no simple cause-and-effect relationship, however. Studies also
show that once sensory cues have triggered a great white shark's feeding mode, the shark is liable to launch a strike against a target even if
it is just a floating square board tethered to a research vessel.

In many if not most cases, sharks don't use their vision to scout for
prey initially, but instead pay attention to acoustic cues and odors. But
it stands to reason that once those sensory stimuli have drawn a shark's
interest and the shark swims closer to a potential prey item, visual
information may ratchet up the shark's curiosity to a point that triggers active feeding behavior. That information might include colors,
glinting metallic fixtures, and other features of swimwear, wet suits,
flippers, and other aquatic paraphernalia. Without the equivalent of
a gigantic white-shark aquarium that would allow controlled testing
of a smorgasbord of variables, researchers can probe for answers only
by piecing together bits of data gleaned from records like the ISAF
data set. Meticulously sifting through records of 159 great white
attacks documented between 1876 and 1995, George Burgess found
that nearly 90 percent of the victims were wearing clothing (including
wet and dry suits) that was primarily black, gray, or blue. A little over
27 percent had yellow, gold, or a similar hue ("yum-yum yellow") as a
secondary color. In fact, in ISAF data nearly two-thirds of the attacks
were on people wearing a high-contrast combination of black and yellow, white, blue, or orange. No attacks were associated with clothing
that was predominantly green, white, silver, orange, or purple, and
less than 2 percent involved brown, tan, or rust-colored apparel. In
the visual world of a large predatory shark, color combinations that
contrast strongly underwater, making them easy to see, may help
stack the deck in favor of a feeding attempt.

In general, scientifically validated information on precise triggers
of shark attacks is hard to come by. Beyond the issue of color patterns,
other after-the-fact observations are that a preponderance of attacks

have been directed at solitary humans and at those who are making noise or splashing, as a lone swimmer might. Attacks tend to occur in the early morning or at twilight, when visibility in the water is limited, although some shark species, such as great whites, tiger sharks, bull sharks, and lemon sharks, will feed whenever prey are available. In coastal areas, attacks also seem to be associated with onshore winds, the reduced salinity that develops when rainfall has been high, and the presence of bait fish or gurry dumped from a fishing vessel. Eighty percent of the attacks noted by the ISAF have occurred in water that was no more than five feet deep.

Rarely, a single large shark will attack several people in sequence—the *Jaws* scenario. The Russian couple at Cape Hatteras were hit this way, and in the previous year three triathletes, two middle-aged men and a woman, were out for a training swim in the dawn surf off Gulf Shores, Alabama, when a bull shark set upon the men in turn. After an initial bump, the shark tore off the fingers on the right hand of one man, then left his thrashing quarry to attack the second swimmer, biting him on the right arm and hip. Then the bull shark returned to its first target, who was still in the water. After inflicting several more wounds, the shark took the man's right arm in its mouth and held on even while the frantic swimmer was making his way to shore. The two were struggling in water only inches deep when the arm finally broke off. In some quarters the encounter resurrected the enduring myth of a "rogue" shark bent on capturing human prey, but observations of wild sharks have revealed that sequential attacks are often the way sharks feed, when they can. Ghastly as such encounters are from a human point of view, from the shark's perspective, that innate behavior boosts its chances of survival. If a hungry shark isn't successful on its first strike, doesn't get enough, or realizes it has made a mistake, it makes sense to go after another potential victim nearby. Like all good predators, sharks are adapted to take full advantage of opportunities to feed, because the next chance may not come along for a while.

A shark must also somehow arrive at the decision to strike at potential prey, based on the complex sequence of sensory stimuli their brains can process. "I think sharks in general get into a heightened level of feeding excitement—a mind-set where they're on edge, alert, specifically attuned to their cues," says Burgess. "It's what all predators do. As more cues come in, the signals get the shark more and more excited. And so under those circumstances they're more likely to make quick, even rash, decisions to go get what they want, because their nervous system is primed to rock 'n' roll. And that rock 'n' roll may ultimately be set off by a splash at the water's surface, vibrations, or the glint of something. Any number of things they might interpret as their final cue to go for their feeding rush."

"Tell me about sand tigers," I say to George. I've been hearing stories of sand tiger sharks being highly aggressive toward divers along the Virginia coast, especially in the spring, and I've heard that there is increasing concern about them in Australia and some other places. Since sand tigers are dedicated fish eaters, the tales are puzzling. Yet after great whites, bull sharks, and tiger sharks, on the ISAF list, sand tigers have achieved the number four spot for attacks on humans.

Burgess responds with a nod. "Sand tigers apparently don't like to be too close to human beings under water. And they are *very* predisposed to go after speared fishes. We've had a lot of reports of sand tigers chasing humans right up to the boat. I think that's a species where some attacks are not feeding attacks but agonistic behavior towards humans."

Agonistic behavior has nothing to do with capturing food. It is a hostile response to a perceived threat, like a person shaking a fist at someone who hurls an insult. By Burgess's reckoning, only a small percentage of shark attacks are agonistic, though the chance for growth in that statistic is steadily increasing as people find more ways to enter the world of sharks.

The rising popularity of shark tourism may be a case in point, although expert opinion differs on this question. Reef sharks, like the Caribbean reef, lemon sharks, blacktips, and even nurse sharks, have been known to attack divers and snorkelers who violate what the shark apparently perceives to be its personal space. It is possible that having an unnaturally large number of sharks in a given space can spook some animals into behaving aggressively.

"Forty sharks swimming around a frozen piece of chum is not a natural situation, any way you look at it," opines Burgess. On some tourist dives, clients in scuba gear sit in a circle while staff divers set out a ball or Popsicle-like skewers of frozen fish (a "chumsicle"), which reef sharks then tear apart. "It's no different than watching a feeding at Sea World. Reef sharks virtually never feed like that in a wild setting. It's artificial behavior."

The ISAF includes about two dozen cases of shark handlers or their clients being bitten. "One guy was a handler on a feeding operation," Burgess recalls. "When they dropped the chum ball down, he went to attach it to the anchor. Meanwhile the boat was revving its engine, like Pavlov's bell, to attract the sharks. Suddenly he saw a Caribbean reef go down and start doing belly flops on the sand, then come up really fast. That's a typical agonistic display. Caribbean reef sharks tend to get on edge. Then he saw this thing shoot up and grab him on the leg. He was in the hospital for weeks."

Listening to George, I can't help thinking of Bimini, where only two months earlier Bev and I had watched amazed at the fluid, precise movements of reef sharks as they fed on chunks of fish tossed from a boat. It had been a scientific, not a tourist operation, but we'd been overwhelmed nonetheless. I could understand why other people might want to see that beauty, and some, perhaps most, experienced researcher-divers do not see controlled chumming situations as particularly dangerous. At the first-ever Pan-African Shark Conservation Conference in Cape Town, South Africa, Andy Cobb, a South African naturalist and dive master who has led unbaited shark dives since 1981, told me that in general he is opposed to shark baiting, preferring instead to take a small number of clients to places where sharks aggregate naturally. His clients enter the water only after Cobb thoroughly indoctrinates them about the animals' habits and life histories, and are allowed to do nothing that might disturb them. In situations where a dive operator must (or elects to) attract sharks with a chumsicle, it is Cobb's view that doing so is generally safe because it focuses the sharks on the food and mimics natural situations in which several sharks converge on a central food source such as a dead whale. Shark scientist Wes Pratt, who has spent three decades diving with sharks as part of his research on shark behavior, also views well-executed tourism dives as basically safe.

At Mote Marine Laboratory in Sarasota, Bob Hueter cautiously weighs in on the controversy. In places like Florida, he says, shark dives are problematical because of the close proximity of so much human activity to places where sharks may be fed. But he also can quote statistics gathered by an association of tourist dive operators in the Bahamas, where Caribbean reef sharks predominate and shark dives are a lucrative business. Affirming that "this is an extremely controversial subject" among shark researchers, Hueter says that the dozen operations working from 1973 to 2000 reported an impressive safety record. In twenty-one thousand shark dives, only eight customers out of over 240,000 were bitten. During the same twenty-seven-year period, operators reported forty injuries to dive staff, who interact with sharks more closely. Hueter also is quick to point out that there is virtually no scientific data on how tourist dive operations affect the *sharks*.

"We know that in an artificial feeding environment like this, there are probably some effects on natural dominance relationships among the reef sharks," Hueter says. "In an undisturbed reef setting, Caribbean reef sharks may move from one reef habitat to another— and we don't know how these feeding operations alter that. For instance, we need to ask if sharks can essentially be entrapped at feeding stations because that's where the easy food is, and so curtail their normal migrations. Does organized feeding at particular sites affect their mating behaviors? We don't know the answers to questions like these."

Sharks that become accustomed to feeding on chumsicles may not get the proper nutrition, especially if they are fed so routinely that they stop hunting their natural prey. One concern is the temptation for cost-conscious operators to offer the sharks spoiled or diseased fish or a diet deficient in nutrients. "We know from studies of natural feeding that a reef shark weighing one hundred to one hundred fifty pounds would capture three to six pounds of fish a week," Hueter points out. "With the tourism operations, some sharks may get a lot more than that, which could unnaturally accelerate their growth or their nutrition could suffer."

Commercial feeding operations also raise questions about long-term ecological impacts. If sharks congregate regularly around the feeding sites in unnaturally large numbers, the influx might well perturb the natural structure of the reef community, where normally only a few apex predators are present. Certain sharks have high site fidelity, moving onto and off the reef in a predictable way that correlates with their normal feeding pattern—often staying farther offshore at mid-day and coming in to feed in the early morning and again at dusk. When a feeding operation attracts more large sharks to an area, especially reef sharks whose instinctive responses to unnatural situations seem to include agonistic behavior, people like George Burgess worry that the number of shark attacks on humans there might increase. The sharks might also learn to associate people with feeding. The ISAF records one case of a woman tourist who was bitten on the head by a reef shark when she visited a feeding area on a nonfeeding day. Was the shark somehow frustrated when the human in the water wasn't accompanied by food? Did its body language give warning signs that the diver missed?

From 1994 to 2000 in the Bahamas, the number of shark dives tripled over the number recorded in the previous twenty years, yet there has been no increase in unprovoked attacks there and ISAF statistics for the area have remained flat. At this writing, the Bahamian government estimates that over 250,000 people have participated in shark dives in its waters, spending money there that cannot be overlooked. In response, conservation efforts in the Bahamas are thriving, and shark long-lining there has essentially been outlawed.

"My sense is that there may be a balance to be achieved here.

Shark dives aren't all bad, but it's up to the industry to ensure that the conservation and educational benefits of tourist dives outweigh the negatives," says Bob Hueter. "A high-quality operation can educate hundreds of thousands of people about shark conservation. That's a huge benefit."

Some sharks, particularly carcharhinids, signal by their body language when they're distressed. Common signs include jaw movements that resemble yawning, hunching the back, dropping the pectoral fins. Reading such warnings from a shark, the way one might back off when a dog growls, isn't something we humans instinctively do. George Burgess himself once antagonized lemon sharks in the Bahamas, when he decided to see what would happen if he obstructed the swimming path of some young lemons moving back and forth through a gully. The little lemons were disquieted by the large man in their path and started swimming anxious circles around him. "It was really interesting, a complete change in their behavior," he recalls. "Then I looked over and saw this large pregnant female lemon, a seven-footer, heading straight for me." The shark veered away only when Burgess lunged at her, flailing his arms in a display he hoped she would interpret as counterposing strength. "I could just see the headlines, 'Shark attack scientist attacked by sharks,' because I was stupid enough to get in their way."

If the ruse hadn't been successful, Burgess would have been guilty of overtly provoking a shark attack. Provoked attacks include those on divers or snorkelers who are bitten after "petting" a shark or grabbing its tail or a fin. Also in Burgess's "S for Stupid" file are attacks on spearfishers or divers who swim along trailing a stringer of fish or a bag of shellfish. In a case several years ago off Virginia Beach, a sand tiger was attracted to a pair of scuba spearfishers who had been diving on a wreck and were transferring a fish to a stringer in about forty feet of water. Mistaking one diver's left hand—which was inside a glove slathered with fish blood and slime—for a fish, the shark closed its mouth on the hand, then quickly let go when it discovered its error. The hand was mangled, nonetheless. The diver's lack of judgment was compounded by the fact that he had observed sand tigers cruising around the wreck all afternoon.

For all the attack statistics that crowd the ISAF files, none come from analysis of data gathered scientifically. You can't orchestrate a shark attack. Details must be plumbed from the memories and perceptions of victims or bystanders. By contrast, boatloads of experiments have explored just about every conceivable antishark strategy, from beach meshing to chemical repellents, electromagnetic fields, and chain-mail divewear.

My 2000 trip to South Africa included a lesson on meshing. The Natal Shark Board has been in charge of beach meshing in Durban since 1964, and early on a cool May morning Assistant Director Geramy Cliff took me and several other fishery scientists out on one of the board's launches to observe crews hauling back the nets. We left the dock just as the sun was rising, and cruised along the oceanfront in the shadows of the tall hotels that line Durban's famous white-sand bathing beaches. Ahead of us, the six-man crews of two board launches were already hauling in large mesh nets by hand. These crews are black Africans, as Shark Board crews always have been. The nets are set about a mile from the beach and actually fish in midwater with space above and below them. The nets are staggered and so do not form a continuous wall, keeping sharks at bay. Rather, they function to reduce the risk of shark attack by catching sharks and reducing the size of the local population. About one-third of the sharks are captured on the *inside* of the nets. Every morning seventeen Shark Board launches ply the KwaZulu-Natal coast, hauling and repairing nets at all the heavily used beaches.

"The nets are pulled in winter during the sardine run," Cliff tells us. "Otherwise the bycatch of dolphins following the sardines is very high at that time. In other seasons we shorten the netted area from forty-five to twenty-nine kilometers to reduce the bycatch of sea turtles and marine mammals. There hasn't been any increase in shark attacks."

The Shark Board is also experimenting with drum lines—simple floats with large baited hooks to catch larger (and more dangerous) sharks. Such lines do not usually catch sea turtles or marine mammals and have been adopted in many places, such as Australia, as an alternative to beach meshing. Sharks killed by Shark Board efforts are used for educational programs; the live ones are tagged and released. The annual cost of the operation is $2.5 to $3 million.

Because sharks favor solitary prey, other antishark strategies designed for personal use have taken aim at the shark's keen sensory responses to certain chemicals, odors, and electric fields. In the wake of the *Indianapolis* disaster, the U.S. Navy rushed to develop Shark Chaser, a mixture of copper acetate and black dye meant to mimic a chemical exuded by decaying shark carcasses—according to seafaring lore, a sure shark repellent. Hurriedly added to every sailor's survival gear, the concoction showed itself in follow-up experiments to be essentially useless. A second potential repellent was formulated based on researcher Eugenie Clark's observation that sharks were put off by body fluids of the Red Sea Moses sole. The active ingredient in the sole's secretions was a whitish, detergentlike substance called pardaxin, which could repel small sharks in a laboratory setting, though exactly how it bothered the sharks has never been discovered. At the Bimini shark lab, a team led by Sonny Gruber tested a detergent brew called SDS (for sodium dodecyl sulfate) on captive lemon sharks; he and others have tried the same or similar stuff on blue sharks and wild great white sharks as well. Some people have tried squirting sharks with toxin-loaded syringes. In the early 1990s, a South African enterprise developed a battery-operated device called the shark POD—for Protective Oceanic Device. Designed to deter sharks by irritating their sensitive electroreceptors, the POD generates a twenty-foot field of electromagnetic energy around the person wearing it. More recently, an Australian entrepreneur has begun marketing a smaller device, called Shark Safe, which is supposed to operate on the same principle. It sells for about four hundred dollars.

The only problem with these and other antishark devices is that, insofar as experiments—and experience—have been able to demonstrate, none of them can be counted on to work consistently. Devices like Shark Safe and the POD seem to have a deterrent effect only in encounters where the human tester has well-scripted control of the circumstances. When Ken Goldman was working with great whites off Australia, he observed a telling POD encounter. Curious to see how effective the device might be, Ken and his Australian colleagues baited one with a chunk of tuna and attached it to a three-foot pole dangling over the side of their skiff. The bait soon attracted a great white shark, which instead of turning away made its feeding rush right through the POD's electromagnetic field. When its jaws closed around the POD, the shark—thrashing wildly and in obvious distress—was unable to release it because the electric current stimulated a continual contraction of its jaw muscles. The shark finally bit the POD in two, swallowed the half in its mouth, and disappeared back into the Pacific Ocean.

The practical requirements for a chemical repellent—that it be potent at a concentration of a hundred parts per billion (of seawater), function in a range of warm to cool water temperatures, and be rapidly deployable as a nondispersing cloud around the user—have also turned out to be formidable. New chemical candidates are proposed from time to time, including a class of compounds called saponins, which marine creatures as lowly as sea cucumbers have evolved as antipredator defenses.

Fortunately, most of the seventy-five or so people attacked by sharks each year will escape serious injury. ISAF data have recently begun to provide insights on the best approaches for treating shark bite victims, essentially improving the odds that victims of severe attacks will survive. One discovery is that fresh wounds that are not immediately closed tight with stitches or staples are less likely to become infected; another is that medical personnel should order lab tests for *Vibrio* bacteria, potentially dangerous microbes that seem to be common in the mouths of sharks.

New grist for the ISAF mill is also being provided by modern tools for interpreting historic oceanographic information. Computerized tide calculations are an example. Created by oceanographers concerned with tracking physical changes in the oceanic environment, the computer programs allow anyone who knows the date, location, and approximate time of a shark attack to find out what the tide was when the incident occurred. "We're plugging in data from every ISAF case where the information is available, going back sixty years or more," says Burgess. "In most cases, we're finding that sharks are attacking on the highest high tides and the lowest low tides. And for some species, there seems to be a real lunar periodicity."

The upshot may eventually be the ability to forecast, for some coastal areas, when shark encounters are most likely.

I wonder, though, about expending resources to forecast shark encounters. Right now, it's possible to say with certainty that every year in some places, such as along the beaches of Florida's Volusia County, a handful of the millions of people who swim there will meet up with a few of the sharks—whose numbers overall are in decline— that inhabit those waters. It's a given, like hurricane season in the south and earthquakes in California and grizzly bears in Alaska. As in all such situations, those of us who choose to be in such places assume the risk, however infinitesimal, that along with finding pleasure and beauty we will meet up with a natural force beyond our control. One evening I tuned in to watch television personality Larry King interview the Alabama athlete who had lost his forearm to a bull shark. King asked the man if his experience had led him to hate sharks. Gesturing with his stump, the man didn't hesitate, replying matter-of-factly that he found nothing to hate. Sharks lived in the water, always had, and he had chosen to put himself there. Sharks are incredible animals, I think he said. It seemed like the most rational of answers.

9   The Shark Pharmacy

"Shark cartilage." On a spring morning in 1993, my anger rose as I read the words on the pill bottle in an airport drugstore. Coming down with a cold and looking to buy some vitamin C, I realized with a jolt that I was beholding the newest threat to sharks, and a powerful one at that. My shark monitoring program in the mid-Atlantic had been coming up increasingly empty each summer—the sharks just didn't seem to be there anymore—and now hawkers of shark cartilage pills were springing up like malevolent toadstools, proclaiming the powdered tissue the latest cure for cancer, spurring fisheries in many parts of the world to target sharks more intensively than ever. A major impetus for the hype had been the previous year's best-seller *Sharks Don't Get Cancer* by I. William Lane, an entrepreneurial biochemist and nutritionist who almost single-handedly stirred up a shark-cartilage frenzy by, as he told reporters, "taking research to the people." What he had not told "the people," including tens of thousands of cancer sufferers willing to try virtually anything to stay the progress of their disease, was that reputable researchers agreed that pulverized shark skulls and spines were worthless. Meanwhile Lane, his son, and others were selling the stuff for as much as $130 a pound.

Eight years after my first encounter with shark cartilage pills, I have arrived at the Penn Stater Conference Center Hotel late for a meeting with Carl Luer, one of the world's most respected experts on the shark immune system. Both of us are presenting papers at the annual meeting of the American Elasmobranch Society, over which Carl also is presiding this year and which is being held in a sprawling conference center operated by Pennsylvania State University in the picturesque town of State College. This year also, an estimated fifty thousand cancer-stricken Americans will down shark cartilage preparations, which still retail for about a hundred dollars a pound. As in the early 1990s, those tablets and powders are ground up shark cartilage, high in protein and calcium, and I. William Lane is still selling the stuff, although his company now promotes it as an aid "for maintaining joint health and mobility." The shark cartilage/cancer-cure enterprise, he has recently been quoted as saying, was merely part of "a faddish industry." But it seems to me that, as the French like to say, the more things change, the more they stay the same.

As the shift in Mr. Lane's business model suggests, though, there has been a curious evolution in the way shark-product entrepreneurs pitch their wares, and Carl Luer almost certainly has had something to do with that. A biochemist of impeccable scientific credentials, and director of the Marine Biomedical Research Program at Mote Marine Laboratory near Sarasota, Florida, he has spent the last twenty-plus years meticulously sorting fact from fiction when it comes to the nature of shark defenses against disease. It hasn't been easy, because sharks and their relatives are so different from every other group of animals on Earth. There's been the aggravation of seeing his work cited—not to mention creatively reinterpreted—by shark cartilage purveyors hoping to adorn their products with scientific cachet. And from the standpoint of public education, Luer's job has been and continues to be an uphill push, because of the common and amazingly persistent belief that sharks are almost magically impervious to cancer and other afflictions—and thus are candidates for being ground up and packaged into pills, potions, and powders touted as beneficial not only for cancer but for ailments ranging from arthritis to dandruff.

Such misconceptions notwithstanding, as I hustle down a corridor to the emptying meeting room where Carl is already speaking earnestly into Bev's tape recorder, I'm well aware that he and his colleagues are beginning to map the terra incognita of sharks' disease-fighting weapons. It turns out that, after all, sharks may have some gifts to offer humankind. And if they *do* exist, those boons for human health, yours and mine, won't come from fast-money, grind 'em up and sell 'em schemes, because the questions that lead to meaningful answers don't have anything to do with big profits or grinding up animals to fill bottles with useless pills. Here are some of the important ones: Are the 450,000-year-old chondrichthyan immune defenses really as primitive as researchers once imagined—or have they just been underappreciated? What is the scientifically defensible approach to finding out whether substances like shark cartilage or liver oils or shark-anything-else have medically useful properties? Where in this convoluted, emotion-laden subject does wisdom lie?

When we think of resistance to disease, we usually think of the immune system. But if you want to know something about the shark immune system, you can't go to a bookshelf and pull out a tome on the subject. That book doesn't exist, perhaps because we are only at the brink of being able even to name all the system's components, let alone understand what they do. And until very recently, efforts to describe the shark immune system were molded by what we know about our own elaborate body defenses.

To wit, the human immune system, a mammalian one, is anchored in the marrow of large bones like the breastbone and femur, in the spleen, and in the thymus, structures that produce an array of defensive white blood cells including a subset called lymphocytes. Bone marrow is the source for lymphocytes known as B cells, which do not directly combat invading pathogens. Instead, B cells manufacture antibodies—proteins that patrol the bloodstream and inactivate potentially harmful microbes that have not yet infected body cells. Another term for antibody is immunoglobulin, and so antibodies are labeled Ig; humans have five major types. By contrast, other important components of the human immune system are T lymphocytes, or T cells, soldiers that attack body cells that are already infected or that have turned cancerous. A T cell identifies these abnormal body cells by way of receptors that stud its surface like antennae. Some T cells also help mobilize antibody defenses. T cells come from the thymus, a small organ at the base of the neck. The spleen is yet another major player in the immune system and its functions include cleansing the blood of debris and serving as a site where lymphocytes multiply into counterattacking armies when a pathogen invades.

These core immune system organs are buttressed by a bodywide network of lymphatic vessels that link lymph nodes located in strategic places like the armpits, neck, and groin. Because of the way lymphatic vessels are built, cancer cells and pathogens such as bacteria and viruses can rather easily enter them and use them as highways through the body. Assorted defensive cells, including "killer" T cells that destroy cancer cells, lurk in lymph nodes where, if all goes well, they intercept and destroy the enemy. Conversely, when the defenders are overwhelmed or evaded, the body develops an infection or cancer gains a foothold.

In simple terms that's how the human immune system works, and for a long time a shark's internal physical and chemical defenses looked meager by comparison. Not having a bony skeleton, sharks and their kin lack bone marrow. Yet shark blood is well supplied with white blood cells and antibodies. The latter come from B cells inside the shark's spleen, which, like our own, is tucked up against the stomach. Sharks also lack a lymphatic system, and for decades dissections of sharks yielded little unequivocal evidence for a thymus either. In fact, Carl Luer and several of his coworkers were the first to definitively trace the development of the shark thymus and pin down its functions, as part of a larger search for anything that could explain sharks' apparent ability to fend off cancer. Whenever one talks about shark immunity, cancer is just about always the first subject to come up.

Carl has been explaining all this, leaning forward intently in a molded plastic chair, elbows propped on a service table littered with napkins and plastic cups. He periodically stabs the air with an index finger for emphasis. "It's *always* been known that sharks *do* get cancer, but the incidence is very low." A federally sponsored tumor registry created in 1965 to track reports of cancers in lower animals has recorded forty cases of tumors in sharks and other elasmobranchs, plus or minus. Carl, a skeptic by nature, doubts even that number. "Opinions differ, but in my view there've been maybe half a dozen legitimate cancer tumors identified in sharks since 1965, mostly skin cancers, though of course we don't know how many go unseen or unreported."

Cancer is a genetic disease that starts when the DNA instructions for replicating a given type of cell go awry. This transformation can happen in various ways, but common causes are damage to the cell's DNA (from radiation or free radicals, for example) or mutation triggered by an external agent such as a chemical carcinogen. Cells normally have mechanisms for repairing altered DNA. When DNA repair isn't effective, and when the immune system then fails to dispose of the malfunctioning cell or cells, cancer becomes a threat. Accordingly, the likelihood an animal will develop cancer may relate to how efficiently its cells can fix damaged DNA, how effectively its immune system detects cancerous cells, or both.

In Luer's laboratory at Mote, he says, "we initially wanted to see if we could do something experimentally to induce tumors so we could study that process, and we tried some potent carcinogens, including aflatoxin [a natural by-product of a fungus that infests peanuts]. But we couldn't even get precancerous changes." That work drew some attention when it was reported, but as it happens, mutations do not turn up in shark DNA as frequently as in that of mammals and one hypothesis—largely untested—is that the shark mutation rate is so low because sharks have evolved unusually efficient DNA repair.

Superefficiency may be a hallmark of the elasmobranch immune system as well.

Luer did his early investigations of the shark-cancer conundrum in the 1980s. As the 1990s got under way in the wake of the explosion of research on immune function sparked by the advent of HIV and AIDS, he and other researchers began focusing on what a shark's immune defenses really look like. In effect, they were asking that first, key scientific question, not realizing at the time that their effort would overturn some entrenched views on shark immunity.

"When we started researching the scientific literature on immunity in elasmobranchs," Carl is explaining, "we saw right away that some of it was right, some was wrong, and some was confusing. One problem was that everybody was trying to interpret findings in sharks in terms of what we knew in humans. So initially, we had to stop and ask ourselves, what's *really* known?" Luer's group began by reexamining the immune cells detectable in an elasmobranch's bloodstream: four major classes of antibodies, including one, IgM, shared with humans; B and T cells; and a smattering of white blood cells that have roles in inflammation, the body's generalized, first response to tissue damage. That part, Luer remembers, was relatively easy.

"Anybody who has any knowledge of blood cells can look at a sample of shark blood and say, 'Oh yeah, those are lymphocytes,'" he recalls. "So the next question was, Where are they being made? Because sharks don't have bone marrow, everybody said they must be made in the spleen." Another possible source for some lymphocytes was the thymus. Up to that time, however, thousands of elasmobranchs dissected in research laboratories around the world had produced only scant evidence for that organ; a small, lumpy mass of thymus tissue had been found in fetuses of a few species and seemed to vanish as the animals grew to maturity, rather like the way a human embryo loses its tail as it develops into a fully formed baby. The consensus among researchers was that a meaningful version of this crucial immune system element had simply never evolved in sharks.

Not knowing what they would find, Luer and his coworkers at Mote decided to challenge the conventional wisdom. In effect they embarked on a thymus hunt, although at first the search would take the Mote team down a series of blind alleys. "Like everybody else," confesses Luer, "we started out looking for the thymus in the wrong place," namely, associated with muscle to the rear of a shark's head, near its gills, where the fetal thymus is located. In animals more than a few days or weeks old, this target tissue flattened and folded inward, all but disappearing. Eventually, however, over the course of five years of painstaking dissections, the team discovered ribbonlike swaths of thymus in juveniles and adults, sandwiched deep within layers of head muscle. In species after species they examined—including bull sharks, sandbars, tiger sharks, nurse and lemon sharks, horn sharks, and great hammerheads, as well as skates, rays, a guitarfish, and a sawfish—they could trace how the once unified mass of immune system tissue had bifurcated, different parts of it migrating into the interior layers of head muscles as the animal matured. Now, says Luer with a grin, "we've looked in twenty-three species and we find it in the same locations in every one." Under a microscope, each section of thymus reveals unmistakable evidence of what Luer calls "the shark version of T cells."

It's still not known what elasmobranch T cells do, and their functions may be far different from those of human T cells. That would make sense, for they are T cells for the disease challenges a shark faces, not those we confront. Molecular studies led by Gary Litman at the University of South Florida and Martin Flajnik at the University of Maryland are uncovering the chemical makeup of genes that encode the T cell receptors, the antennae that allow the cell to detect potentially harmful foreign entities in the shark's body. One receptor gene that has been analyzed in detail is remarkably similar to the equivalent gene for a human T cell receptor; our mammalian bodies still carry this relic, an immunity gene (and maybe more than one) that arose in the earliest sharks and lives today in their descendants. It's a connection between us and them that has survived 450 million years. We might also be glimpsing our ancient beginnings in the other major element in immune responses, the antibody system. Although the operating rules for the shark antibody-producing system differ from ours in some important ways (such as how genetic instructions for building antibodies are organized), in their basic outlines the two versions of antibody-making machinery are very much alike, and shark and human antibodies share numerous features. So another of the basic insights we are gaining from exploring the immune functions of sharks is a deeper appreciation of our own immunological inheritance from the earliest jawed vertebrates.

The fundamental differences are just as striking. For instance, sharks have evolved a means for producing antibodies that may better prepare them for meeting disease challenges than ours prepares us. The details are complex, but basically our immune system is set up to make millions of different antibodies sensitive to millions of different invaders. The only prerequisite is that we must be exposed to a given pathogen before the system can gear up for a counterattack, and that response takes time, sometimes many days or several weeks. Sharks, by contrast, are less well equipped than we are to make as many *different* antibodies, but their immune system is already poised against certain pathogens, probably ones they commonly encounter in the sea. One might say we have more kinds of immunological bullets at our disposal, but sharks enter the world with some big guns already loaded. In this sense, a shark's options for responding effectively to a disease threat may be much more efficient than our own.

Spleen, thymus, B and T cells. By 1995 scientists like Carl Luer had begun to be able to tick off in sharks the parts we think of as necessary for a more-than-primitive immune system. More recently Luer and a handful of others have turned their attention to two unique features of elasmobranch anatomy, the epigonal organ and the organ of Leydig. These structures don't exist in higher vertebrates, but most sharks and their relatives have one or both. The "epigonal," as Luer calls it, is a large, obvious organ adjacent to an elasmobranch's reproductive tract, while the Leydig organ sits just under the outer layer of the esophagus. The provocative thing about both is that microscopically they look a lot like bone marrow. "When I took comparative anatomy," Luer recalls, "I was taught 'that's the epigonal, we have no idea what it does.' Now we know that it makes immune cells. We're convinced it's a bone marrow equivalent." Carl Luer's pleasure in this conclusion is palpable. "And what this means," he continues, "among other things, is that elasmobranchs are the earliest phylogenetic group of animals to have all the components that are necessary for an adaptive immune system. You don't find those elements in any living animal lower than them."

A mammal's bone marrow makes B cells, which produce antibodies, but in adult cartilaginous fishes most B cells seem to be cranked out by the Leydig and epigonal organs. Evidence to substantiate this hypothesis comes from the appealing little clearnose skates (*Raja eglanteria*), and as with a lot of the research being carried out today on elasmobranchs, sophisticated methods for identifying genes are propelling rapid advances in our understanding. Using stretches of DNA that have been engineered to probe for specific genes, researchers have found signs that this skate's cells sequester a range of immune cell genes. In short, in laboratories at Mote and elsewhere, sharks and their kin are meeting modern molecular biology and are giving up millennia of disease-resistance secrets.

Some cells of the immune system are specialized for disposing of or destroying other body cells that are diseased or unneeded—the body's cellular castoffs, as well as its attackers. Carl Luer hypothesizes that the epigonal organ may have evolved to facilitate the transition to inactivity that occurs in a shark's gonads when a mating cycle is completed, a time when the organs that make eggs and sperm rest. It's a phenomenon that frees the shark from having to take in energy to support body parts that aren't functioning for long periods. "I have a lot of harebrained ideas," Luer shrugs. "Some of them I have evidence for, and some I don't. But it kind of makes sense that these could be tissues that evolved originally to help the reproductive organs go fallow when they're not needed."

Bonnethead sharks, *Sphyrna tiburo,* are peculiar little hammerheads common in the warm waters off the Florida coast. Unlike other *Sphyrna* species, they don't have a hammer-shaped head, but one that is broad and rounded like the blade of a garden shovel. However, it's their cream-colored epigonal tissue that has come to intrigue Carl Luer, along with some collaborating researchers, in the hunt for anti-cancer weapons. When a bonnethead's epigonal cells are grown in culture, a substance the cells exude—chemically undeciphered at this writing—has a marked capacity to inhibit the growth of several types of cancerous cells. As Carl Luer describes the work, his right index finger thunks the table for emphasis.

"From the very beginning, [thunk] we've been showing 80 to 90 percent inhibition at very low concentrations. *Both* cell lines [thunk], very high inhibition. Every single time [thunk] with every single animal we did [thunk]."

Despite all the high-tech tools research laboratories now have at their disposal, it can be difficult to coax shark cells to live in a petri dish, and one of Luer's methods is to grow the epigonal cells initially under what he calls "elasmobranch conditions," in a culture medium that is high in urea and salt. Then, when the cells have excreted whatever substance (or substances) they make as part of their normal operations, the medium's chemical composition is adjusted in a dialysislike process that yields more of a mammalian mix. This "mammalization" of the experimental brew is crucial; otherwise, if mammalian cancer cells exposed to the medium were to die, it would be impossible to know if they were killed by an anticancer factor or simply by the toxic (to mammals) urea-infused soup in which a shark's cells thrive. When two different experimental lines of cancer cells (which can be purchased like frozen soup from laboratories that maintain them) were exposed to the Mote group's "shark-conditioned medium," the epigonal factor—whatever it is—strutted its anticancer stuff. Later, a scientist at a private research institute tried the shark-conditioned medium on lymphoma cells. "Our stuff zapped that material, too," says Luer. "What impressed him was that our stuff was *more* effective than the chemical being used to treat lymphoma patients. Now that doesn't mean that we have any information on the possible side effects of the shark-conditioned medium, but it's interesting."

A patent on the bonnethead medium is pending, and the next step for the Mote group will be to begin the process of determining the nature of its active ingredient, which may be a protein resembling an interleukin. Interleukins belong to a class of chemicals called cytokines that can alter a cell's activities and are already used to treat certain human cancers. Results have been mixed; even when they are effective, interleukins are not cures, and nothing extracted from a shark is likely to be either. "That's not what this stuff is going to do," Luer hastens to add. "The best thing we can hope is that down the road we can come up with a drug that effectively knocks a cancer down to where it can be handled in other ways. The real aim of our work on cytokines is to understand how the runaway proliferation of cancer cells is regulated. And we've got a start on that."

For the moment, "shark epigonal-organ factor" hasn't yet splashed across headlines as the next anticancer miracle. It may never do so. And while Luer and his coworkers would be delighted if their pioneering studies will one day yield medical benefits, like me and other shark researchers they are edgy about the potential for abuse of information that emerges from research on sharks and cancer. The most egregious example is the miasma of misunderstanding, misrepresentation, and hype that still surrounds the subject of shark cartilage.

Down two flights of flagstone stairs from the room where Bev and I have been talking with Carl Luer, a poster session is proceeding. Scientific posters are, more or less, the written equivalents of oral presentations in the meeting rooms upstairs, and usually a poster's author is present for part of the allotted session to discuss the work reported and answer questions. My interest has been piqued by a poster reporting a commercial company's findings with respect to the efficacy against certain cancers of a semipurified decoction of shark cartilage.

This afternoon none of the poster's authors is present, leaving me with no one to query about its content, or about the press release issued by their employers a few days earlier. In the release, the sponsoring commercial enterprise, the Canadian biopharmaceutical firm AEterna Laboratories Inc., announced that its scientists had "discovered" potent antiangiogenic activity in molecules isolated from a compound they named Neovastat—a liquid distillation of shark cartilage. In the preceding sentence I have placed the word *discovered* in quotes because cartilage—any cartilage, from any vertebrate, from cattle to squirrels to people—has been known for at least twenty-five years to deter angiogenesis, the formation of blood vessels. In fact, anticancer claims for shark cartilage have their roots in an early 1980s study by MIT researchers Anne Lee and Robert Langer, which found that the cartilage seemed to inhibit angiogenesis, blocking the development of small blood vessels that a growing tumor needs for its supply of oxygen and nutrients. In addition to servicing the tumor, such new blood vessels may become highways for the cancer's spread, the metastasis that makes cancer so deadly.

Which cartilage protein (or proteins) is the specific deterrent to angiogenesis, nobody knows. And the only thing special about shark cartilage in all this is that it is relatively plentiful in the animal's body. About 6 percent of a shark's body weight is cartilage, compared to about 1 percent in a human or a calf. Lee and Langer used shark cartilage only because it was easy to come by in quantity.

AEterna's web site indicates that the company purchases processed shark cartilage from "industrial producers" who in turn obtain their raw material from shark fishers, who were already selling the fins and meat from their shark catch and now have found an additional product to market, the skeletons they formerly threw away. In other words, AEterna, and enterprises that market food supplements and other products derived from shark cartilage, contribute further to the financial push for unfettered harvesting of sharks and other cartilaginous fishes. A Costa Rican shark fishery that exploded in the early 1990s in part to supply I. William Lane's shark cartilage factory in that country has since gone bust because the local shark populations were decimated. Likewise a fishery in the Cocos Islands.

So what are my questions for the absent poster authors? Among other things, I'd like to know how many raw shark skulls and spines it takes to make, say, a liter of Neovastat. The company reports that about one hundred skeletons are required to yield enough sufficiently purified Neovastat to "treat" (experimentally) a cancer patient for one year. As I do the mental math—for, say, twenty thousand cancer patients, that would amount to 2 million dogfish a year—Neovastat is entering clinical trials to test its efficacy in people afflicted with advanced forms of lung and kidney cancer, as well as multiple myeloma, a blood cancer. Several hundred patients have been recruited for the trials, many, if not most of them, probably desperate for an effective treatment for their disease. At any given time, in the United States alone, several hundred *thousand* patients with advanced forms of various cancers are undergoing chemotherapy. As these facts accumulate, they beg the question of the present and foreseeable status of the population of spiny dogfish off South America, which reportedly is the source of AEterna's shark cartilage. Today those little sharks are being killed in an aggressive, unmanaged fishery, essentially as fast as they can be caught—just as they were in the North Atlantic. For those of us who have worked extensively on the issues, our experience with such fisheries is that many fish populations, and those of long-lived sharks in particular, cannot long sustain the slaughter. It is worth remembering that a female spiny dogfish must live for twelve to twenty years before she can even begin to breed, and then only produces a litter every other year. AEterna's chirpy press releases simply note that the South American stocks are "abundant." For now.

It may be true that AEterna's cartilage comes from sharks that are harvested in what is called a full-utilization fishery: every part of the animal, including fins, meat, and now its cartilage skeleton, is sold commercially, so none of the sharks are killed specifically for their cartilage (as many are for their fins, in other places). The tricky issue, though, is that the more parts of a shark that people can be paid to pile up on a dock, the harder it is for scientists to make a case for sustained long-term management and conservation. There is simply too much money to be made in the short run, and the interests allied against slowing the shark-killing pace are powerful.

As I write this, no well-designed, unbiased scientific study has confirmed ingested shark cartilage to be of any significant human health benefit, let alone a cancer treatment. Nor have scientists at the National Cancer Institute been able to confirm any long-term beneficial effects. Clinical trials there hint that drinking slushy, fishy-tasting Neovastat "milk shakes" twice a day may have prolonged the lives of some kidney cancer patients for a few months, but nothing more.

What is it in cartilage that inhibits the development of blood vessels, stunting the growth of tumors? According to Carl Luer, nobody has yet determined that fundamental bit of knowledge, or if they have, they have not made the finding public. He himself is collaborating on a project to chemically define the biologically active molecules in cartilage, trying "to specifically identify material that might be useful in antiangiogenic applications." Such a definitive biochemical analysis would be well worth having, especially from the sharks' point of view. Clever biochemists have managed to develop synthetic versions of many natural compounds, most notably taxol, the cancer-fighting drug first discovered in yew trees. As a result, the world still has yew trees, plus a potent weapon against uterine and ovarian cancer.

Efforts to develop another antiangiogenesis, anticancer weapon, based on a substance found in sharks, stand in stark contrast to the mass-processing of skeletons for cartilage. Searching for natural antibiotics in the mid-1990s, Michael Zasloff, a senior scientist with the Genaera Corporation, was analyzing tissues from spiny dogfish when he came across, first in the stomach and then even more abundantly in the liver, a substance that readily killed bacteria and also was active against fungi and protozoa. The chemical was identified as an aminosterol, a water-soluble steroid, and in addition to killing off pathogens it showed the ability to block blood vessel growth. Zasloff and his coworkers named it squalamine and with little public fanfare launched a program to develop a synthetic version that would be as effective as the shark variety. It was the yew tree/taxol model, applied to a potentially useful substance from sharks. When I ask Carl about it, his expression visibly brightens.

"To me," says Carl Luer, "this squalamine work is good stuff. It's been done in a very responsible way. They learned from the animal, but aren't relying on it to supply the substance. And that's an important difference from, say, the food supplement folks out there. They're not even attempting to understand what they have. It's a very different focus."

Since discovering squalamine, the Genaera team has identified seven more aminosterols in shark liver, at least some of which kill or inhibit microbes. Squalamine itself is being clinically evaluated for its effects on a type of virulent lung cancer, on ovarian cancer, and on some other tumors. It is being tested in combination with other chemotherapeutic drugs, because that is how it would likely be prescribed if it gains approval for widespread use. Like Neovastat, though, the best that can be said for now is that the synthetic squalamine appears to have shrunk tumors in perhaps a quarter of the patients who have taken it, and perhaps helped prolong their lives by several months.

Now and then new or reformulated products appear on the shelves of the shark pharmacy, representing some commercial entity's hopes for cashing in on the shark mystique. In parts of Scandinavia, entrepreneurs have taken to marketing pills containing an extract of Greenland shark liver, a lipid known chemically as a triacylglycerol, as a curative for morning sickness. A few years ago an article by Eugenie Clark in *National Geographic* reported that in Japan, capsules filled with squalene, the shark liver oil, were being promoted for their general health benefits and, predictably, as a restorative for male sexual vigor. It's not clear how much, if any, real science informs these business ventures. On the other hand, responsible researchers in university and private laboratories are continuing to examine shark tissues for known and new substances that might come to be useful in human medicine.

In 1975 a scientist named Jack Burke from the Medical College of Virginia went out on several of my long-lining cruises to obtain fresh shark blood so he and some colleagues could test its effects on a type of lung cancer called Lewis lung carcinoma. A scientific paper they published the next year reported that the blood serum of sandbar sharks inhibited the growth of tumor cells that had been transplanted into lab mice. Burke passed away not long afterward, and I never heard of any more studies along those lines. When I queried Carl Luer about the work, all he could come up with was a battered photocopy of the research report. Apparently, in the end the study didn't lead anywhere, scientifically. Maybe the cancer cells died simply as a result of being bathed by the high urea and salt in a sandbar's blood. Or maybe Burke's coauthors just went on to different, more readily answerable questions.

"In the end, we really still don't know why sharks have such a low incidence of cancer." Carl has another appointment and is summing up. "And frankly I don't think there's any one explanation. I do think their immune system is involved, and I still have my hunch about their DNA repair mechanisms being very efficient. I think that their liver is very good at detoxifying harmful substances. The high urea and TMAO content of their body fluids may be involved, and there are other things that we may not even recognize yet. And in thinking about all this, it's important to remember that the immune system of sharks appears to have evolved to a point and then changed very little, because they achieved a system that works for them in their environment."

So we have found that sharks do get cancer, but very rarely, and they may have a low incidence of other diseases as well. Apparently they owe this stalwart health to an immune system that in many ways is simpler than ours, but tremendously effective for the life sharks live. More importantly, our improving grasp of elasmobranch immune defenses is leading to the discovery of compounds that may help establish a new line of defense against human cancers and other diseases. The issue is whether, as Carl Luer says, in this remarkable process of learning from sharks, we can discipline ourselves to limit the killing.

Like my colleague, I am a realist. As unsustainable shark fisheries decimate one stock after another, the crass sellers of shark cartilage, liver oils, and other substances will do what they've always done and move on to the next "miracle." And as legitimate treatments from shark tissues are discovered, I wonder: To what avail is this work if, in the process, shark populations are plundered to the point where they can no longer meet the pharmaceutical demand? Isn't it more responsible for researchers to learn which shark compounds are biologically effective in controlling human disease, then bring to bear the immense power of modern biochemistry and genetic engineering to manufacture them in quantity? Then the sharks' gifts to our species can improve generations of human lives. It seems to me that this is where wisdom lies.

10   *Man Eats Shark*

In the summer of 1991, off the Virginia coast, Captain Tony Penello stands in the wheelhouse of the ninety-foot *Anthony Anne*, chain-smoking as he steers her into the wind. This old wooden trawler is the spitting image of the *Cape May*, the vessel Jack Casey and I used in 1961, with thick oak planking, fo'c'sle, and a sturdy mast of Maine white pine. Now, thirty years later, we are hauling line off Smith Island Shoal. "Here comes the first buoy!" Tony bellows, his rich baritone carrying easily over the din of the rumbling longline winch. Clad in a worn T-shirt and baggy green pants, Tony is a big man, quick to laugh and large of heart, with forty years' fishing experience, nearly all of it on the *Anthony Anne*. She is his second home and, after his family, the love of his life, meticulously chipped and repainted after each winter's trawling in the rough North Atlantic. For the past several summers he has volunteered his time and his vessel to my VIMS shark project, so that we may continue our long-term shark monitoring.

As the winch retrieves line and the hooks appear one by one, Tony steadies the ship's course and shakes his head. "Doctor Jack, it's a damn shame," is all he can say, echoing exactly what I am thinking. Down on deck I am at the rail removing each gangion as it comes up empty on the dripping longline. Steve Branstetter, the post-doc who saved me from going overboard in the Canary Islands, stands by to tag or gaff sharks that might be caught. This day we are fishing stations visited regularly since my shark research program off Virginia was established in 1973, and our gear is basically identical to that we used on the *Cape May*. But now, having somehow managed each summer since to survey shark populations in these waters, I have become deeply concerned about the future of sharks not only off the Atlantic coast of the United States, but globally as well.

No sharks appear. Steve looks bored. In fact, no sharks have been captured at more than one-third of our stations, where ten years earlier we would have been assured of sharks on every set. In 1980, we averaged fifteen sharks per set with at least three species represented. Now our hooks bring up three animals at most, and typically only a single species. Leaning over the gunwale, I find myself looking in vain for species that once were common, like duskies and sand tigers. Not that the void is a surprise. After the movie *Jaws* appeared in the mid-1970s, in the United States the recreational fishery for sharks exploded. Tournaments proliferated as dauntless anglers strove to land the largest shark and amass the greatest cumulative shark poundage per day. After being photographed with their catches and perhaps removing the jaws as trophies, the fishers left the carcasses to rot. Tons of dead sharks were toted off to dumps from southern New England to Texas. A few clubs such as the Virginia Beach Sharkers established tournament regulations designed to limit the number of animals killed, but they were notable exceptions. By 1985 our survey data had uncovered a 50 percent decline in some shark populations, and from then on the downward skid had so accelerated that many shark species had declined by what I estimated to be 75 to 90 percent.

Other factors besides shark-fixated recreational fishers had also been at work. In the early 1980s, many sharks were killed as bycatch on longlines set for swordfish along the edge of the continental shelf.

In addition to open-ocean sharks like makos and blues, this fishery took thousands of large coastals like duskies and sandbars. Then, just as government managers began to take notice of overfishing in the swordfishery and impose tight regulations, the infrastructure developed to market and transport shark fins from fishing ports around the world to markets in Hong Kong, Singapore, and Taiwan. Fin cartilage provides the basis for shark fin soup, a much valued entrée in Asian restaurants, and finning became the straw that finally broke the camel's back. By the close of the 1980s, along the east coast of the United States the price of shark fins had risen from less than a dollar to twenty dollars or more a pound. With this economic incentive, many long-liners began to target sharks exclusively for their fins, each year killing as many sharks as they could haul aboard for the few seconds it takes to slice the fins away.

As a commercial fisherman, Tony Penello from time to time had his disagreements with government regulators, but on the following he had been outspoken. If there ever was any question of how such abundant stocks of large animals could implode so quickly in a time of modern fisheries management, the answer had become obvious. Those charged with legal responsibility for managing the taking of sharks from the seas off the eastern United States didn't give a damn. Until the mid-1980s, sharks were of low value compared to bony fishes such as flounder, cod, or tuna, all of which *were* being managed (albeit, in my judgment, poorly). Sharks hadn't mattered because nobody was making much money off them, and so in ten short years, from 1981 to 1991, populations of large sharks along the Atlantic coast of the United States totally collapsed.

All of which begs a couple of other questions as the barren longline winds onto a huge spool on the *Anthony Anne*'s steel deck. Why did the numbers of sharks in the slate-green ocean here fall so rapidly, and does it matter?

At the outset, a shark's life strategy has two dangerous soft spots. One is their vulnerability to fishing pressure due to their slow growth, late maturity, long life span, and few young. It's not a fish's way of doing things, it's an elephant's or a turtle's or a human's. I sometimes contrast sharks with the croakers that swim into the mouth of the tidal creek on which I live. The Atlantic croaker, a mundane little fish that emits a throaty grunt when caught, may mature in a year or two and then lay hundreds of thousands of eggs every year thereafter. A lot of bony fishes follow this pattern, in which most of the babies die before their first birthday, swept away by currents or becoming meals for other marine animals. Only about one in ten thousand newborn croakers survives. By contrast, of the eight or ten pups born to a mother sandbar shark—herself at least thirteen years of age before she bears young—perhaps 50 percent will survive that vulnerable first year. The mother shark has made what ecologists call a "heavy parental investment" in her young. Yet the croaker has a much higher natural rate of increase than the shark, a statistic that encompasses a slew of factors: how long it takes a species to reach sexual maturity and to begin to have young, how many young survive, how often the adults reproduce, and the maximum age a species can attain—which determines roughly how many times an individual can reproduce in its lifetime. Some bony fishes can increase their populations by 50 to 100 percent in a single year. Because of their late maturity and demanding parental investment, in the best of circumstances sharks' natural increase rates can be on the order of around 10 percent per year for smaller species, and only 2 percent a year for larger ones, like sand tigers and duskies, which tend to grow and mature the slowest. Along the continental slope, where the ocean is perpetually cold (around 38° F), the pace at which sharks living there grow is even more sluggish, making them even more vulnerable to overfishing.

A second Achilles' heel for sharks is their inability to compensate for heavy fishing by doing what many bony fishes do: shifting gears to produce more young faster. Remove a lot of croakers from an area and suddenly the survivors are less crowded and encounter less competition for food. The changes can trigger faster growth, which means earlier sexual maturation as well as a boost in the number of eggs females produce. Most sharks haven't evolved this kind of response. The single most important factor controlling how fast their numbers increase is simply how many breeding females there are.

One of the curious and scientifically revealing features of sharks is that most species form rings on their vertebrae, which are much like the annual ring of a tree. As in a tree trunk, the rings reflect seasonal changes in growth, and so they make it possible to check whether there actually might be some growth compensation in sharks. In my laboratory a graduate student named Tom Sminkey did just this, comparing vertebrae from sandbar sharks caught at the beginning of the 1980s, when their precipitous decline in Chesapeake Bay was starting, with the vertebrae of sandbars captured a decade later after overfishing had literally decimated the population to between 10 and 20 percent of its former abundance. Sminkey found a slight growth increase after the decline, but no evidence that the sharks were starting to breed at a younger age. There also was no chance that females could have begun bearing more pups, because the number of babies a mother shark can carry is determined by the size of her uteri. The only compensation effect we could see was better survivorship of baby sandbar sharks during their first couple of years, and that was because the shark fishery also had nearly wiped out sand tigers, blacktips, tiger sharks, bull sharks, and other large species who dine on smaller sharks.

Although fishers who want to earn a living catching sharks should take into account how fast the animals can reproduce and rebound from heavy fishing pressure, the overall record on that score hasn't been very good. Neither have most fishers taken into account the natural ecological role of larger sharks. In ecosystems where sharks are among the apex predators, that job description places them at the center of ecological balance because of the way food energy flows in nature. The arrangement is usually cast as a pyramid. Its broad base, the foundation of the food web, consists of life-forms that use sunlight as their basic fuel, essentially capturing the sun's energy in chemical bonds in their bodies. These "producers"—in the sea, for the most part, vast pastures of microscopic phytoplankton—become food for a smaller biomass of larger creatures, whose bodies in turn feed an even smaller group of still larger animals, and so on up through a series of feeding levels that end at the pyramid's apex. It's a precarious perch. The laws of thermodynamics decree that the energy that was originally made tangible in the tiny bodies of phytoplankton is progressively eroded the higher one goes on the pyramid, because food not only gets converted into body parts (which can be eaten by others) but also is used as operating fuel. Like engines, animals lose a great deal of the energy they consume as heat. In general, only about 10 percent of the food energy available at one level can be transferred in the form of edible biomass, which is why fewer and fewer "consumers" can be accommodated higher in the pyramid. As a practical matter, this means that ecosystems can support fewer large animals than smaller ones, very few apex predators like makos and tiger sharks, and only a handful of "superpredators" like great whites, which can eat other large sharks. In the deep ocean, so little food energy is available that an apex predator can't survive. This is why, in a world ocean that in places is more than seven miles deep, large sharks live no deeper than three thousand to six thousand feet, except in areas where producers are unusually abundant.

Although their numbers are few, one thing apex predators do for ecosystems is help weed out the members of prey populations who are old, sick, less fit. From this vantage point, all of our planet's great predators, or the ones that remain, are agents of natural selection— the Darwinian broom that deftly sweeps away all but the fittest in each natural environment. Wolves once served this role throughout much of North America, as have lions on the African savanna, and although sharks' predatory work is much harder to observe, it stands to reason that sharks must be the wolves and lions of the sea. There's no reason to believe that the fundamentals of ocean ecosystems are any different than they are on land. When humans remove a top predator or severely deplete its numbers, as they are now doing with sharks, more lower-level predators survive, and proceed to eat a larger share of *their* prey. That upsets the predator-prey balance at lower feeding levels. The result is a cascade of disturbed ecological relationships, all evolved over countless millennia, all sundered in what amounts to a blip in time.

What man puts asunder might be hard to put right. For example, mathematical modeling of the ecological relationships of a Hawaiian reef showed that the impact of removing tiger sharks could be profound. The numbers of tiger shark prey, such as monk seals, sea turtles, seabirds, would surge, but small tuna and jacks, which are the common food of seabirds, would almost disappear. On the other hand, small bottom fishes, which tuna and jacks would no longer be around to eat, would undergo a population explosion. In effect, the ecosystem would be knocked out of kilter, with unknown long-term consequences. Modeling of intensive taking of blue sharks (for their fins) in the central Pacific suggested that it would take decades before balance could be restored. Skeptics like to dismiss models as hypothetical, as many have done with global warming. But at the very least, even if we ignore concerns about ocean ecosystems, models are warnings that in the long run if we want to keep sharks in the sea, we can remove them from it only in a sustainable way. In fact, though, we don't need theoretical predictions to tell us what might happen in a lot of places where sharks are being pursued with no holds barred. In an age of fisheries on an almost unimaginable scale, we've already got the answers.

The recent history of fishing enterprises that target sharks and their kin is a tale of unmitigated disaster and unheeded lessons about how many fish there really are in the sea. If the sea were transparent, fishers might long ago have been forced to take into account, and reckon with, the fact that you can't fish for anything, let alone sharks, without some restraint. But time and again fisheries have sprung up and then mushroomed with management nowhere in sight, and time and again fishers have gone belly-up after plundering shark stocks to the point of collapse. Consider, for example, how in the late 1930s off California, fishers began pounding the soupfin shark (*Galeorhinus galeus*).

They were mainly interested in the sharks' liver oil, which is high in vitamin A and at the time was part of the formula for preparations ranging from cosmetics to hemorrhoid creams. Between 1937 and 1941 the price of *G. galeus* liver oil soared from fifty dollars a ton to two thousand dollars. The result was a free-for-all as fishers, each with an expensive boat to pay for, tried to catch the sharks before the other guys did. In 1939 landings in the fishery peaked at over 4,000 tons, but by 1944, as more and more fishers had rushed in to get a piece of the action, the catch had plummeted to less than 290 tons because there were so few of the little soupfins left to catch. All this happened in the space of seven years, and three-quarters of a century later *G. galeus* still is not plentiful along the California coast. This species may live sixty years and takes ten to fifteen years to mature, so its demise under heavy fishing pressure should have come as no surprise. In the 1990s in Australia, the same animal (called the school shark there) was declared overfished even though able managers have been monitoring it for decades.

The litany of fishers going for the big payoff, and of failed shark fisheries, goes on and on: porbeagles across the North Atlantic; spiny dogfish in the North Atlantic and in the northeast Pacific; Pacific angel sharks and common threshers off California; basking sharks off western Ireland in the latter half of the nineteenth century, and again between 1950 to 1975, off Norway between 1960 and 1980, off Vancouver Island, Canada, in the 1950s, and elsewhere. Rays and skates haven't been immune to the human penchant for excess either, because the larger species tend to be sharklike in their growth rates and natural increase. Once upon a time one sizable species, the common skate, was indeed common in the Irish Sea and other parts of the northeast Atlantic. But in large measure because European diners relish skate wings and are willing to pay for them, overzealous fishing virtually wiped the common skate out of those waters. For a long time, nobody really noticed that the larger animals were disappearing because dutifully published fishery statistics did not enumerate different species, only totals—and smaller species that replenish their numbers faster held their own. Only when catch data were

analyzed in detail was the common skate's dismal fate discovered—
too late.

Too late is becoming a common phrase in the vocabulary of global
shark conservation, especially with regard to large species that, like
the common skate, are taken in what managers call mixed fisheries—
ones where the bulk of the fish caught are short-lived, fast repro-
ducers, but which include significant numbers of long-lived, slow-to-
mature elasmobranchs. A mixed fishery can keep going for many years
on the strength of species that can easily compensate for their losses,
while the sharks, rays, and skates are steadily, stealthily being wiped
out. For them, this scenario may be the greatest threat of all, putting
the lie to the comfortable notion that fisheries with declining catches
will end when the economic return diminishes enough, and before
they can drive species to extinction.

The threat is even greater for sharks and their relatives taken as
bycatch—the fisher's expression for unwanted fish that usually are
culled from nets and jettisoned dying or dead. So many barndoor
skates were trapped in the North Atlantic groundfishery for cod, had-
dock, and other fishes that the species has been proposed for listing
under the U.S. Endangered Species Act. It is another case of fishers
apparently not being aware that they were essentially killing off an
entire stock of one fish while they were going after another. If it were
not for long-term survey data collected on NMFS research cruises
and by the Canadian Department of Fisheries and Oceans, no one
would have noticed that the number of barndoor skates left in the
ocean had dropped by 95 percent.

Worldwide, there are precious few fisheries that do not claim
sharks, skates, or rays as bycatch, and in the vast majority of cases
nobody is keeping track of which ones or how many. In fact, as many
as half of all the elasmobranchs killed by humans may meet their end
this way, in what amounts to a completely unrecorded mass destruc-
tion of sharks and their relatives. What scant data exist don't bring
much cheer; for instance, the logbooks kept by observers on Atlantic
swordfish boats show a drastic decline in the number of makos being
caught (though no pregnant females, fortunately), and sparse records

on blue sharks trace a serious decline in their numbers also. A major issue in this regard is the shark fin trade, and it is also one of the more grotesque arenas in which shark meets man.

I ate shark fin soup once, on a research trip to Japan—the same one that had taken me to Nago harbor to see whale sharks eating shrimp poured out of buckets. The soup, which seemed to be a concoction of chicken broth laced with the translucent, noodlelike fin cartilage, wasn't my menu choice. I was being served as an honored guest at a dinner hosted by scientists working for the Japanese Fisheries Agency, which lobbies tirelessly against international regulations of shark fisheries—or of any fisheries, for that matter. And it is the bycatch of sharks in international longline fisheries, where deck crews equipped with well-sharpened knives whack the fins off sharks and throw the bloodied carcasses (or fatally maimed animals) overboard, on which much of the shark fin trade is based.

The respected international wildlife conservation organization WildAid has been gathering statistics on the fin trade that go back thirty years. The numbers neatly track the evolution of shark fin soup from a pricey gourmet item available only to moneyed diners, to a commodity that can be afforded routinely by the burgeoning Asian middle classes. The major fin suppliers are based in China, Taiwan, Singapore, the United Arab Emirates, Japan, and India. The trade is centered in Hong Kong, where the fins taken in fisheries around the world find their way to brokers who sell them—generally dried, frozen, or salted—mostly to Asian buyers. According to WildAid, in 1999 Hong Kong brokers booked a little over 14 million pounds of fins, up from 5.3 million pounds in the early 1970s, then reexported nearly all of it (13.7 million pounds). A shark's fins make up no more than about 5 percent of its total body weight. Assuming that sharks weigh forty pounds on average, then 14 million pounds of fins works out to 280 million pounds of shark in a single year—or about 7 million animals, more or less—many, if not most, killed for their fins alone.

The demand for shark fin comes mainly from China and other

countries with large Chinese populations. In the late 1990s, when end users in the United States were purchasing about ninety thousand pounds of shark fins per year, China's share totaled 6.6 million pounds, all to satiate its internal market demand for shark fin soup and other fin products. Those Chinese consumers were responding to entrenched cultural factors, as well as to the allure of access to a supposed luxury. An authority on this is a Singapore conservationist named Tony Wu, who has written that "shark fin has never been about practicality or nutrition. Perhaps more than anything it has been a symbol of extravagance and wealth . . . a way of honoring one's guests, while demonstrating that one has 'made it.'" Wu notes that $8.99 all-you-can-eat shark fin buffets are now common in Asian cities, and some Asian airlines have offered shark fin soup as part of in-flight meals. Some people also market or use shark fin preparations as aphrodisiacs; polls show that a small percentage of Chinese believe that sharks regrow fins that have been lopped off. Wu and others are doing what they can to educate consumers about the realities of finning, apparently with some success. Recently a consortium of restaurateurs from Bangkok's Chinatown district sued WildAid for $2.5 million, charging that an anti–shark fin soup advertising campaign mounted by the group had slashed their business by 50 percent. For those who make huge profits from the fin trade, lawsuits also are a way of raising the ante for antifinning efforts.

Being increasingly controversial, but valuable and easy to conceal among the whole fishes in a vessel's hold, shark fins often are not recorded by the country in which they are landed. They may, however, appear in the trade statistics of Singapore or Hong Kong when they are first imported there. A friend of mine, the British conservationist Sarah Fowler, recently discovered large imports of shark fins to Hong Kong from the European Union (EU), imports that were at odds with official EU landings data suggesting that shark finning was not widespread among Europe's commercial fishers. The discrepancy was resolved when Fowler discovered that the large Spanish longline fleet had been neglecting to report their sizable take of shark fins. In fact, Fowler's sleuthing showed that finning is rampant on vessels of

several EU countries, a situation that she and her European colleagues are working to end.

Finning is not only cruel and unethical; my own view is that dis-
carding a doomed, finned shark is a terrible waste in a world where
millions of humans lack for protein. The practice also is contrary to
the United Nations Food and Agriculture Organization (FAO) guide-
lines for responsible fisheries. Even in places like the United States,
however, where antifinning sentiment runs relatively high, the economic rewards of finning have spawned efforts to continue it. For
example, in the early 1990s finning was outlawed in U.S. fisheries in
the Atlantic and off California, but the Central Pacific Fishery Management Council refused to enact a similar ban in Hawaii even
though at the time, landings of blue shark fins (bycatch from the tuna
and swordfish longline fisheries) were expanding exponentially. The
council attributed its decision not to enact antifinning regulations
to "cultural differences," but the fact that some powerful council
members had direct financial stakes in the longline fishery suggested
another possible explanation. In 1998, of the ninety thousand–plus
blue sharks caught by Hawaii-based commercial long-liners, more than
fifty-five thousand of the animals were finned. Under pressure from
scientists and activists, in 2000 Hawaii's legislature banned the landing of shark fins without carcasses, thereby mandating that at least the
entire animal would be used. Eventually the U.S. Congress laid the
dispute to rest by prohibiting finning in all U.S. entities, and one by
one, countries including Canada, Australia, Brazil, and even the Sul-
tanate of Oman have followed suit. Encouraging as these develop-
ments are, however, other major players whose vast fleets reap large
profits from the fin trade—nations such as Indonesia, Taiwan, Japan,
and India—haven't shown much interest in enacting or enforcing a
finning ban.

For the most part, international leadership in the conservation of
Earth's sharks has come from the World Conservation Union, also
known as the International Union for the Conservation of Nature

(IUCN), based in Gland, Switzerland. The IUCN's members include countries, governmental agencies, and nongovernmental organizations. Best known for its Red List, a global assessment of species facing extinction, the organization sponsors a series of Specialist Groups that provide scientific advice to national and international management agencies charged with negotiating the terms by which different countries will harvest at-risk plants or animals, or trade in products derived from them. The go-between status of IUCN scientists often places them in venues where the people who want unfettered access to resources lock horns with those who want to conserve them—that is, to use them, but in a sustainable way. The meetings' outcomes generally are shaped by depressing reports on the decline of fishes and other wildlife on the one hand, and on the other by counterattacks from the advocates of "maximum use." I spent most of the summer of 1997 getting a joyless education in the maximum-use philosophy as it is being applied to sharks and other elasmobranchs all over the world.

The first occasion was a June meeting of the Convention on International Trade in Endangered Species, or CITES, in Harare, the capital of Zimbabwe. On the docket were issues ranging from the trade embargo on African elephant ivory to a similar prohibition involving the shells of endangered hawksbill sea turtles that were being stockpiled in Cuba in the hope that they could one day be sold to buyers in Japan. I was there as part of a delegation representing the IUCN's Shark Specialist Group (SSG) that included Sonja Fordham, a specialist in fisheries at the Ocean Conservancy in Washington, D.C., and Merry Camhi, a scientist with the Audubon Society's Living Oceans Program. Composed of volunteer scientists and conservationists, the SSG was formed in 1991 in response to international worry over rapidly declining stocks of sharks and their relatives. Sonja has been one of the most effective voices in opposing the irresponsible management of New England fisheries for spiny dogfish and other species. Merry is the main author of many of the group's proposals and opinion statements. Sonny Gruber served as the group's first chair, and since 1997 Sarah Fowler and I have been cochairs.

As its name implies, CITES is an agreement signed by about 150 countries to protect wild animals and plants from overexploitation through international trade. Depending on the degree of threat, species can be listed under one of three CITES appendices. Appendix I lists species threatened with extinction and for which no trade is allowed. Appendix II is for species at lower risk in which trade is subject to strict regulation and monitoring. The third appendix contains listings provided by individual countries for species protected within their borders, and for which cooperation to control trade is requested from other CITES parties. A two-thirds majority of the parties must vote for listing or delisting species on Appendix I or Appendix II.

In 1994, when the drastic decline in shark stocks was becoming apparent, the CITES Animals Committee was charged with preparing a report on the status of international trade in sharks. In Harare this report (largely based on work done by the SSG) was slated to be presented for approval by the entire conference. In addition, the United States had nominated several species of sawfishes for listing under Appendix I. Sawfishes are large, sharklike rays that once flourished in tropical waters, including places such as the Florida Everglades and the Gulf of Mexico. Like all sawfish species in the world, their numbers have plummeted, in part because their elongated sawlike snouts (rostra) get entangled in virtually any sort of fishing gear and the animals drown. Their situation is dire, with some species close to extinction.

Even so, the U.S. proposal was defeated after debate drawn along predictable political lines—a perfect example of the time-honored stratagems employed by those who want free access to the world's resources for their private gain. Much to the chagrin of Japanese conservationists, Japan and its allies, including Norway and a consortium of Latin American countries, are opposed to CITES becoming involved in fisheries issues regardless of whether species are endangered. Representatives of those countries united to defeat the sawfish proposal by claiming that sawfishes are not threatened by international trade (a CITES criterion), so their conservation should be a local concern. In a sense, the numbers were on their side. If international trade statistics are difficult to collect even for some common sharks, trade data on the already rare sawfishes are nonexistent. As I know from personal experience, it's easy enough to find sawfish saws for sale in Southeast Asian curio shops, and of course the animal's large fins are highly valued in the fin trade. But since no one tracks the trade, there is no hard evidence that it even exists.

Other proposals came and went, buffeted by the same maneuvering. Flyers attacking an IUCN position opposing the reopening of trade in hawksbill turtle shells were stuffed in delegates' mailboxes in the wee hours of the morning when a vote would be taken, leaving the Marine Turtle Specialist Group with little chance to rebut the claims. In other cases, false reports were circulated that key discussion sessions had been canceled, an attempt to prevent conservation advocates from showing up. Such antics could be dismissed as sophomoric if the stakes weren't so high.

Initially, sharks would seem to fare a little better at this particular meeting. The Animals Committee report was revealing, detailing how vulnerable sharks are to overharvest, their historical declines, and the paucity of reliable data on the international trade in shark products. It also identified the need for an international action plan for the conservation and management of sharks. After the report was presented and circulated, debate on its acceptance began, with most comments positive until a delegate from Japan—the head of the agency that had fed me shark fin soup—rose to offer the opinion that sharks in general grow faster and are not as vulnerable as the report suggested. In what was clearly a coordinated attack, his words were echoed by delegates from other, smaller countries in Southeast Asia and elsewhere, all of which trade heavily with Japan and receive Japanese foreign aid. When the opposition finished, I rose to present an "intervention" on behalf of the IUCN—basically a position statement supporting the report. The intervention pointed out factual errors in the Japanese presentation, and documented the real and present threat to shark stocks worldwide and the need to monitor international trade.

When the vote was taken, the shark report was approved by a comfortable margin, and on that day it seemed as though real progress might be made in the drive to limit the taking of sharks to levels that can be sustained. One outcome was a charge to the FAO to prepare an IPOA—an International Plan of Action—for the conservation and management of sharks, and after two years of regional consultations a plan was approved by the FAO Committee on Fisheries. It provided a framework for the development of shark assessments and official shark plans to be implemented by FAO member states. Yet, as of 2001, only nine of the eighty-seven coastal member states with shark populations had submitted their reports, and the vast majority of members had not even begun. Of the reports that *were* submitted, many were superficial and essentially useless. At this writing, the shark IPOA seems at best to have increased awareness of the need for global elasmobranch conservation, but because compliance with it is largely voluntary, it has done little to foster the intelligent management sharks need. At worst, the IPOA process has become a convenient delaying tactic for countries like Japan that vehemently oppose CITES control of the trade in shark fins and other elasmobranch products.

A week or so after departing Zimbabwe, I was in Sabah, Malaysia, in the Sandakan fish market watching men in seaboots and rubber aprons rushing about with carts overflowing with fishes off-loaded from boats ranging from outrigger canoes to sailing junks and small motor trawlers. Gulls wheeled and traffic buzzed down the narrow streets, and for an ichthyologist the sensory riot of shapes and colors of the passing fishes was exhilarating. Sabah sits on the northern tip of the huge island of Borneo, smack in the middle of the greatest fish— and shark—biodiversity on Earth, the Indo-Malaysian archipelago.

I was being given a tour of the fish market by Rachel Cavanaugh and Scott Mycock, two young field biologists working for Sarah Fowler under a grant from Britain's Darwin Initiative. They were in Sabah as part of a pilot project to document the kinds and relative numbers of sharks, skates, and rays being landed in the local fisheries. Both were infused with enthusiasm for the natural world they were studying, energetically pointing out species after species of sharks and rays lying in rows on fishmongers' trays.

"These are the three most common sharks," Rachel instructed. "The whitecheek shark [*Carcharhinus dusummieri*], the milk shark [*Rhizoprionodon acutus*], and the scalloped hammerhead. And the most abundant stingrays are those over there, the blue-spotted stingray [*Dasyatis kuhlii*] and the sharpnose stingray [*Himantura gerrardi*]." Scott chimed in that "over the past year we have documented thirty-four species of sharks and thirty-five rays here, of which twenty-three were new records for Sabah." In other words, local fishers were showing up in the Sandakan market with species that had never been officially recorded in the waters of northern Borneo.

I commented that with the exception of a few large stingrays, all of the animals we were seeing were small to middling in size. There were no large fish, sharks or otherwise.

"Oh, they keep everything," Scott responded. "Nothing is thrown back."

The words became a burden as I glanced over at a small trawler, its crew off-loading baskets of anchovies and shrimp and tossing yard-long sharks up on the dock. I was reminded of Chachalacas, an artisanal fishing village on the east coast of Mexico where I had spent time helping Ed Heist, another of my doctoral students, gather shark tissues so he could establish the genetic relatedness of different populations of sandbar sharks and other shark species in the western North Atlantic. There, the barefoot Mexican fishermen with their brightly painted *pangas* had so efficiently stripped local waters of sharks that few large specimens of any species remained. The larger sharks, for the most part, are the individuals that breed, keeping the population going. Though they are probably ten thousand miles apart, Chachalacas and Sandakan confirmed my sense that, small in scale and charming as the world's artisanal fisheries may seem, they are becoming devastating for sharks.

Fishers worldwide are simply taking and keeping too much. Data assembled by the prominent fishery biologist Daniel Pauly and his colleagues strongly suggest that the world's fisheries are "fishing down the food web." That is, their catches increasingly consist of fish from lower down on the feeding pyramid—small fish, because most of the larger species have been overfished and now are uncommon or rare. In places like Sandakan this phenomenon is painfully obvious.

Rachel pointed out a pair of male stingrays lying belly-up on a table. Of equal size, they looked virtually identical except that one was mature with large calcified claspers and the other was immature, his claspers small and soft. "People have always thought these were the same species," she said. "But Peter Last [an Australian expert on batoids] has shown that actually only one of them is a cowtail stingray [*Pastinachus sephen*]. The other one is undescribed." That is, one of the rays on the table, which would shortly become someone's supper, is completely unknown to science.

I replied that at the rate the stingrays were being landed, the unknown one might be gone before it was officially recognized, the fate other biologists fear is befalling the plants and animals of tropical rain forests. As with the biota of rain forests of Brazil and Costa Rica and elsewhere, the full diversity of elasmobranchs in biologically rich Southeast Asia is still a mystery. Unless scientists get to these places and runaway fisheries are managed, there is a serious risk that we will lose species of sharks and rays before we even know they exist.

The Borneo river shark (an as yet unnamed shark in the genus *Glyphis*) is a large requiem shark that for decades was known only from a single specimen in a Vienna museum. It was thought to be extinct until Scott and Rachel rediscovered it in the lower reaches of Borneo's Kinabatangan River, near a remote village called Abai. We had visited this village several days earlier, meeting a local fisherman named Zul where a dirt road ended at the river, and running in his outboard-driven mahogany-plank canoe up through the rain forest for two and a half hours. The turbid river was broad, tidal freshwater, and the shark appears to use it as a pupping and nursery ground. Beyond that, virtually nothing is known of the river shark's life and biology. The villagers told us that the river sharks come seasonally and that although they are not common, neither are they rare.

With Rachel and Scott and their rediscovered river sharks, I had a fleeting sense that there might yet be hope for the world's sharks and rays. But at a meeting of the Brazilian Elasmobranch Society three years later, Sarah Fowler and I heard familiar, discouraging tales. The scalloped hammerhead, hit hard by the pelagic longline fleet, is in severe decline off northern Brazil, while in waters off southern Brazil several smaller sharks and rays have been decimated by trawling. The Brazilian guitarfish (*Rhinobatos horkelii*) has been listed as critically endangered on the IUCN Red List. In the Amazon, unregulated export of baby river stingrays for the aquarium trade may threaten the existence of several native species.

Everywhere elasmobranchs swim, mounting evidence of severe losses stacks up against small signs of hope. In 2001, Cape Town, South Africa, hosted the first pan-African conference on shark conservation. Arranged by the International Fund for Animals, the meeting was attended by representatives of virtually every coastal African nation, a measure of those countries' concern about the problems confronting the sharks in their waters. Participants ranged from minor government bureaucrats to specialists in shark biology like myself, and the issues with which we all grappled were typical. Most reported the unbalanced scales of expanding fisheries and declining stocks, and virtually all the developing countries bemoaned the dearth of financial resources for shark research and management and the lack of enforcement of fisheries regulations. Nigeria, Sudan, and other countries are plagued by foreign longline and trawler fleets poaching and otherwise fishing illegally in their waters, removing huge catches of all sorts of fishes, including sharks and rays. Many African countries lack even the legislative framework to regulate fisheries in their waters, and several seem mired in unending civil wars. In places like these, where the ship of state is foundering, going with it is any radar screen upon which shark management might have appeared. International cooperation, vital because migrating sharks are oblivious to political boundaries, is another major problem, not only in Africa but wherever sharks cross imaginary political lines in the sea. And yet despite these towering difficulties, when the participants boarded their planes and trains out of Cape Town, they had unanimously taken the first step toward the formation of a pan-African working group for shark management and conservation. It remains to be seen whether this group will be able to take all the other steps that will be needed to secure a future for sharks that swim along African coasts.

Captain Durand Ward steers the sleek aluminum crew boat into the wind, jogging first to port and then to starboard, keeping the incoming longline close to the starboard bow. Ward, tireless with a well-trimmed salt and pepper beard and graying temples, comes from a long line of Virginia seamen, his great-grandfather having served on the CSS *Virginia* (or *Merrimack* if you are a Yankee) during its famous battle with President Lincoln's *Monitor*. The *Bay Eagle*, at sixty-five feet VIMS's largest research vessel, in 2001 serves as our principal long-lining platform. The *Anthony Anne* is gone, gutted by a shipyard fire and committed to a grave in the deep, resting on the bottom as part of an artificial reef at the Chesapeake Light Tower, twelve miles off the Virginia coast. Gone too is Tony Penello, dear friend and mentor to so many, struck down by lung cancer, the result of the chain-smoking endemic to a multitude of fishers who spend the early dark hours alone, standing watch. Tony went to great lengths to prepare the *Anthony Anne* so that she would meet government regulations that would allow the boat to be scuttled for an artificial reef. Having been a high-line trawlerman for several decades, he said the sea and the fish had been good to him and he wanted to give something back. Now, as we haul back this longline set, the sea and this reef are yielding up some signs of encouragement that sandbar sharks may be responding to stricter management, and their abundance slowly increasing. Jason Romine removes a taut gangion from the line and hands it back to Christina Conrath; hand over hand she hauls up a twenty-pound juvenile sandbar, grabs the shark carefully in front of the first dorsal, and carries it back to a table on the rear deck. There she removes the hook with a pair of pliers, measures and tags the shark, and tosses it back into the sea where it streaks away. With the help of others, the two graduate students tag and release six sandbars on this set—an improvement over the three that we would average before the new management measures were put in place in the mid-

1990s, but well below the fourteen or fifteen that we would have taken in the 1970s.

In the shelter of long-needed regulations by the National Marine Fisheries Service, declines in most east coast shark populations have halted and some species, such as sandbars, have begun to recover, albeit slowly. Dusky sharks and some other species are now completely protected and if captured must be released. Even so, to date there is no clear evidence that they are coming back. Part of the problem in this regard is that half of the dusky sharks caught on a longline will die while they dangle there, unable to swim and ventilate their gills, slowly suffocating while a fisher waits to haul in the line. A "released" dead shark is still dead. I do not know if in my lifetime I will ever again see those sleek and beautiful animals in anything like the bounty they once could claim.

Epilogue

A vision of sharks once again thriving in the sea originally drew me to put my understanding of sharks and their multifaceted universe on paper for an audience wider than the one that reads scientific journals. I, for one, won't ever relinquish that vision, and I now spend much of my professional energy trying to focus attention on the worsening plight of sharks all over the world. In 1986, data from the twenty-plus years I spent monitoring the fluctuations, then the crash, of shark populations off the mid-Atlantic coast of the United States became the red flag signaling that fisheries for sharks in U.S. waters desperately needed management if the animals were to survive. Even then, it took seven years, until 1993, for the National Marine Fisheries Service to implement regulations to address the problem. Their progress was hampered to some extent by bureaucratic red tape, but even more significantly by legal maneuvering and other opposition by the fishers who stood to gain financially—or so they thought—from continuing to fish until the last shark was caught.

If most species of sharks remain depleted in U.S. waters, where at last they have come under serious management, what fate awaits the vast majority of elasmobranchs being subjected to intensive harvesting globally, with no controls whatsoever? There's no doubt that most are overfished, at the very least. Fishers have removed them from the sea so rapidly that the remaining small populations can provide only a meager take, compared to a more gradual but ultimately larger harvest that proper management could sustain. Although many fishers close their eyes to the fact, in the long run overharvesting, and practices such as finning, result in a truly huge financial loss, not to mention the squandering of food resources. Powerful economic and political forces drive the process; the world's massive industrial fisheries represent billions of dollars sunk into ships and equipment, an investment that in the account books of investors can be profitably recouped only if vessels catch as many fish as possible as quickly as possible. Yet, because the fish simply are not there in numbers the account books demand, since the 1980s the vast international fleets of long-liners and factory trawlers have operated at a loss, kept afloat only by government subsidies. Humankind has already outstripped the sea's capacity to produce fish, and because there are so many vessels vying for the same shrinking resource, few can make a profit.

Industrial fishers aren't the only problem. Artisanal fisheries centered on small boats in coastal communities all over the world have proliferated at such a rate that they also have become a major threat to sharks. Again, the story is too many fishers and too many boats.

What are the chances that some kinds of sharks, or many, will go extinct? Some scientists argue that it is impossible to drive widely distributed coastal shark species, like sand tigers and the handsome duskies that used to be regular visitors to the Virginia coast, to extinction. I believe they are wrong—that there is a point of no return at which remnants of populations become so few that there are not enough breeders to continue. We may be on the brink of finding out just where that point is.

If extinction does come to some sharks, for the most part it will come silently—no startling bang to seize our attention, just a series of whimpers. Here and there, in the waters of Africa and Brazil, Borneo and Virginia, and a thousand other places where sharks have endured for 450 million years, one day, quite possibly when no one is keeping watch, there simply won't be enough of a particular population to reproduce anymore and it will be consigned to memory and specimen jars in museums. And when, one by one, the populations of a given shark confront such a moment, the entire species will be lost. We're beginning to see more and more of these life-or-death moments.

Not all the news is bad. While the threat that some sharks will go extinct is real, in a growing number of places people are recognizing that such losses are not inevitable. Great white sharks now are protected off California, South Africa, and parts of Australia, as are whale sharks in the waters of the United States, Australia, the Philippines, and India. Protection also has come to sand tigers in the United States and South Africa, and in Australia, where they were once nearly extirpated—in large measure by divers who used spearguns armed with exploding heads to slaughter the animals for sport. These examples don't really begin to address larger problems, such as wanton finning and massive lethal bycatches, but I'd like to think that at least some of these protections are coming about because we humans are beginning to realize what we stand to lose if we don't act on behalf of sharks, and soon. For those of us whose lives have been bound up with sharks, whether for work or out of curiosity or sheer fascination, the loss will be of creatures intricately adapted for their world and way of life—sensing things we can only try to imagine, generation upon generation carrying out rituals and rhythms of procreation seen in no other fish. Collectively we will lose yet another piece of the diverse tapestry of life on Earth. At a more basic level, ecosystems will lose apex predators crucial to their balance, a valuable and sustainable source of food will have been wasted, and sooner or later humanity will likely suffer the consequences of both.

Finally, if the foregoing are not reasons enough to keep sharks in our world, I offer two more. First, because our species is the only one to concern itself with ethics, isn't it simply unethical to extinguish entire species of our fellow creatures out of ignorance, arrogance, or stubborn greed? And beyond the question of ethics, each of us—all of us—arrived in this world with an inheritance that included seas rich with living creatures, not the least of which are the sharks. Entrusted with the care of so much biological wealth, don't we all bear a responsibility to do what we can to pass on that inheritance, whole and undiminished, to the generations who will follow?

Appendix

Table 1: Shark Evolution at a Glance

Era	Period	Epoch	Millions of Years Ago	Major Events
CENOZOIC	QUATERNARY	Recent	Includes present day	Modern humans arise. Sharks become major targets of fisheries and increasingly threatened or endangered
		Pleistocene	1.6	
	TERTIARY	Pliocene	5	Human lineage appears
		Miocene	25	Modern shark groups present
		Oligocene	45	Third shark radiation / Modern mammals appear and diversify
		Eocene	57	
		Paleocene	65	Mass extinctions
MESOZOIC	CRETACEOUS		135	Large open-ocean sharks arise / Hybodont lineage disappears
	JURASSIC		180 / 200 / 205	Rays, skates arise / Modern sharks (neoselachians) arise
	TRIASSIC		250	Dinosaurs, first mammals

Table 1: Shark Evolution at a Glance (cont.)

Era	Period	Epoch	Millions of Years Ago	Major Events
PALEOZOIC	PERMIAN		290	Mass extinctions, holocephalans stethacanthids, ctenacanths dwindle or disappear
	CARBONIFEROUS		320 355	Second great shark radiation; hybodont sharks and holocephalans arise
	DEVONIAN		410	Mass extinctions Sea level rises Sharks diversify: cladodonts, stethacanthids, ctenacanths, xenacanths
	SILURIAN		438	First bony fishes First jawed fishes
	ORDOVICIAN		455 510	Oldest shark scales First (jawless) fishes
	CAMBRIAN		540	Animals with a notochord arise
	PRECAMBRIAN		3.5 billion years ago	Life evolves on Earth

Table 2: The Players

Orders and Families of Galeomorphs

Heterodontiformes
  Heterodontidae   bullhead sharks

Orectolobiformes
  Brachaeluridae   blind sharks
  Ginglymostomatidae   nurse sharks
  Hemiscylliidae   bamboo sharks
  Orectolobidae   wobbegongs
  Parascylliidae   collared carpet sharks
  Rhincodontidae   whale sharks
  Stegostomatidae   zebra sharks

Lamniformes
  Alopiidae   thresher sharks
  Cetorhinidae   basking sharks
  Lamnidae   mackerel sharks
  Megachasmidae   megamouth sharks
  Mitsukurinidae   goblin sharks
  Odontaspidae   sand tiger sharks
  Pseudocarcharidae   crocodile sharks

Carcharhiniformes
  Carcharhinidae   requiem sharks
  Hemigalidae   weasel sharks
  Leptochariidae   barbeled hound sharks
  Proscylliidae   finback catsharks
  Pseudotriakidae   false catshark
  Scyliorhinidae   catsharks
  Sphyrnidae   hammerheads
  Triakidae   houndsharks

Orders and Families of Squalomorphs

Hexanchiformes
  Chlamydoselachidae   frilled sharks
  Hexanchidae   cow sharks

Echinorhiniformes
  Echinorhinidae   bramble sharks

Squaliformes
  Centrophoridae   gulper sharks
  Dalatiidae   cookiecutter sharks
  Etmopteridae   lantern sharks
  Oxynotidae   rough sharks
  Somniosidae   sleeper sharks
  Squalidae   dogfishes

Squatiniformes
  Squatinidae   angel sharks

Pristiophoriformes
  Pristiophoridae   saw sharks

Orders and Families of Batoidea

Torpediniformes
  Hypnidae   coffin rays
  Narcinidae   numbfishes (electric rays)
  Narkidae   sleeper rays
  Torpedinidae   torpedo rays

Pristiformes
  Pristidae   sawfishes

Rhiniformes
  Rhinidae   wedgefishes

Rhyncobatiformes
  Rhinobatidae   guitarfishes, shovelnose rays
  Rhyncobatidae   sharkfin guitarfishes

Rajiformes
  Arhynchobatidae   softnose skates
  Rajidae   skates

Myliobatiformes
  Dasyatidae   stingrays

Gymnuridae	butterfly rays
Hexatrygonidae	sixgill stingrays
Myliobatidae	eagle rays, manta rays, devil rays, cownose rays
Platyrhinidae	thornback guitarfishes
Potamotrygonidae	river stingrays
Urolophidae	stingarees
Urotrygonidae	longtail round stingrays
Zanobatidae	panrays

Acknowledgments

In this book we have attempted to weave together the many threads of the lives of sharks and rays—their fascinating biology, their long past, and their uncertain future. Any endeavor that tries to cover such an extensive landscape requires the help, counsel, and support of scores of individuals. We have been exceptionally fortunate that so many shark researchers, conservationists, and others were willing to give of their time and talent to this project.

Because we wanted readers to be able to see how scientists have learned and are continuing to learn about sharks, our plan for this book depended on the cooperation of scientists in the field who allowed us to follow along as they pursued their research. First and foremost, these colleagues included Dick Lund and Eileen Grogan in the fossil fields of Bear Gulch in Montana; Shelley Applegate in the fossil beds of El Cién in Baja California; Sonny Gruber at his remarkable shark lab in Bimini; Jeff Carrier and Wes Pratt in the nurse shark mating lagoons of the Dry Tortugas; George Burgess at the International Shark Attack file at the University of Florida in Gainesville; and Ken Goldman tracking salmon sharks in Prince William Sound, Alaska. The latter work would not have been possible without the help of Scot Anderson, Charlie Stock, Matt Miller, Dave Branshaw, Dave Anderson, and Bill Steffan. Carl Luer contributed a depth of knowledge and a library of research articles on the subject of shark immunity. Phil Motta and Bob Hueter provided key insights in the areas of shark feeding strategies and attacks on humans, respectively. Richard Peltier and Natalia Slobodskaya shared personal experiences with shark attacks; we will always remember their grace and courage.

During our sojourn in Bimini with Sonny Gruber, graduate student Allan Grant not only deepened our understanding of the sharks there but literally came to our rescue when a sudden diving mishap threatened our visit with disaster. Mari Gruber and the Bimini lab staff deserve special thanks for their hospitality, logistical support, and the best conch fritters and the only pica stew we ever ate. In the Tortugas, Kyler MacIntyre educated us about the possibilities offered by the National Geographic Society's Crittercam and warned us of black rats scuttling in the bushes at night.

The research and discoveries of dozens of scientists around the world inform and enrich the stories of sharks we have tried to tell here. Of special value were the science and friendship of Gregor Cailliet, Jack Casey, José Castro, Eugenie Clark, Guido Dingerkus, Scott Eckert, Bill Hamlett, Tom Hoff, Peter Klimley, Doug Markle, John McCosker, John McEachran, John Morrissey, Sandy Moss, Colin Simpfendorfer, Greg Skomal, and Mathias Stehmann. Juan Sabalones arranged for observations of shark swimming speeds at the Baltimore Aquarium. NASA scientists Dennis Bushnell and Mike Walsh were central to the studies of shark hydrodynamics that we discuss here. This book also benefits tremendously from classic studies of shark sensory systems and behavior carried out by Perry Gilbert and Don Nelson. "Uncle" Henry Bigelow, Bill Schroeder, and Stewart Springer provided advice and inspiration to Jack Musick when he was a neonatal Harvard graduate student interested in sharks.

Shark research and conservation are international endeavors. Mexican colleagues whose scientific work is reflected here include Ramon Bonfil, Leonardo Castillo, Fernando Marquez, and Carlos Villavincenzo. Peter Last, John Stevens, and Terry Walker are Australian scientists whose studies of sharks and other elasmobranchs are yielding vital information about shark diversity and ecology. We would like to thank our Japanese colleagues Hideki Nakano, Sho Tanaka, Tooru Taniuchi, and Kazunari Yano for their kind hospitality; Senzo Uchida was particularly helpful in our whale shark observations in Okinawa. In South Africa, Jeremy Cliff and Sheldon Dudley of the Natal Shark Board organized a revealing morning aboard net boats that monitor the anti-shark meshing of beaches. Conservationist and dive master Andy Cobb provided thought-provoking insights into shark-dive tourism there.

Special thanks are due to our colleagues in the IUCN Shark Specialist Group (SSG): Cochair Sarah Fowler; Treasurer Sonja Fordham; Deputy Chair Merry Camhi; Regional Vice Chairs Alberto Amorim, Leonard Compagno, and Hajime Ishihara; and Program Officer Rachel Cavanaugh. Several scientists mentioned above are also members of the SSG. Others with SSG affiliations who have helped in our endeavors are Scott Mycock and Amy Brautigam. Carl Safina, founder of the Audubon Society's Living Oceans Program, has provided advice and friendship for several years. The Audubon Society, Ocean Conservancy, International Fund for Animal Welfare, and WildAid each devote major resources to outreach and public education with respect to rampant overfishing and practices such as finning, which are putting more and more shark species at risk. The World Wildlife Fund's TRAFFIC program has done invaluable work in tracking trade in shark products.

One of us, Jack Musick, has devoted his professional life to the study of shark ecology at the Virginia Institute of Marine Science at the College of William and Mary. A plethora of current and former graduate students and postdoctoral fellows doing shark research there have made (and continue to make) lasting contributions to our understanding of the lives of sharks. Those whose efforts directly touch this book include Heidi Banford, Steve Branstetter, Christina Conrath, Jim Colvocoresses, Wes Dowd, Julia Ellis, Jim Gelsleichter, Ken Goldman, Dean Grubbs, David Hata, Ed Heist, Richard Kraus, Ed Lawler, Marta Nammack, Bill Raschi, Jason Romine, Tom Sminkey, and Chris Tabit. All have devoted days and nights at sea setting and hauling back longline gear, setting buoys, baiting hooks, stripping baits, applying tracking tags, and doing the dissections and statistical analyses that have allowed VIMS to become a globally recognized center for shark research.

Several other individuals and entities have provided essential support for that program. The individuals include our colleague and collaborator John Graves, assistant directors Gene Burreson and Bob Byrne, and VIMS directors Bill Hargis, Frank Perkins, and Don Wright. Crucial funding for the VIMS shark program has come from the Virginia Marine Resources Commission, with special thanks due to William Pruitt and Jack Travelstead, who clearly understand the vital role sharks play in coastal ecosystems and how much there remains to learn about them. Monies from the federal Wallop-Breaux, Sea Grant, and Saltonstall-Kennedy programs also have been key to sustaining VIMS shark studies. Bill Hogarth of the National Marine Fisheries Service is owed a special debt of gratitude for providing funding for our shark work in recent years.

Most research on sharks gets started on a boat, and research vessels require skippers who understand the special requirements of setting and hauling back longlines, handling large, dangerous fish for tagging and release, and myriad other tasks—including dealing with scientists—that go far beyond mere "fishing." Without captains Tony Penello (*Anthony Anne*), Durand Ward (*Bay Eagle*), Jack Lewis (*Pathfinder*), and Charles Machen (*John Smith*), and port captain George Pongonis, more than thirty years of VIMS research cruises would have been difficult or impossible.

The idea for writing a shark book that focused both on the animals and on the researchers and the research process rolled around in our heads for several years. Only when Bev McMillan broached the subject to John Thornton of the Spieler Agency did that seed blossom into a carefully crafted plan, and only when Erika Goldman of Times Books/Henry Holt saw the promise did the plan become a formal project. To them we offer thanks for your trust in our proposal and, later, for believing that we would indeed get the job done.

As with nearly all books, there are a few people whose contributions tend to be submerged in the final product, though they were absolutely essential. At VIMS, Gloria Rowe typed and later keyboarded years of shark research reports. Melanie Miller Harbin took on the daunting job of keyboarding drafts of several chapters, among other thankless tasks. At the eleventh hour, Consuelo Goldman and Diana Wagnitz literally saved part of the manuscript from electronic oblivion. Sean Azarin sacrificed family time to further the cause of meeting a publishing schedule and was a continual source of long-distance moral support. Kate Musick and Susanna Musick have endured their father's lifelong fascination with sharks and, even as small children, aided and abetted in wading through piles of shark guts. They also helped keep the Musick-McMillan household going during the weeks of travel this book entailed.

The Shark Chronicles includes many details of shark biology and behavior. Many of the researchers named in the preceding paragraphs have contributed advice and comments on technical matters, for which we are deeply grateful. We alone are responsible for any errors of fact or interpretation that may remain. Our sincere apologies to those deserving souls whom we have inadvertently omitted from these acknowledgments.

Index